60 HIKES
WITHIN 60 MILES

3rd Edition

SALT LAKE CITY

Including Ogden, Provo, and the Uintas

60 HIKES WITHIN 60 MILES: SALT LAKE CITY

Copyright © 2008, 2012, and 2019 by Greg Witt
All rights reserved
Printed in China
Published by Menasha Ridge Press
Distributed by Publishers Group West
Third edition, first printing

Editor: Ritchey Halphen
Cover and interior design: Jonathan Norberg
Maps and elevation profiles: Scott McGrew and Greg Witt
Photos: Dallin Witt, except as noted
Proofreader: Emily Beaumont
Indexer: Galen Schroeder/Dakota Indexing

Front cover: Lone Peak (see Hike 42, page 191), photo by Dennis Coello; *back cover:* (top) the Living Room (see Hike 13, page 74); (bottom, left–right) Lofty Lake (see Hike 58, page 266); Mount Olympus (see Hike 24, page 119); Sunset Peak (see Hike 36, page 167); photos by Dallin Witt

Library of Congress Cataloging-in-Publication Data

Names: Witt, Greg, 1952– author.
Title: 60 hikes within 60 miles : Salt Lake City including Ogden, Provo, and the Uintas / Greg Witt.
Other titles: Sixty hikes within sixty miles
Description: Third edition. | Birmingham, Alabama : Menasha Ridge Press [2019]
Identifiers: LCCN 2019000151 | ISBN 978-1-63404-132-4 (pbk.) | ISBN 978-1-63404-133-1 (ebk.)
Subjects: LCSH: Hiking—Utah—Salt Lake City—Guidebooks. | Salt Lake City (Utah)—Guidebooks.
Classification: LCC GV199.42.U73 W58 2019 | DDC 796.5109792258—dc23
LC record available at lccn.loc.gov/2019000151

MENASHA RIDGE PRESS
An imprint of AdventureKEEN
2204 First Ave. S., Ste. 102
Birmingham, Alabama 35233

Visit menasharidge.com for a complete listing of our books and for ordering information. Contact us at our website, at facebook.com/menasharidge, or at twitter.com/menasharidge with questions or comments. To find out more about who we are and what we're doing, visit blog.menasharidge.com.

Dedication

For all Utahns who work to preserve the Salt Lake City area's natural beauty. It's because of you that this is the place.

60 HIKES WITHIN 60 MILES
3rd Edition

SALT LAKE CITY

Including Ogden, Provo, and the Uintas

Greg Witt

MENASHA RIDGE PRESS
Your Guide to the Outdoors Since 1982

60 Hikes Within 60 Miles: Salt Lake City

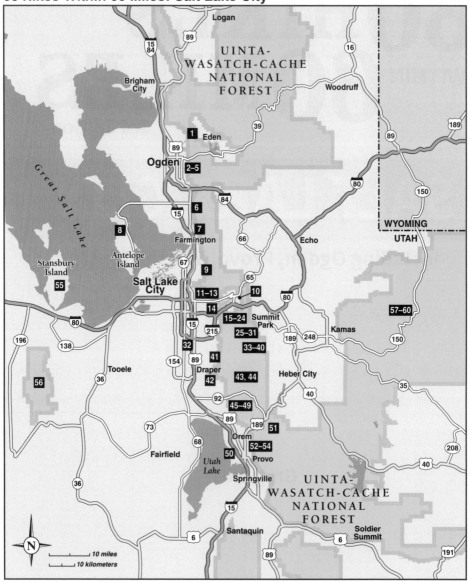

TABLE OF CONTENTS

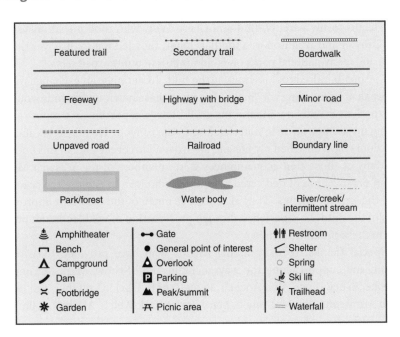

ACKNOWLEDGMENTS

A project of this magnitude goes from concept to print with the contributions of many. I'm thankful for the energetic and talented team at Menasha Ridge Press, who approached me about writing a Salt Lake City hiking guide. I was somewhat reluctant at first, but through their encouragement, vision, and support, *60 Hikes Within 60 Miles: Salt Lake City* became a reality.

Thanks to Sheryl McGlochlin, whose energy and enthusiasm are infectious. She has introduced many of these hikes to hundreds of locals and is always eager to share a favorite hike with friends like me.

I'm appreciative of the staff at Weber Pathways, who have created a hiking legacy for the Ogden area through their efforts to promote, plan, and preserve trails.

I'm grateful to Alan and Kristine Colledge, with whom I've shared gallons of Gatorade and miles of terrain across the Wasatch, the Colorado Plateau, and the Grand Canyon.

Thanks to my parents, Bud and Claire Witt, who took me on hikes in Mill Creek Canyon and Brighton as a toddler. Later, they led me to discover the Sierra Nevada and many national parks on fabulous cross-country road trips.

I've met hundreds of hikers along the trail. Sometimes our exchange was nothing more than "g'morning" or "hello." But often these newfound friends would share their experiences with me: identifying a wildflower, reporting on a moose sighting, or telling me about a favorite waterfall just up the canyon. Their insights and love of the outdoors have enriched my life and are woven into every hike in this book.

Many of those trail acquaintances were members of the Wasatch Mountain Club, an organization of dedicated volunteers who love to explore the scenic wonders of the area mountains. They also deserve much of the credit for improving the quality of the outdoor experience through preservation of wild lands and providing access to these pristine reaches.

Special thanks to many hiking friends who have provided ideas, encouragement, and support along the way, including Phil Schow, Mark McGuire, Bart Hamatake, Bruce Bown, Ben Adcock, Peter Tennis, David Crowther, Jim Rasband, Vaughn Armstrong, Jim McDonald, Mary Baxter, Jack Welch, Al Christy, Jim Driggs, Harlan Hatfield, and Dennis Hoagland.

I always cherish the time I've spent on these and other Utah trails with my children, Heather, Blair, Lindsey, Dallin, and Tessa. I look forward to sharing many more trail miles with my grandchildren, Hannah, Isaac, Alden, and Grant.

My deepest gratitude goes to my wife, Elain, my best friend and eternal trail companion. Her sustaining belief, encouragement, and love have guided me through this project and every other aspect of my life. She joined me on many of these hikes, but I wish she could have joined me on every one. If she had, this would have been a far more elaborate book.

—*Greg Witt*

Welcome to Menasha Ridge Press's 60 Hikes Within 60 Miles, a series designed to provide hikers with the information they need to find and hike the very best trails surrounding metropolitan areas.

Our strategy is simple: First, find a hiker who knows the area and loves to hike. Second, ask that person to spend a year researching the most popular and very best trails around. And third, have that person describe each trail in terms of difficulty, scenery, condition, elevation change, and other categories of information that are important to hikers. "Pretend you've just completed a hike and met up with other hikers at the trailhead," we told each author. "Imagine their questions; be clear in your answers."

An experienced hiker and writer, Greg Witt has selected 60 of the best hikes in and around the Salt Lake City metropolitan area. Witt provides hikers (and walkers) with a great variety of hikes—all within roughly 60 miles of Salt Lake—from urban strolls on city sidewalks to aerobic outings in the High Uintas. This third edition includes not only several new hikes but also additional sections and new routes for some existing hikes.

You'll get more out of this book if you take a moment to read the Introduction, which explains how to read the trail listings. The Topographic Maps section (page 4) will help you understand how useful topos are on a hike and will also tell you where to get them. And though this is a where-to, not a how-to, guide, readers who have not hiked extensively will find the Introduction of particular value.

As much for the opportunity to free the spirit as to free the body, let these hikes elevate you above the urban hurry.

All the best,
The Editors at Menasha Ridge Press

Alaska is our biggest, buggiest, boggiest state. Texas remains our largest unfrozen state. But mountainous Utah, if ironed out flat, would take up more space on a map than either.
—**Edward Abbey,** *A Voice Crying in the Wilderness*

The Wasatch Mountains loom over the Salt Lake City skyline.

Photo: Joe Guetzloff/Shutterstock

With mountains on every side, Utah's Salt Lake Valley offers a greater variety of dramatic and awe-inspiring day hikes than any major metropolitan area in the United States. Nestled below the western flank of the Rockies, Salt Lake City provides ready access to a stunning array of alpine lakes, snow-draped mountain peaks, fragrant evergreen forests, deep canyon waterfalls, granite towers, and flowered cirques.

Within 60 miles of Salt Lake City lie thousands of square miles of national forest, national wilderness areas, state parks, and designated recreation areas to explore. But it takes accurate and dependable information to select the best hiking adventure for you. Within minutes of a bustling urban center, you can immerse yourself in the history of early miners, the Pony Express, the Donner Party, or Mormon pioneers. With a little planning you can summit one of a dozen 11,000-foot peaks sprinkled throughout the region. You can find solitude in flickering aspen groves, shaded canyons, and pristine wilderness. Whether you're lacing up boots, stepping into running shoes, or strapping on snowshoes, Salt Lake City is a premier destination for hikers.

About the Hikes

It would have been easy to catalog 60 hikes near Salt Lake City from the hundreds of hiking trails in the area. But the ultimate challenge in writing this book was to pinpoint the *absolute best* of those hikes: the most enjoyable, inspiring, intriguing, and accessible of the bunch. You'll quickly discover that every hike has a wow factor: a memorable destination, a glistening lake, a mesmerizing stream, a breathtaking view, or a soothing canyon.

The 60 hikes that made the list had to both captivate the attention of young hikers and challenge the endurance of seasoned ones. The hikes needed to reflect the diversity of the mountain, valley, and canyon terrain in the area. And with fuel costs rising, I wanted to reveal hikes that were nearby and easily accessible to the 1.7 million people who live within 60 miles of Salt Lake City.

Faced with the challenge of selecting the best hikes in the Salt Lake area, I assembled a powerful and compelling list in less than an hour. But the book really demanded a more rigorous process. So I distributed my best-hikes list to dozens of area hikers, rangers, scoutmasters, youth leaders, mountain bikers, rock climbers, dog walkers, trails advocates, and city recreation officials. I sought their suggestions on which hikes to include, asking them to advise which routes offered the best trailhead access and best overall experience. Their input was exciting to receive and proved invaluable. Surprisingly, we achieved a high level of consensus on which hikes to include—in fact, the 60 hikes included here are about 90% consistent with my original list.

To present the most accurate information possible, I rehiked each trail to take distance measurements, determine GPS coordinates, measure elevations, and clarify trail markings. My goal was simple: create a trustworthy, authoritative trail guide that would provide years of valuable hiking pleasure.

When *60 Hikes Within 60 Miles: Salt Lake City* was first published in 2008, it instantly became the best-selling hiking guide in Utah and the essential trail guide for thousands of hikers in the Wasatch. For that I am grateful, and it's been especially enjoyable to be on the trail and run into hikers who have a well-used, dog-eared copy of *60 Hikes* in their pack.

The big challenge came with the opportunity to publish this third edition. Sure, there were updates to include—new trailhead amenities, increased entrance fees, new access roads. But dare I take out one of my favorite hikes? And if so, which new hikes are worthy of inclusion in the latest edition?

If you're already familiar with the previous two editions of *60 Hikes,* I think you'll be pleased with the new additions as you put this new edition to the test. If you're picking up this book for the first time, rest assured that you're heading to some of the most beautiful and magical places in the West. Most of all, I have loved the challenge of selecting these hikes and providing every detail to make your adventure memorable.

Just 60 hikes, though? *Hardly.* At last count, it was closer to 120 hikes organized into 60 profiles. Most of these hikes, as are most Wasatch trails, are interconnected. Each hike profile describes a particular route and also allows for a variety of options, extensions, and spur trails. In addition, the Nearby Activities mentioned at the end of most trail descriptions often reveal short hikes leading to hidden waterfalls, short interpretive trails, or points of historical or geological interest. Most of these activities consist of walks that are less than 1 mile round-trip, while the 60 hikes are 1 mile or more in length. If you're a novice hiker and want to build your speed and stamina, you may want to start with some of the Nearby Activities.

These hikes appeal to a wide variety of skill levels and interests. Of the featured trips, about 31% are considered easy, 47% are moderately difficult, and 22% are strenuous. They range in distance from 1 mile on Buffalo Peak to 16 miles on Ben Lomond. Elevation change ranges from −58 feet on the Jordan River Parkway to +5,460 feet on Lone Peak. Though all of these trips are described as day hikes, many can be adapted to overnight backpacking. You'll find that *60 Hikes* has something for everybody.

REGIONS

The hikes in this book are organized by area in relation to Salt Lake City: north, central, south, east, and west. Conveniently, these areas also match county lines, as most county boundaries are defined by mountain ridges. Most of the hikes are in the Wasatch Mountains, which run north and south, with the vast majority of the area's population living on the slopes and valleys to the west of the range.

Within each county, hikes are organized geographically, from generally north to south. Here's a quick overview of each region:

North (Weber County) These hikes are easily accessed from Ogden, about 35 miles north of Salt Lake City. Ogden's historical roots as a junction on the transcontinental railroad have been overshadowed in recent years by its emergence as a center of outdoor recreation. The alpine peaks that hosted downhill and super-G events at the 2002 Winter Olympics are also great hiking destinations in the summer. Favorite Weber County hikes include Ben Lomond to the north and beautiful Waterfall Canyon to the south, just minutes from the city center.

North (Davis County) Immediately north of Salt Lake City, Davis County is traditionally known for farming communities such as Bountiful, Farmington, and Fruit Heights, which rest on the alluvial plain at the base of smaller Wasatch peaks. But it also offers some great canyon hikes, such as the ones in Farmington and Adams Canyons. Davis County has more square miles of Great Salt Lake than it has land area, and Antelope Island is the ideal place to explore the wonders of the lake on dry ground.

Central (Salt Lake County) It's fitting that more than half of the 60 hikes are right in Salt Lake County. These hikes offer easy access to glacial canyons, alpine lakes, and snowcapped peaks. You'll be amazed how close wilderness areas are to the heart of the city. Salt Lake's pioneer history unfolds along celebrated trails and the Pony Express route. You'll find adventure waiting in each of the seven canyons that have shaped, nourished, powered, and built Salt Lake City since 1847. Most hikers can

Predictable snowfall guarantees a wide variety of creeks and streams across the Wasatch.

find enough opportunities in Big Cottonwood Canyon alone to feed their passion for a year or more. Some of the more popular hikes in the central Wasatch include Grandeur Peak, Brighton Lakes, and Doughnut Falls.

South (Utah County) To the south of Salt Lake City, Mount Timpanogos watches over Utah County. Dozens of canyons flank "Timp," and waterfalls cascade down all sides. Provo and American Fork Canyons offer exceptional recreational opportunities year-round. But while Timp is arguably the best hike in northern Utah, you don't want to overlook such Utah County jewels as Silver Lake and Stewart Falls.

West (Tooele County) With so much to enjoy in the Wasatch, you can see why most locals overlook the desert to the west. But the Stansbury Mountains and the Deseret Peak Wilderness Area, with its rugged terrain and 11,031-foot centerpiece, simply can't be ignored. Views stretch across the Bonneville Salt Flats and into Nevada. It's a straight shot out I-80, just 35 miles to the west.

East (Summit County and Uintas Mountains) The Uintas, which include Utah's highest peaks, lie directly east of Salt Lake City, beyond the Wasatch Mountains. The Mirror Lake Scenic Byway provides easy access to picturesque basins and forests of spruce and fir. You can climb 11,943-foot Bald Mountain in less than an hour or spend days on end in the alpine heaven known as Naturalist Basin.

Let *60 Hikes* be a starting point. Let it inspire your own adventure on a road less traveled. Maybe you'll discover a hidden waterfall or encounter a mysterious field of white columbine. Wasatch trails are notoriously unmarked, and maybe with enough experience you'll discover you don't need trail signs to have a great hike. If a family of moose is blocking the trail, you may find a parallel trail over the ridge. If the trailhead parking lot is full, you can often take a shorter, steeper trail to the summit from another trailhead. The possibilities are endless—and you'll have the time of your life exploring them.

See you on the trail!

60 HIKES BY CATEGORY

REGION Hike Number/Hike Name	Page #	Mileage	Difficulty	Steep	River/Stream	Lakes	High Altitude	Scrambling
NORTH (Weber County)								
1 Ben Lomond	18	16	S					
2 Ogden River Parkway	22	6.8	E		✓			
3 Mount Ogden (via Snowbasin Gondola)	26	3.1	E					
4 Malans Peak (via Taylor Canyon)	30	5.0	M	✓	✓			
5 Waterfall Canyon	34	2.6	M		✓			
NORTH (Davis County)								
6 Adams Canyon	40	3.6	M	✓	✓			
7 Farmington Creek Trail	44	2.6	M		✓			
8 Frary Peak	48	6.6	M	✓				
9 Kenney Creek Trail	53	4.5	M	✓	✓			
CENTRAL (Salt Lake County)								
10 Mormon Pioneer Trail	60	9.1	M		✓			
11 City Creek Canyon	65	3–12	E		✓			
12 Red Butte Garden	70	2–4	E		✓			
13 The Living Room (with Red Butte Extension)	74	2.3	E					
14 Jack's Mountain	78	2.6	M	✓				
15 Lambs Canyon	82	4.0–6.0	M		✓			
16 Mount Aire	87	3.8	M	✓	✓			
17 Grandeur Peak (via the Western Ridge)	91	6.8	S	✓				
18 Pipeline Overlook (via Rattlesnake Gulch)	95	3.3	E					
19 Grandeur Peak (via Mill Creek Canyon)	99	5.4	M		✓			
20 Desolation Trail to Salt Lake Overlook	103	4.8	M					
21 Gobblers Knob (via Alexander Basin)	107	4.4	M	✓			✓	
22 Mill Creek to Park City Overlook (Including Murdock Peak)	111	5.2	M		✓			
23 Neffs Canyon	115	5.5	S		✓			
24 Mount Olympus	119	7.0	S	✓				✓
25 Dog Lake	123	4.6	E			✓		
26 Desolation Lake	127	6.6–8.2	M			✓		
27 Mount Raymond (via Butler Fork)	131	8.0	S		✓		✓	✓
28 Broads Fork	135	4.5	M	✓	✓			
29 Doughnut Falls	139	1.4	E		✓			✓
30 Lake Blanche	143	5.8	M		✓	✓		

REGION Hike Number/Hike Name		Page #	Mileage	Difficulty	Steep	River/Stream	Lakes	High Altitude	Scrambling
31	Willow Heights	147	1.5	E		✓	✓		
32	Jordan River Parkway	151	11.0	E		✓			
33	Great Western Trail (Guardsman Pass to Clayton Peak)	155	2.2	M				✓	
34	Lake Solitude (via the Silver Lake Interpretive Trail)	159	3.5	E			✓		
35	Brighton Lakes	163	4.5	M			✓		
36	Sunset Peak	167	4.2	E				✓	
37	Cecret Lake	171	1.6	E			✓		
38	White Pine Lake	175	9.8	M		✓	✓	✓	
39	Pfeifferhorn (via Red Pine Lake)	179	7.0–10.0	S	✓		✓	✓	✓
40	American Fork Twin Peaks	183	2.2	M				✓	✓
41	Bells Canyon	187	8.4	S	✓	✓			
42	Lone Peak	191	12	S	✓			✓	✓
SOUTH (Utah County)									
43	Silver Lake	198	4.4	M		✓	✓		
44	Box Elder Peak	203	9.8	S	✓	✓		✓	✓
45	Timpanogos Cave National Monument	206	3.0	M					
46	Mount Timpanogos (via the Timpooneke Trail)	210	14.8	S		✓		✓	
47	Emerald Lake and Mount Timpanogos (via Aspen Grove)	214	13.6	S		✓	✓	✓	
48	Stewart Falls	219	3.6	E		✓			
49	Battle Creek Falls	223	1.6	E		✓			
50	Provo River Parkway	227	15	E		✓			
51	Big Springs Hollow	232	5.0	E		✓			
52	Buffalo Peak	237	1.0	E					
53	Squaw Peak	241	7.0	M	✓	✓			
54	Y Mountain	245	2.2	M	✓				
WEST (Tooele County)									
55	Stansbury Island	252	9.5	M					
56	Deseret Peak	256	8.5	S	✓	✓		✓	

(continued on next page)

DIFFICULTY RATINGS		
E = Easy	M = Moderate	S = Strenuous

REGION Hike Number/Hike Name	Page #	Mileage	Difficulty (E/M/S)	Steep	River/Stream	Lakes	High Altitude	Scrambling
EAST (Summit County and Uintas Mountains)								
57 Naturalist Basin	262	12.0–18.0	S		✓	✓	✓	
58 Lofty Lake Loop	266	4.1	M			✓	✓	
59 Fehr Lake Trail	270	3.4	M			✓	✓	
60 Bald Mountain	274	3.0	M				✓	

DIFFICULTY RATINGS		
E = Easy	M = Moderate	S = Strenuous

Hikes by Category (continued)

REGION Hike Number/Hike Name	Page #	Mountain Biking	Road Biking	Waterfalls	Winter	History	Kids	Dogs	Popular
NORTH (Weber County)									
1 Ben Lomond	18	✓							
2 Ogden River Parkway	22		✓		✓		✓	✓	✓
3 Mount Ogden (via Snowbasin Gondola)	26	✓					✓		
4 Malans Peak (via Taylor Canyon)	30								
5 Waterfall Canyon	34			✓	✓				✓
NORTH (Davis County)									
6 Adams Canyon	40			✓					
7 Farmington Creek Trail	44			✓					
8 Frary Peak	48				✓				
9 Kenney Creek Trail	53								
CENTRAL (Salt Lake County)									
10 Mormon Pioneer Trail	60	✓				✓			
11 City Creek Canyon	65		✓		✓	✓	✓	✓	✓
12 Red Butte Garden	70			✓	✓	✓	✓		
13 The Living Room (with Red Butte Extension)	74							✓	
14 Jack's Mountain	78				✓			✓	
15 Lambs Canyon	82								

REGION Hike Number/Hike Name	Page #	Mountain Biking	Road Biking	Waterfalls	Winter	History	Kids	Dogs	Popular
16 Mount Aire	87							✓	
17 Grandeur Peak (via the Western Ridge)	91							✓	
18 Pipeline Overlook (via Rattlesnake Gulch)	95	✓			✓			✓	✓
19 Grandeur Peak (via Mill Creek Canyon)	99	✓			✓			✓	✓
20 Desolation Trail to Salt Lake Overlook	103							✓	
21 Gobblers Knob (via Alexander Basin)	107								
22 Mill Creek to Park City Overlook (Including Murdock Peak)	111	✓						✓	
23 Neffs Canyon	115					✓		✓	
24 Mount Olympus	119								✓
25 Dog Lake	123	✓			✓				
26 Desolation Lake	127	✓							✓
27 Mount Raymond (via Butler Fork)	131								
28 Broads Fork	135								✓
29 Doughnut Falls	139			✓	✓		✓		✓
30 Lake Blanche	143								✓
31 Willow Heights	147				✓		✓		
32 Jordan River Parkway	151		✓		✓	✓	✓	✓	✓
33 Great Western Trail (Guardsman Pass to Clayton Peak)	155						✓		
34 Lake Solitude (via the Silver Lake Interpretive Trail)	159	✓					✓		✓
35 Brighton Lakes	163						✓		✓
36 Sunset Peak	167						✓		✓
37 Cecret Lake	171						✓		✓
38 White Pine Lake	175	✓							
39 Pfeifferhorn (via Red Pine Lake)	179								
40 American Fork Twin Peaks	183								
41 Bells Canyon	187			✓					
42 Lone Peak	191								
SOUTH (Utah County)									
43 Silver Lake	198			✓					
44 Box Elder Peak	203								
45 Timpanogos Cave National Monument	206					✓			✓
46 Mount Timpanogos (via the Timpooneke Trail)	210			✓					✓
47 Emerald Lake and Mount Timpanogos (via Aspen Grove)	214			✓					✓
48 Stewart Falls	219			✓			✓	✓	✓

(continued on next page)

REGION Hike Number/Hike Name	Page #	Mountain Biking	Road Biking	Waterfalls	Winter	History	Kids	Dogs	Popular
SOUTH (Utah County) *(continued)*									
49 Battle Creek Falls	223			✓			✓	✓	
50 Provo River Parkway	227	✓	✓	✓			✓	✓	✓
51 Big Springs Hollow	232				✓				
52 Buffalo Peak	237						✓	✓	
53 Squaw Peak	241								✓
54 Y Mountain	245						✓		✓
WEST (Tooele County)									
55 Stansbury Island	252	✓		✓					
56 Deseret Peak	256							✓	
EAST (Summit County and Uintas Mountains)									
57 Naturalist Basin	262							✓	✓
58 Lofty Lake Loop	266							✓	
59 Fehr Lake Trail	270						✓	✓	
60 Bald Mountain	274						✓		✓

Hikes by Category (continued)

REGION Hike Number/Hike Name	Page #	High Summits	Scenic	Year-Round	Solitude	Wildlife	Wildflowers	Regular Workouts	Runners
NORTH (Weber County)									
1 Ben Lomond	18	✓							
2 Ogden River Parkway	22	✓	✓					✓	✓
3 Mount Ogden (via Snowbasin Gondola)	26	✓							
4 Malans Peak (via Taylor Canyon)	30	✓							
5 Waterfall Canyon	34								
NORTH (Davis County)									
6 Adams Canyon	40	✓							
7 Farmington Creek Trail	44								
8 Frary Peak	48	✓	✓		✓				
9 Kenney Creek Trail	53	✓							

REGION / Hike Number/Hike Name	Page #	High Summits	Scenic	Year-Round	Solitude	Wildlife	Wildflowers	Regular Workouts	Runners
CENTRAL (Salt Lake County)									
10 Mormon Pioneer Trail	60				✓				
11 City Creek Canyon	65		✓			✓		✓	✓
12 Red Butte Garden	70		✓	✓		✓	✓		
13 The Living Room (with Red Butte Extension)	74		✓				✓		
14 Jack's Mountain	78	✓	✓						
15 Lambs Canyon	82			✓		✓			
16 Mount Aire	87	✓							
17 Grandeur Peak (via the Western Ridge)	91	✓			✓				
18 Pipeline Overlook (via Rattlesnake Gulch)	95	✓	✓						✓
19 Grandeur Peak (via Mill Creek Canyon)	99	✓							
20 Desolation Trail to Salt Lake Overlook	103	✓							
21 Gobblers Knob (via Alexander Basin)	107	✓					✓		
22 Mill Creek to Park City Overlook (Including Murdock Peak)	111	✓							
23 Neffs Canyon	115			✓					
24 Mount Olympus	119	✓							
25 Dog Lake	123								
26 Desolation Lake	127								
27 Mount Raymond (via Butler Fork)	131	✓							
28 Broads Fork	135	✓							
29 Doughnut Falls	139								
30 Lake Blanche	143	✓							
31 Willow Heights	147			✓			✓		
32 Jordan River Parkway	151			✓				✓	✓
33 Great Western Trail (Guardsman Pass to Clayton Peak)	155	✓							
34 Lake Solitude (via the Silver Lake Interpretive Trail)	159		✓			✓			
35 Brighton Lakes	163		✓						
36 Sunset Peak	167		✓						
37 Cecret Lake	171		✓			✓	✓		
38 White Pine Lake	175		✓						
39 Pfeifferhorn (via Red Pine Lake)	179	✓	✓						
40 American Fork Twin Peaks	183	✓	✓						
41 Bells Canyon	187				✓				
42 Lone Peak	191	✓	✓						

(continued on next page)

REGION Hike Number/Hike Name	Page #	High Summits	Scenic	Year-Round	Solitude	Wildlife	Wildflowers	Regular Workouts	Runners
SOUTH (Utah County)									
43 Silver Lake	198		✓			✓			
44 Box Elder Peak	203	✓	✓		✓	✓			
45 Timpanogos Cave National Monument	206		✓						
46 Mount Timpanogos (via the Timpooneke Trail)	210	✓	✓				✓		
47 Emerald Lake and Mount Timpanogos (via Aspen Grove)	214	✓	✓				✓		
48 Stewart Falls	219		✓						
49 Battle Creek Falls	223			✓					
50 Provo River Parkway	227			✓				✓	✓
51 Big Springs Hollow	232			✓					
52 Buffalo Peak	237	✓			✓				
53 Squaw Peak	241	✓							
54 Y Mountain	245	✓	✓					✓	
WEST (Tooele County)									
55 Stansbury Island	252		✓	✓	✓				
56 Deseret Peak	256	✓	✓						
EAST (Summit County and Uintas Mountains)									
57 Naturalist Basin	262		✓			✓	✓		
58 Lofty Lake Loop	266		✓				✓		
59 Fehr Lake Trail	270		✓						
60 Bald Mountain	274	✓	✓				✓		

Welcome to *60 Hikes Within 60 Miles: Salt Lake City.* If you're new to hiking or even if you're a seasoned trekker, take a few minutes to read the following introduction. We'll explain how this book is organized and how to get the best use out of it.

About This Book

Utah is unparalleled in its natural diversity, and the wide variety of flora, fauna, and landscapes that surrounds the Salt Lake Valley is on proud display in this book. From the grassy slopes of Antelope Island to the granitic cliffs of the Cottonwood Canyons, we've made every effort to showcase the incredible assortment of vistas that you can access within just an hour of this city.

Given the sheer volume of hiking options in the area, winnowing the field down to just 60 was a challenge. Hikes were selected for their unique ecology, physical challenges, and rewarding views. Many of these hikes, such as those in the High Uintas, offer a level of isolation and serenity that seems almost unfathomable when you're in the bustling urban core of Salt Lake. Others offer rapid getaways: hikes you could take over a long lunch or quickly attempt after a full day in the office.

Regardless of what type of hike you're looking for, you've got dozens of options—all within a quick drive of the city.

How to Use This Guidebook

The following information walks you through this guidebook's organization, making it easy and convenient to plan great hikes.

OVERVIEW MAP, REGIONAL MAPS, AND MAP LEGEND

Each hike's number appears on the overview map, opposite the table of contents; in the table of contents itself; at the beginning of each regional chapter, which has its own overview map and list of hikes; and in the hike profiles themselves. The regional maps provide more detail than the main overview map, bringing you closer to the hikes in that chapter. As you flip through the book, a hike's full profile is easy to locate by watching for the hike number at the top of each left-hand page.

A map legend that details the symbols found on the trail maps follows the table of contents, on page vii.

TRAIL MAPS

A detailed map of each hike's route appears with its profile. On each of these maps, symbols indicate the trailhead, the complete route, significant features, facilities, and topographic landmarks such as creeks, overlooks, and peaks. But despite the high quality of the maps in this guidebook, we strongly recommend that you always carry an additional map, such as the ones noted in each entry's Key Information listing for Maps.

ELEVATION PROFILES

In addition to a trail map, each hike description includes this graphical element. The elevation profile represents the rises and falls of the trail as viewed from the side, over the complete distance (in miles) of that trail. On the diagram's vertical axis, or height scale, the number of feet indicated between each tick mark helps you visualize the climb. To prevent flat hikes from looking steep (and vice versa), varying height scales provide an accurate image of each hike's climbing challenge.

THE HIKE PROFILE

Each hike contains a brief overview of the trail, a description of the route from start to finish, key at-a-glance information—from the trail's distance and configuration to contacts for local information—GPS trailhead coordinates, and directions for driving to the trailhead. Each profile also includes a map (see Trail Maps, previous page) and elevation profile (see above). Many hikes also include notes on nearby activities.

IN BRIEF

Think of this section as a taste of the trail, a snapshot focused on the historical landmarks, beautiful vistas, and other sights you may encounter on the hike.

KEY INFORMATION

The information in this box gives you a quick idea of the statistics and specifics of each hike.

DISTANCE & CONFIGURATION *Distance* notes the length of the hike round-trip, from start to finish. If the hike description includes options to shorten or extend the hike, those round-trip distances will also be factored here. *Configuration* defines the trail as a loop, an out-and-back (taking you in and out via the same route), a figure eight, a balloon (a loop with an out-and-back section), or some other layout.

DIFFICULTY The degree of effort that a typical hiker should expect on a given route. For simplicity, the trails are rated as *easy, moderate,* or *strenuous.*

SCENERY A short summary of the attractions offered by the hike and what to expect in terms of plant life, wildlife, natural wonders, and historical features.

EXPOSURE A quick check of how much sun you can expect on your shoulders during the hike.

TRAIL TRAFFIC Indicates how busy the trail might be on an average day. Trail traffic, of course, varies from day to day and season to season. Weekends typically see the most visitors.

TRAIL SURFACE Indicates whether the trail surface is paved, rocky, gravel, dirt, boardwalk, or a mixture of elements.

HIKING TIME How long it takes to hike the trail. A slow but steady hiker will average 2–3 miles an hour, depending on the terrain.

DRIVING DISTANCE Listed in miles from the southernmost intersection of I-15 and I-80. Not that you'd necessarily want to start from here every time, but the mileages should give you a good general estimate of travel times to the trailheads.

ELEVATION CHANGE This numerical range shows the elevation at the trailhead and the high or low point on the trail.

ACCESS Fees or permits required to hike the trail are detailed here and noted if there are none; always check ahead for the latest information, though. Trail-access hours are listed here as well.

MAPS Resources for maps, in addition to those in this guidebook, are listed here. (As previously noted, we recommend that you carry more than one map—and that you consult those maps before heading out on the trail.)

FACILITIES Alerts you to restrooms, water, picnic tables, and other basics at or near the trailhead.

WHEELCHAIR ACCESS Lets you know whether there are paved sections or other areas where one may safely use a wheelchair.

CONTACT Listed here are phone numbers and website addresses for checking trail conditions and gleaning other day-to-day information.

LOCATION Where you'll find the trailhead, either generally or specifically. Full street addresses are provided where applicable.

COMMENTS Here you'll find assorted nuggets of information that don't fit into any of the above categories, such as whether or not dogs are allowed on the trails.

DESCRIPTION

The heart of each hike. Here, the author provides a summary of the trail's essence and highlights any special traits the hike has to offer. The route is clearly outlined, including landmarks, side trips, and possible alternate routes along the way. Ultimately, the hike description will help you choose the hikes that are best for you.

NEARBY ACTIVITIES

Look here for information on things to do or points of interest: nearby parks, museums, restaurants, and the like. Note that not every hike has a listing.

DIRECTIONS

Used in conjunction with the GPS coordinates (see next section), the driving directions will help you locate each trailhead.

GPS TRAILHEAD COORDINATES

Along with the driving directions, the trailhead coordinates—the intersection of latitude (north) and longitude (west)—will orient you from the trailhead. In some cases, you can drive within viewing distance of a trailhead. Other hiking routes require a short walk to the trailhead from a parking area.

This guidebook presents latitude and longitude in degree–decimal minute format. For example, the GPS trailhead coordinates for Hike 1, Ben Lomond (page 18), are as follows:

N41° 19.236' W111° 53.933'

The latitude–longitude grid system is likely quite familiar to you, but here's a refresher:

Imaginary lines of latitude—called *parallels* and approximately 69 miles apart from each other—run horizontally around the globe. The equator is established to be 0°, and each parallel is indicated by degrees from the equator: up to 90°N at the North Pole, and down to 90°S at the South Pole.

Imaginary lines of longitude—called *meridians*—run perpendicular to latitude lines. Longitude lines are likewise indicated by degrees. Starting from 0° at the Prime Meridian in Greenwich, England, they continue to the east and west until they meet 180° later at the International Date Line in the Pacific Ocean. At the equator, longitude lines are also approximately 69 miles apart, but that distance narrows as the meridians converge toward the North and South Poles.

To convert GPS coordinates given in degrees, minutes, and seconds to degrees and decimal minutes, as shown above, divide the seconds by 60. For more on GPS technology, visit usgs.gov.

Topographic Maps

The maps in this book have been produced with great care and, used with the hike text, will direct you to the trail and help you stay on course. That said, you'll find superior detail and valuable information in the U.S. Geological Survey's 7.5-minute-series topographic maps (or topo maps for short). At mytopo.com, for example, you can view and print free USGS topos of the entire United States. Online services such as Trails.com charge annual fees for additional features such as shaded relief, which makes the topography stand out more. If you expect to print out many topo maps each year, it might be worth paying for such extras. The downside to USGS maps is that most are outdated, having been created 20–30 years ago; nevertheless, they provide excellent topographic detail. Of course, Google Earth (earth.google.com) does away with topo maps and their inaccuracies . . . replacing them with satellite imagery and its inaccuracies. Regardless, what one lacks, the other augments. Google Earth is an excellent tool whether you have difficulty with topos or not.

If you're new to hiking, you might be wondering, "What's a topo map?" In short, it indicates not only linear distance but elevation as well, using contour lines. These lines spread across the map like dozens of intricate spiderwebs. Each line represents a particular elevation, and at the base of each topo a contour's interval designation is given. If, for example, the contour interval is 20 feet, then the distance between each contour line is 20 feet. Follow five contour lines up on the same map, and the elevation has increased by 100 feet. In addition to the sources listed previously and in Appendixes A and B (see pages 278 and 279), you'll find topos at major universities, outdoors shops, and some public libraries, as well as online at national map.gov and store.usgs.gov.

Weather

Salt Lake City experiences a wide range of temperatures and climatic conditions in its dry, four-season climate. While weather is often the single most important factor in deciding when to enjoy any given hike, many of the 60 hikes in this book can be enjoyed year-round. Note, however, that most of the hikes in this guide lie within the Wasatch and Uinta mountain ranges, and during winter that means that trailheads are often inaccessible, trails are covered with snow, and avalanche dangers may be present.

Because many hikes in the Wasatch and Uintas are at a high elevation, you'll find that in their short season, some of them offer a great way to beat the heat on the valley floor. In general, the temperature decreases about 3–5° with every 1,000 feet of elevation gained.

The chart on the next page lists average temperatures and precipitation by month for Salt Lake City. For each month, "Hi Temp" is the average daytime high in degrees Fahrenheit, "Lo Temp" is the average nighttime low, and "Rain or Snow" is the average precipitation in inches.

MONTH	HI TEMP	LO TEMP	RAIN or SNOW	MONTH	HI TEMP	LO TEMP	RAIN or SNOW
JAN	37°F	20°F	1.4"	JUL	92°F	62°F	0.7"
FEB	43°F	24°F	1.3"	AUG	90°F	61°F	0.8"
MAR	52°F	31°F	1.9"	SEP	80°F	51°F	1.3"
APR	62°F	38°F	2.0"	OCT	66°F	40°F	1.6"
MAY	72°F	46°F	2.1"	NOV	50°F	30°F	1.4"
JUN	83°F	54°F	0.8"	DEC	39°F	22°F	1.2"

Source: USClimateData.com

Water

How much is enough? Well, one simple physiological fact should convince you to err on the side of excess when deciding how much water to pack: a hiker walking steadily in 90° heat needs approximately 10 quarts of fluid per day—that's 2.5 gallons.

A good rule of thumb is to hydrate prior to your hike, carry (and drink) 6 ounces of water for every mile you plan to hike, and hydrate again after the hike. For most people, the pleasures of hiking make carrying water a relatively minor price to pay to remain safe and healthy. So pack more water than you anticipate needing, even for short hikes.

If you find yourself tempted to drink found water, do so with extreme caution. Many ponds and lakes encountered by hikers are fairly stagnant, and the water tastes terrible. Drinking such water presents inherent risks for thirsty trekkers. Giardia parasites contaminate many water sources and cause the dreaded intestinal disturbance giardiasis, which can last for weeks after ingestion. For more information, check with the Centers for Disease Control and Prevention: cdc.gov/parasites/giardia.

In any case, effective treatment is essential before using any water source found along the trail. Boiling water for 2–3 minutes is always a safe measure for camping, but day hikers can consider iodine tablets, approved chemical mixes, filtration units rated for giardia, and UV filtration. Some of these methods (for example, filtration with an added carbon filter) remove bad tastes typical in stagnant water, while others add their own taste. As a precaution, carry some means of water purification to help in a pinch and if you realize that you've underestimated your consumption needs.

Clothing

Weather, unexpected trail conditions, fatigue, extended hiking duration, and wrong turns can individually or collectively turn a great outing into a very uncomfortable one at best—and a life-threatening one at worst. Thus, proper attire plays a key role in staying comfortable and, sometimes, in staying alive. Here are some helpful guidelines:

➤ **Choose silk, wool, or synthetics for maximum comfort in all of your hiking attire**—from hats to socks and in between. Cotton is fine if the weather remains dry and stable, but you won't be happy if that material gets wet.

➤ **Always wear a hat,** or at least tuck one into your day pack or hitch it to your belt. Hats offer all-weather sun and wind protection as well as warmth if it turns cold.

➤ **Be ready to layer up or down** as the day progresses and the mercury rises or falls. Today's outdoor wear makes layering easy, with such designs as jackets that convert to vests and pants with zip-off or button-up legs.

➤ **Wear hiking boots or sturdy hiking sandals with toe protection.** Flip-flopping along a paved urban greenway is one thing, but never hike a trail in open sandals or casual sneakers. Your bones and arches need support, and your skin needs protection.

➤ **Pair that footwear with good socks.** If you prefer not to sheathe your feet when wearing hiking sandals, tuck the socks into your day pack; you may need them if the weather plummets or if you hit rocky turf and pebbles begin to irritate your feet. Plus, in an emergency, you can adapt the socks into mittens in case you lose your gloves.

➤ **Don't leave rainwear behind,** even if the day dawns clear and sunny. Tuck into your day pack, or tie around your waist, a jacket that is breathable and either water-resistant or waterproof. Investigate different choices at your local outdoors retailer. If you're a frequent hiker, you'll ideally have more than one rainwear weight, material, and style in your closet to protect you in all seasons in your regional climate and hiking microclimates.

Essential Gear

Today you can buy outdoor vests that have up to 20 pockets shaped and sized to carry everything from toothpicks to binoculars. Or, if you don't aspire to feel like a burro, you can neatly stow all of these items in your day pack—none of these hikes should necessitate carrying much more than that (except perhaps a camera bag if you prefer a dedicated camera to a smartphone for taking pictures). The following list showcases don't-hike-without-them items, in alphabetical order, as all are important:

➤ **Extra clothes:** rain gear, wide-brim hat, gloves, and a change of socks and shirt.

➤ **Extra food:** trail mix, granola bars, or other high-energy foods.

➤ **Flashlight or headlamp** with extra bulb and batteries.

➤ **Insect repellent.** For some areas and seasons, this is vital.

➤ **Maps and a high-quality compass.** Even if you already know the terrain well and you have a GPS device or smartphone, don't leave home without these—digital devices have limited battery life, after all, so you shouldn't rely on them exclusively on the trail. If you're also using GPS, double-check its guidance against that of your maps and compass. If you're using your phone rather than a dedicated GPS unit, turn off Wi-Fi, data syncing, and roaming to extend battery life on the trail; if your phone has a removable battery, bring a spare just in case.

➤ **Pocketknife and/or multitool.**

➤ **Sunblock.** Be sure to check the expiration date on the container.

➤ **Water.** As we emphasize more than once, it's prudent to bring more than you think you'll drink. Depending on your destination, you may want to bring a container and iodine or a filter for purifying water in case you run out.

➤ **Whistle.** This little gadget could be your best friend in an emergency.

➤ **Windproof matches and/or a lighter,** as well as a fire starter.

First Aid Kit

In addition to the aforementioned items, the ones that follow may seem daunting to bring along for a day hike. But any paramedic will tell you that the products listed here—in alphabetical order, because all are important—are just the basics. The reality of hiking is that you can be out for a week of backpacking and acquire only a mosquito bite. Or you can hike for an hour, slip, and suffer a bleeding abrasion or broken bone. Fortunately, these listed items collapse into a very small space. Convenient prepackaged kits are also available at your pharmacy or online.

➤ **Adhesive bandages**

➤ **Antibiotic ointment** (Neosporin or the generic equivalent)

➤ **Athletic tape**

➤ **Blister kit** (such as Moleskin/Spenco 2nd Skin)

➤ **Butterfly-closure bandages**

➤ **Diphenhydramine (Benadryl or generic),** in case of allergic reactions

➤ **Elastic bandages or joint wraps**

➤ **Epinephrine in a prefilled syringe (EpiPen),** typically by prescription only, for people known to have severe allergic reactions to hiking mishaps such as bee stings

➤ **Gauze** (one roll and a half-dozen 4-by-4-inch pads)

➤ **Hydrogen peroxide or iodine**

➤ **Ibuprofen (Advil) or acetaminophen (Tylenol)**

Note: Consider your intended terrain and the number of hikers in your party before you exclude any article cited above. A botanical-garden stroll may not inspire you to carry a complete kit, but anything beyond that warrants precaution. When hiking alone, you should always be prepared for a medical need. And if you are a twosome or with a group, one or more people in your party should be equipped with first aid material. It's also important that anyone who has any allergies or prescription medication needs (including dosages), to make sure that information is known or accessible to other members of your hiking group.

General Safety

The following tips may have the familiar ring of your mother's voice as you take note of them.

➤ **Let someone know where you'll be hiking and how long you expect to be gone.** Give that person a copy of your route, particularly if you're headed into an isolated area. Let him or her know when you return.

➤ **Sign in and out of any trail registers provided.** Don't hesitate to comment on the trail condition if space is provided; that's your opportunity to alert others to any problems you encounter.

➤ **Don't count on a cell phone for your safety.** Reception may be spotty or nonexistent on the trail, even on an urban walk—especially one embraced by towering trees.

➤ **Always carry food and water, even for a short hike.** And again, bring more water than you think you'll need.

➤ **Ask questions.** Public-land employees are on hand to help.

➤ **Stay on designated trails.** Even on the most clearly marked trails, you usually reach a point where you have to stop and consider in which direction to head. If you become disoriented, don't panic. As soon as you think you may be off-track, stop, assess your current direction, and then retrace your steps to the point where you went astray. Using a map, a compass, and this book, and keeping in mind what you have passed thus far, reorient yourself and trust your judgment on which way to continue. If you become absolutely unsure of how to continue, return to your vehicle the way you came in. Should you become completely lost and have no idea how to find the trailhead, remaining in place along the trail and waiting for help is most often the best option for adults and always the best option for children.

➤ **Always carry a whistle,** a precaution that we can't overemphasize. It could be a lifesaver if you get lost or hurt.

➤ **Be especially careful when crossing streams.** Whether you're fording the stream or crossing on a log, make every step count. If you're unsure whether you can maintain your balance on a log, ford the stream instead: use a trekking pole or stout stick for balance, and *face upstream as you cross.*

9

If a stream seems too deep to ford, don't chance it—whatever is on the other side isn't worth the risk.

➤ **Be careful at overlooks.** While these areas may provide spectacular views, they're potentially hazardous. Stay back from the edge of outcrops, and make absolutely sure of your footing; a misstep could mean a nasty or possibly fatal fall.

➤ **Standing dead trees and storm-damaged living trees pose a significant hazard to hikers.** These trees may have loose or broken limbs that could fall at any time. While walking beneath trees, and when choosing a spot to rest or enjoy your snack, *look up.*

➤ **Know the symptoms of subnormal body temperature, or hypothermia.** Shivering and forgetfulness are the two most common indicators of this stealthy killer. Hypothermia can occur at any elevation, even in the summer, especially when the hiker is wearing lightweight cotton clothing. If symptoms develop, seek shelter, hot liquids, and dry clothes as soon as possible.

➤ **Likewise, know the symptoms of heat exhaustion, or hyperthermia.** Lightheadedness and weakness are the first two indicators. If you feel these symptoms, find some shade, drink some water, remove as many layers of clothing as practical, and stay put until you cool down. Marching through heat exhaustion leads to heatstroke—which can be fatal. If you should be sweating and you're not, that's the signature warning sign. Your hike is over at that point: heatstroke is a life-threatening condition that can cause seizures, convulsions, and eventually death. If you or a hiking partner is experiencing heatstroke, do whatever you can to get cool and find help.

In summary: Plan ahead. Watch your step. Avoid accidents before they happen.

Flora and Fauna Precautions

Hikers should remain aware of the following concerns regarding plant life and wildlife, described in alphabetical order.

BLACK BEARS Though attacks by black bears—the only ursine species found in Utah—are uncommon, the sight or approach of a bear can give anyone a start. If you encounter a bear while hiking, remain calm and avoid running. Make loud noises to scare off the bear, and back away slowly. In primitive and remote areas, assume bears are present; in more-developed sites, check on the current bear situation prior to hiking. Most encounters are food-related, as bears have an exceptional sense of smell and not particularly discriminating tastes. While this is of greater concern to backpackers and campers, day hikers who want to enjoy a lunchtime picnic or munch on an energy bar on the trail should likewise remain aware and alert.

BLACK FLIES Though certainly annoying, black flies aren't dangerous: the worst they'll cause is an itchy welt. They are most active mid-May–June, during the day,

Lightning and Avalanches

These are the two most deadly natural hazards in Utah. The best way—the only way, really—to protect yourself from them is to avoid the areas and conditions under which they're most likely to occur. Always observe posted warnings, check weather advisories, watch local conditions, and use a healthy dose of common sense before venturing into the backcountry.

Though most summer hikes in the Wasatch take place in favorable weather under cloud-free skies, there's always a chance of an afternoon thunderstorm rolling in. If you see a storm approaching, or if you can see lightning or hear thunder, the risk of a life-threatening lightning strike is already elevated. Especially loud and frequent thunder means that electrical activity is approaching, increasing the risk of lightning injury or death. If the time delay between seeing the lightning and hearing the thunder is less than 30 seconds, you're in danger.

No place is absolutely safe from a lightning strike, but some places are safer than others. Seek covered shelter as quickly as possible. Avoid being on or near ridgelines, mountain peaks, exposed slopes, open fields, isolated trees, communications towers, ski lift supports, metal fences, or water.

While climbers, backcountry skiers, and snowmobilers are the most likely avalanche victims in Utah, snowshoers and recreational hikers can also be at risk. Avalanches can occur on any slope given the right snow conditions, but they're most likely to occur in areas where they've occurred in the past, particularly near steep, barren slopes and in the presence of avalanche-scarred terrain. Hikers should observe avalanche warnings and check local advisories before entering the backcountry in winter.

and especially before thunderstorms, as well as during the morning and evening hours. Insect repellent has some effect, but the only reliable way to keep out of the pests' swarming midst is to keep moving.

MOOSE Sightings of moose in Wasatch meadows and canyon drainages are common and generally quite enjoyable—indeed, they make for a great photo op. While moose aren't aggressive, they may charge if they perceive a threat, so never approach or engage a moose.

MOSQUITOES Utah has seen an uptick in cases of West Nile virus in recent years, so hikers should take care to avoid getting bitten by mosquitoes. Late spring and summer are peak mosquito season in Utah. If you plan to hike in an area where these pests are likely be present (read: anywhere close to water), use an insect repellent with DEET, picaridin, oil of lemon eucalyptus, or IR 3535 as the active ingredient.

MOUNTAIN LIONS As more people get into the outdoors and encroach upon wildlife habitat, human encounters with mountain lions (aka cougars or pumas) are bound to increase. Although sightings are extremely rare, these elusive big cats live throughout the Wasatch and Uinta Mountains.

Mountain lions are unlikely to attack adult humans, but in the event of an encounter, make yourself as big and loud as you can: growl, bare your teeth, raise your arms, and fan out your jacket. Act threatening, but also try to give the mountain lion an escape path. Never crouch down or turn your back on the animal, and don't approach it. Don't run away—that can trigger the cat's instinct to chase. Make noise, yell, and throw rocks or anything else you can grab without bending over. Lastly, if you have young children with you, keep them close and even lift them onto your shoulders if you can.

If you're attacked, try to remain standing, as mountain lions will try to bite the neck or head. *Always* try to fight back.

POISON IVY, OAK, AND SUMAC Recognizing and avoiding these plants are the most effective ways to prevent the painful, itchy rashes associated with them. Poison ivy (*bottom left*) occurs as a vine or ground cover, 3 leaflets to a leaf; poison oak (*bottom center*) occurs as either a vine or shrub, also with 3 leaflets; and poison sumac (*bottom right*) flourishes in swampland, each leaf having 7–13 leaflets. Urushiol, the oil in these plants, is responsible for the rash.

Usually within 12–14 hours of exposure (but sometimes much later), raised lines and/or blisters will appear, accompanied by a terrible itch. Try not to scratch, as bacteria under your fingernails can cause an infection and scratching can spread the rash to other parts of your body. Wash and dry the rash thoroughly, and then apply calamine lotion or a similar treatment. If itching or blistering is severe, seek medical attention.

If you knowingly touch poison ivy, oak, or sumac, you have a window of about 15–20 minutes to remove the oil before it causes a reaction. Rinsing it off immediately with cool water (hot water spreads it) is best but impractical on the trail; that said, commercial products such as Tecnu are effective at removing urushiol from your skin. To keep from spreading the misery to someone else, wash not only any exposed parts of your body but also any oil-contaminated clothes, hiking gear, or pets.

Photo: Tom Watson

Photo: Jane Huber

Photo: Norman Tomalin/Alamy Stock Photo

SNAKES Rattlesnakes, cottonmouths, copperheads, and coral snakes are among the most common venomous snakes in the United States, and they typically hibernate October–April. Rattlesnakes like to bask in the sun and won't bother you if you don't bother them.

Rattlesnakes are common on and near trails in the Salt Lake City area, but the ones you'll most likely see while hiking are nonvenomous species and subspecies. The best advice is to leave all snakes alone, giving them a wide berth as you pass, and make sure that all of your hiking companions (including dogs) do the same.

When hiking, stick to well-used trails, and wear over-the-ankle boots and loose-fitting long pants. Don't step or put your hands where you can't see them, and avoid wandering around in the dark. Step *onto* logs and rocks, never *over* them, and be especially careful when climbing rocks. Avoid walking through dense brush or willow thickets.

Photo: Robert Mutch/Shutterstock

TICKS These arachnids are often found on brush and tall grass, where they wait to hitch a ride on a warm-blooded passerby. Adult ticks are most active April–May and again October–November. Among the varieties of ticks, the black-legged tick, commonly called the deer tick, is the primary carrier of Lyme disease.

Wearing light-colored clothing helps you spot ticks before they bite and embed themselves. Insect repellent containing DEET is an effective deterrent. Most important, inspect yourself visually at the end of a hike: check your hair, the back of your neck, your armpits, and your socks.

During your posthike shower, take a moment to do a more complete body check. Use tweezers to remove ticks that have already attached themselves: grasp the tick close to your skin, and remove it by pulling straight out firmly. Do your best to remove the head, but don't twist. Apply disinfectant solution to the wound.

Hunting

A variety of rules, regulations, and licenses governs Utah's hunting types and related seasons. Though hikers generally won't run into problems, they may wish to forgo venturing out during the big-game seasons, when the woods suddenly seem to fill with orange and camouflage.

In Utah, archery hunting season begins in mid-August and firearm hunting season begins as early as mid-September. For more information, visit wildlife.utah .gov (click "Hunting" at the top of the page).

Trail Etiquette

Always treat the trail, wildlife, and your fellow hikers with respect. Below are a few reminders.

➤ **Plan ahead in order to be self-sufficient at all times.** For example, carry necessary supplies for changes in weather or other conditions.

➤ **Hike on open trails only.** In seasons or construction areas where road or trail closures may be a possibility, use the websites and phone numbers in the Contacts line for each of this guidebook's hikes to check conditions before you head out. And do not attempt to circumvent such closures.

➤ **Avoid trespassing on private land,** and obtain all permits and authorization as required. Also, leave gates as you find them or as directed by signage.

➤ **Be courteous to other hikers,** bikers, equestrians, and others you encounter on the trails.

➤ **Never spook wild animals or pets.** An unannounced approach, a sudden movement, or a loud noise startles most critters, and a surprised animal can be dangerous to you, to others, and to itself. Give animals plenty of space.

➤ **Observe the YIELD signs around the region's trailheads and backcountry.** Typically they advise hikers to yield to horses and bikers to both horses and hikers. Per common courtesy on hills, hikers and bikers yield to any uphill traffic. When they encounter mounted riders or horsepackers, hikers may courteously step off the trail, on the downhill side if possible. So that the horse can see and hear you, calmly greet the rider before he or she reaches you, and don't dart behind trees. Also, don't pet horses unless invited to do so.

➤ **Stay on the existing trail, and don't blaze any new trails.**

➤ **Pack out what you pack in, leaving only your footprints.** No one wants to see the trash that someone else has left behind.

Tips for Enjoying Salt Lake City Hikes

Salt Lake City is growing quickly, as is its outdoors scene. As a result, weekends can be hectic in the canyons east of the city—namely Mill Creek, Big Cottonwood, and Little Cottonwood—so consider some of the quieter, farther-afield hikes on weekend days when the weather is particularly pleasant.

In tandem with the minor inconveniences, the growing number of Salt Lake hikers also comes with enormous benefits. The social component of hiking in this city is stronger than ever. Social media groups abound to connect hikers of every skill level to each other, but for those who eschew social media, rest assured that Salt Lake City is extremely friendly and welcoming, so don't be afraid to reach out and connect with other hikers you meet on the trail—and don't be surprised when they reach out and connect with you.

During the winter, thermal inversion layers can form in the valley and trap smog, sometimes for weeks at a time. The inversion layers can go as high as 7,000 feet; thus, in order to escape the choking smog, you'll need to get to a higher altitude. The areas above the inversion layers usually have snow throughout the winter, and snowshoeing can be a wonderful way to enjoy Utah in the wintertime. In winter it's common to have dreary gray skies in the valley but blue skies, full sun, and even warmer temperatures at the higher elevations.

Finally, note that some public lands covered in this book—namely Mirror Lake Scenic Byway and American Fork Canyon—charge entrance/day-use fees that are waived for holders of an **America the Beautiful National Parks and Federal Recreation Lands Pass** ($80 for an annual standard pass or a lifetime Senior Pass). While you might not recoup the cost of the pass just through visits to these two areas, there are also six national parks within a 5-hour drive of the city, so the pass could potentially be a worthwhile investment if you love to hike. For more information, see doi.gov/tourists/get-a-pass, store.usgs.gov/pass, or recreation.gov/pass; the pass is also available through **REI** (rei.com/c/park-passes).

Uinta peaks tower over the valleys below.

NORTH
(Weber County)

Fall colors begin to dot the southern slope of Ben Lomond.

BEN LOMOND HAS the longest, most gentle gradient of any summit trail in the Wasatch. Along the way you're treated to continuous and commanding views in all directions, with a diverse range of vegetation and wildlife.

DESCRIPTION

The best known of the northern Wasatch peaks dominates the skyline over North Ogden. An early pioneer named the peak Ben Lomond because it reminded her of the mountain of the same name in her native Scotland. Years later, W. W. Hodkinson, one of Hollywood's first motion picture moguls, drew inspiration from Ben Lomond when he founded Paramount Pictures in 1914. Hodkinson—who had opened one of America's first movie theaters in Ogden just seven years earlier—designed the studio's iconic logo of a towering, snowcapped peak.

Several routes lead to the Ben Lomond summit, but the North Skyline Trail (which is also a section of the Great Western Trail; see Hike 33, page 155) offers a particularly scenic and varied ascent. Although the North Skyline Trail is a bit longer than the other trails that ascend from the east, it's well traveled, it's reliable, and it offers a wider variety of views along the route, to both the east and west.

From the North Ogden Divide trailhead, cross North Ogden Canyon Road and start making your way up a series of 12 sweeping switchbacks that lead up the north

DISTANCE & CONFIGURATION: 16.4-mile out-and-back

DIFFICULTY: Strenuous

SCENERY: Views of Ogden Valley and Great Salt Lake along the ridgeline, with panoramic views from the summit

EXPOSURE: Partially shaded to saddle, unshaded from saddle to summit

TRAIL TRAFFIC: Light

TRAIL SURFACE: Dirt with rock near summit

HIKING TIME: 8–9 hours

DRIVING DISTANCE: 52 miles from I-15/ I-80 intersection

ELEVATION CHANGE: 6,180'–9,716'

ACCESS: Daily, sunrise–sunset; no fees or permits

MAPS: USGS *North Ogden*

FACILITIES: Restrooms at trailhead but no water

WHEELCHAIR ACCESS: None

CONTACT: 801-625-5112, fs.usda.gov/uwcnf

LOCATION: North Ogden Canyon Road, North Ogden, UT 84404

COMMENTS: Dogs allowed on leash. Be aware that this is a long, dry trail, so make sure to come prepared with plenty of water, food, and sun protection.

side of the mountain over the course of 2.5 miles. As you ascend through a dense cover of Gambel oak, maple, and curly-leaf mountain mahogany, watch out for rattlesnakes, which often enjoy sunning themselves on the south-facing trail.

Beyond the switchbacks, you'll enter a long traverse along the ridge's eastern slope where aspens, bent by heavy snow accumulation, continually lean to the east. This section of trail leads through deer brush (a mountain shrub found throughout the West) and offers generous views of Ogden Valley to the east. Soon the trail enters mature stands of fir and spruce that provide some shade. Along this ridge you'll have views stretching from Morgan County in the south to 9,979-foot Naomi Peak near the Idaho border in the north.

At 4.2 miles from the trailhead and an elevation of 8,240 feet, the trail crosses to the west side of the ridge and yields your first view of the Ben Lomond summit to the northwest. The trail continues straight ahead (northwest) for another 2.3 miles, gaining just over 500 feet in elevation on slopes blanketed with deer brush and dotted with limber pine.

Arriving at the Bailey Springs Trail junction, known locally as just "the saddle," you'll find a large wooden sign with a map showing other trails on the mountain, trail distances, and various points of interest. From this saddle the trail continues to the northwest with the summit in clear view. You're most likely to see mountain goats on rocky slopes at these higher elevations. Above the windswept saddle, krummholz pine and subalpine fir dot the grassy slopes, along with lupine.

In the remaining 1.5 miles and 900 vertical feet to the summit, the trail steepens somewhat, but never enough to become grueling. The final summit approach is accomplished with a well-crafted chain of 28 short switchbacks through outcrops of quartzite, slate, and schist. The well-established trail will take you directly to the summit without your ever having to scramble, boulder-hop, or bushwhack.

Ben Lomond

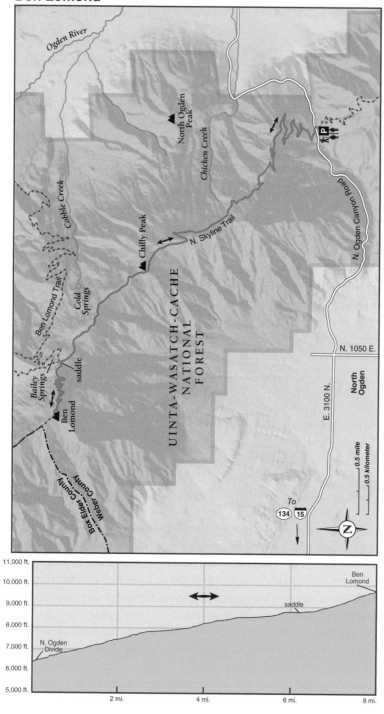

At the 9,712-foot summit, the views stretch out in all directions, with Willard Bay and the Great Salt Lake being the dominant features to the west. Directly to your north is Willard Peak, which at 9,764 feet is the highest point in Weber County and a tad higher than Ben Lomond—a fact that comes as a surprise to many hikers. A straightforward traverse along a trail to the north can lead you on to Willard Peak, adding several hours to an already long day.

Ben Lomond is a classic northern Utah climb: thoroughly enjoyable, yet very different from the southern Wasatch peaks with their high-elevation trailheads and canyon approaches. On the long descent, come prepared with enough water to keep you hydrated. The afternoon sun beats down on the dry, unshaded, south-facing switchbacks that return you to the trailhead.

NEARBY ACTIVITIES

The **Ogden Nature Center** (966 W. 12th St.; 801-621-7595, ogdennaturecenter.org) is a 152-acre wildlife sanctuary and education center. The land is home to mule deer, pheasants, fox, and migrating birds. More than 1.5 miles of walking trails make the sanctuary and ponds accessible. The visitor center features hands-on exhibits, an observation beehive, and The Nest gift shop, with nature-related gifts for all ages.

• •

GPS TRAILHEAD COORDINATES N41° 19.236' W111° 53.933'

DIRECTIONS From the intersection of I-84 and I-15 north of Salt Lake City, drive north on I-15 for 8.7 miles. Take Exit 349 (UT 134/Farr West/Pleasant View), and turn right onto UT 134 South/West 2700 North. Drive 4 miles, during which West 2700 North becomes East 2600 North. Turn left onto North 1050 East, and drive 0.7 mile; then turn right onto East 3100 North, and drive 0.5 mile. East 3100 North becomes North Ogden Canyon Road; continue 2.5 miles to the North Ogden Divide trailhead parking area, on the right.

Waterfowl and spring blossoms bedeck the Ogden River.

THE OGDEN RIVER originates in Ogden Canyon, cuts through Ogden, and flows west toward the Great Salt Lake. Along the way, the Ogden River Parkway connects many of Ogden's most popular parks and recreational venues. The parkway currently extends 3.4 miles, but the most scenic and enjoyable section is the first 1.4 miles, from the mouth of Ogden Canyon to the Ogden Botanical Gardens.

DESCRIPTION

As it emerges from the mouth of Ogden Canyon, the Ogden River still thinks it's a mountain stream. It tumbles and careens off large boulders, its banks lined with the quaking aspens and bigtooth maples common to mountain tributaries. But as it enters the city limits, the river becomes more urban. Its pace slows, and the boulders give way to dirt banks. Towering cottonwoods—characteristic of desert streams—replace the aspens and maples. The Ogden River Parkway parallels the river and captures the transformation.

The best place to start a walk along the parkway is at the canyon-mouth trailhead, across the street from Rainbow Gardens, an Ogden resort and recreation area since 1895. Because there's no parking at the trailhead, you may want to park your car in the large parking lot at Rainbow Gardens, stop by the gift shop for water and

DISTANCE & CONFIGURATION: 6.8-mile out-and-back (recommended section: 4-mile out-and-back)

DIFFICULTY: Easy

SCENERY: River, parks, and mountain views

EXPOSURE: Mostly shaded

TRAIL TRAFFIC: Moderate

TRAIL SURFACE: Asphalt

HIKING TIME: 1–2 hours

DRIVING DISTANCE: 38 miles from I-15/ I-80 intersection

ELEVATION CHANGE: 4,432' at trailhead, with no significant rise

ACCESS: Daily, 1 hour before sunrise–1 hour after sunset; no fees or permits

MAPS: USGS *Ogden*

FACILITIES: Restrooms, water, and other services at trailhead and at various parks along the way

WHEELCHAIR ACCESS: Yes

CONTACT: 801-629-8284, ogdencity.com /461/Parks

LOCATION: Park Boulevard just north of Valley Drive, Ogden, UT 84404

COMMENTS: Dogs are permitted on leash, but skateboarding, horses, and motorized vehicles are not. Bicycle speed limit is 10 mph.

trail snacks, and use the restrooms. Hikers are asked to park in the southwest corner of the parking lot, by the Rainbow trailhead.

Though officially designated as a multiuse trail, the Ogden River Parkway prohibits skateboards and horses. In addition, bicycles have a 10-mph speed limit, which encourages more avid and aggressive cyclists to go elsewhere.

For the first 0.3 mile, the trail is pinned between the river on the right and Park Boulevard on the left. Then the street diverges from the trail, while the path continues to hug the river. The trail stays close to the river throughout, providing frequent opportunities to access the water.

The trail's upper portion maintains a playful, parklike, recreational feel. For the first 2.5 miles, until the parkway crosses Washington Boulevard (US 89), the trail and river link a continuous series of parks, playgrounds, sports fields, George S. Eccles Dinosaur Park, a skateboard park, a rodeo arena, El Monte Golf Course, and Ogden Botanical Gardens.

Park benches every 100 feet or so provide plenty of opportunities to sit and enjoy the river or take a break for a picnic. The string of parks and recreation areas also offers easy access to drinking water and restrooms along the asphalt trail.

At 1 mile from the trailhead, the trail forks—stay to the right, on the river side. At 1.4 miles, you'll arrive at the beautiful Ogden Botanical Gardens. Here you'll have access to water, a public phone, restrooms, and a covered picnic area, making it an ideal spot to stop for a rest, enjoy the gardens, have a picnic, or start back to the trailhead.

If you decide to continue beyond the botanical gardens, the river slows and the parkway takes on a more run-down feeling, passing junkyards, brickyards, old motels, and public storage units. Although the trail remains close to the river, it's often bound by a fence on both sides. The trail finally crosses over a large railroad yard at the 20th Street Bridge, continues around the 21st Street Pond, and then joins

Ogden River Parkway

UINTA-WASATCH-CACHE NATIONAL FOREST

To Ogden

39

0.2 mile
0.2 kilometer

Ogden Canyon Road

Park Boulevard

Valley Drive

Harrison Boulevard

203

203

Ogden River

Ogden Botanical Gardens

Jackson Avenue

39

Monroe Boulevard

Gramercy Avenue

Rodeo Grounds

20th Street

21st Street

24th Street

12th Street

89

Washington Boulevard

89

204

Wall Avenue

204

17th Street

104

53

39

Ogden River

Weber River

4,700 ft.
4,600 ft.
4,500 ft.
4,400 ft.
4,300 ft.
4,200 ft.
4,100 ft.

Washington Boulevard

0.5 mi.   1 mi.   1.5 mi.   2 mi.   2.5 mi.   3 mi.

the Weber River Parkway at the confluence of the Ogden and Weber Rivers in a scenic, shaded setting. The distance from the trailhead to the 20th Street Bridge is 3.4 miles one-way, but you'll find most of the trail's vibrancy and scenic enjoyment in the first 2 miles, making the Botanical Gardens a recommended turnaround point.

The Ogden River merges with the Weber River just east of I-15 and flows another 10 miles, flattening into a wetlands delta that empties into the Great Salt Lake. At the Ogden River Parkway trailhead, hikers can also easily connect with the Bonneville Shoreline Trail for access to some of Mount Ogden's most popular trails.

NEARBY ACTIVITIES

The **Ogden Botanical Gardens** are on the Ogden River Parkway, 1.4 miles downriver (west) from the trailhead at 1750 Monroe Blvd. (801-399-8080, ogdenbotanical gardens.org). An extension program of Utah State University, the gardens, open year-round, feature more than 11 acres of landscaped grounds and facilities for weddings and large group events.

• •

GPS TRAILHEAD COORDINATES N41° 14.202' W111° 55.773'

DIRECTIONS From the intersection of I-84 and I-15 north of Salt Lake City, drive north on I-15 for 3.1 miles; then take Exit 343 for UT 104 East/21st St. Keep right and merge onto UT 104 East, drive 1.8 miles, and then use the middle lane to turn left onto Wall Avenue. After 0.1 mile, turn right onto 20th Street, and drive 1.6 miles. Turn left onto Harrison Boulevard, and drive 0.7 mile. Turn right onto Canyon Road/UT 39, and drive 0.9 mile. Turn right onto Valley Drive; then enter the Rainbow Gardens parking lot, to the left. The trailhead is across the street, at the corner of Valley Drive and Park Boulevard (1900 East).

The Mount Ogden summit viewed from Porky Cirque

Photo: Greg Witt

YOU'LL GAIN MOST of your elevation on the gondola ride, which tops out near a glacial cirque. From here, it's just 20 minutes to the ridgeline. A faint trail follows the ridgeline to the summit, offering sweeping views in all directions.

DESCRIPTION

As with many of Utah's ski resorts, Snowbasin has an appeal that extends far beyond ski season. Summer is a great time to play in the mountains and take advantage of a beautiful setting with available resort features. The same slopes that challenged skiers in the downhill and super-G events at the 2002 Olympic Winter Games test the skills of hikers and mountain bikers in the summer.

You can climb to Mount Ogden's summit from Beus Canyon or Malans Basin on its western slopes. You can also start at the base of the Snowbasin Resort and hike your way up through slopes of Douglas-fir and white fir, although much of the route takes you along resort service roads (4 miles one-way from the resort to the summit).

By riding the gondola to Needles Lodge at 8,710 feet, you can hike to the summit and back in a little more than 2 hours and still have time for mountain biking, an afternoon round of disc golf, or a mountain picnic. The hike to the summit from Needles Lodge is also a good choice for families or less experienced hikers who want to reach a recognizable summit on a trail that matches their experience levels.

DISTANCE & CONFIGURATION: 3.1-mile out-and-back

DIFFICULTY: Easy

SCENERY: Glacial bowl, ridgeline, and great views on all sides

EXPOSURE: No shade

TRAIL TRAFFIC: Moderate

TRAIL SURFACE: Dirt, rock

HIKING TIME: 2–2.5 hours

DRIVING DISTANCE: 44 miles from I-15/I-80 intersection

ELEVATION CHANGE: 8,710'–9,572'

ACCESS: Hike lies on U.S. Forest Service land accessed through Snowbasin Resort. You must buy a ticket to ride the gondola to Needles

Lodge: open June–early October, Saturday and Sunday, 10 a.m.–6 p.m.; rates are $14 adults, $10 ages 7–17, free for children age 6 and younger. Call or check online for the latest information.

MAPS: USGS *Snowbasin, Ogden*

FACILITIES: Restrooms, water, phones, equipment rentals, dining, and shopping at the base in Grizzly Center and at Earl's Lodge; restrooms, water, and phones at Needles Lodge

WHEELCHAIR ACCESS: The trail is not wheelchair accessible, but the gondola is.

CONTACT: 801-620-1000, snowbasin.com

LOCATION: 3925 E. Snowbasin Rd., Huntsville, UT 84317

COMMENTS: Dogs prohibited

During summer the gondola operates Saturday and Sunday; if you hike up, you can ride down at no charge.

The gondola achieves 2,310 feet of vertical lift in about 1.7 miles. In summer, the leisurely ride takes about 18 minutes, in ski season about 15 minutes. After the gondola reaches Needles Lodge, exit the platform and turn left, following the signs that lead you to the Needles Loop Trail and the Cirque Practice Loop to the southwest. You will take the Cirque Practice Loop to the right.

At 0.2 mile from Needles Lodge on the Cirque Practice Loop, you'll see a sign pointing to the Needles Cirque Trail to the ridge. Here you depart the mountain bike trail for a footpath. Follow this faint trail as it switchbacks up this grassy cirque to the ridge. Deer frequently graze in this cirque, and a large patch of snow often remains until midsummer.

Once at the 9,062-foot saddle, you'll enjoy views down Beus Canyon to your west, beyond Hill Air Force Base and stretching far beyond the Great Salt Lake. Mount Ogden lies along the ridgeline to the north and can be recognized by the communications towers on its summit. At this saddle, three unnamed peaks, or knolls, compose the ridgeline between you and the Mount Ogden summit.

A faint trail follows a gentle contour along the western slopes of these first two knolls. Below, you'll see the Beus Canyon Trail winding its way up the dry slopes. Along this part of the trail, you'll be hiking on slopes covered with sage and dotted with an occasional limber pine or subalpine fir. Rattlesnakes frequently bask in the sun on this section of trail, so keep your eyes wide open.

After you round the second knoll, the faint trail has all but vanished. You have two options at this point: drop to a lower visible trail to the left of the third knoll, or ascend the sage slope, crossing over the saddle on the south of the third knoll and

Mount Ogden (via Snowbasin Gondola)

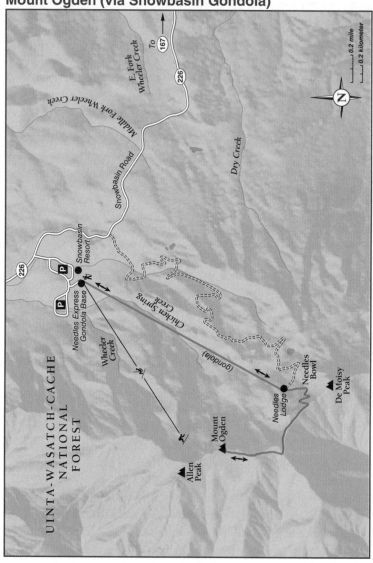

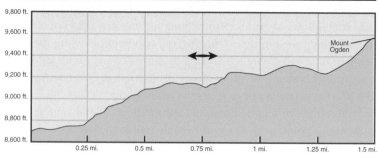

arriving at the saddle to the south of Mount Ogden from the east. Most hikers favor crossing the saddle at this point. As you descend the eastern slope of this third knoll, you arrive at a service road and a concrete bunker that shields some propane tanks.

From here, follow the steep service road that leads to the summit. At 0.2 mile along the service road, take a marked foot trail to your right that ascends the rocky slope to capture the summit. On the 9,572-foot summit, you'll be just a few feet higher than the helipad to your west. You'll have great views in all directions, with some wonderful direct views of Ben Lomond peak to the north and Pineview Reservoir to the east.

NEARBY ACTIVITIES

Snowbasin's summer offerings include an 18-hole disc-golf course and 25 miles of hiking and mountain-biking trails. Special events include moonlit gondola rides and star parties, summer concerts, guided mountain-bike rides and races, outdoor learning excursions, and award-winning dining. Call 801-620-1000 or visit snowbasin .com for events and schedules.

· ·

GPS TRAILHEAD COORDINATES
Needles Gondola Base: N41° 12.945' W111° 51.438'
Needles Lodge: N41° 11.617' W111° 52.440'

DIRECTIONS From the southernmost intersection of I-80 and I-15 in Salt Lake City, drive north on I-15 for 19 miles. Take Exit 324 to continue onto US 89 North in South Ogden, and drive 10.7 miles. Turn right and merge onto I-84 East toward Morgan/Evanston, and drive 4.3 miles. Take Exit 92 for UT 167/Mountain Green/Huntsville, and turn left to cross under I-84; then immediately turn right onto UT 167 North, and drive 1.5 miles. Turn left to stay on UT 167 North, and drive 5.5 miles. Turn left onto UT 226 West, and drive about 3 miles; then turn left to drive into the main Snowbasin parking area. The Needles Gondola departs from the area in front of Grizzly Center.

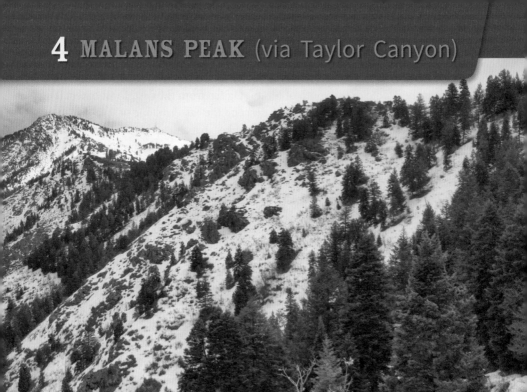

Malans Peak offers ample snowshoeing during the winter.

IN JUST UNDER 2.5 miles, you go from city neighborhoods to brushy bench to a deep canyon and spring-fed creek. Ascending the steep slope, you're rewarded with one of the best views in the area.

DESCRIPTION

It could be argued that Malans Peak isn't so much a peak as it is a rocky outcrop in the foothills of Mount Ogden's western slopes. But the commanding views and the wooded trail leading up the northern slope make this a satisfying hike and a worthwhile destination. You can most easily reach Malans Peak from Taylor Canyon, the large canyon on the north side of Mount Ogden, starting just south of the east end of 29th Street in Ogden.

The peak was named for Bartholomew "Tim" Malan, a prominent Ogdenite. In 1892, Malan and his family carved a road up Taylor Canyon, where they built Malan Heights Resort in the basin between Malans Peak and Mount Ogden. Malan hauled visitors to the hotel in a wagon with a trailing "poke stick" to keep it from rolling backward. Guests received panoramic views, lodging, and meals (including steak) for $6 a week. The hotel burned down in 1906.

Taylor Canyon, which leads to the Malans Peak Trail, is easily accessed from the 29th Street trailhead, which is also a popular access point for Gib's Loop (formerly

DISTANCE & CONFIGURATION: 5-mile out-and-back

DIFFICULTY: Moderate

SCENERY: Deep canyon, natural spring, exceptional views

EXPOSURE: Mostly shaded above bench

TRAIL TRAFFIC: Bench trails are busy; trail from Taylor Canyon to Malans Peak is uncrowded

TRAIL SURFACE: Dirt, rock

HIKING TIME: 2–3 hours

DRIVING DISTANCE: 36 miles from I-15/I-80 intersection

ELEVATION CHANGE: 4,780'–6,980'

ACCESS: Daily, sunrise–sunset; no fees or permits

MAPS: USGS *Ogden*

FACILITIES: Restrooms and water available late spring–early fall

WHEELCHAIR ACCESS: None

CONTACT: 801-625-5112, fs.usda.gov/uwcnf

LOCATION: Buchanan Avenue just south of 29th Street, Ogden, UT 84403

COMMENTS: Dogs allowed on leash

known as the Mount Ogden Exercise Trail), the Bonneville Shoreline Trail, and Waterfall Canyon (see next profile). Joggers and mountain bikers regularly use this network of trails. While often dry and exposed to the sun, the paths along the bench quickly lead to deep, shaded canyons.

From the 29th Street trailhead, follow the trail up the hillside to the east, with signs pointing to the Taylor Canyon South Trail. After 0.2 mile you've reached the Bonneville Shoreline Trail, gained a quick 100 feet of elevation, and taken in a good view of Ogden and the Great Salt Lake. At this junction, turn left and follow the signs leading to Taylor Canyon. After 100 yards along the wide Bonneville Shoreline Trail, the route to Taylor Canyon veers off and up to the right.

The trail leads through sage and Gambel oak into the mouth of Taylor Canyon and up a dry creekbed. At 0.6 mile from the trailhead, the path crosses a bridge to the north side of the creekbed. Soon after, you're engulfed in a beautiful canyon with conifers lining the side slopes. While you may see mountain bikers along the bench trails and even up into Taylor Canyon, few make it into this lush section of the canyon.

Continuing up the canyon, you'll notice that the dry creek suddenly runs with water, but for only about 0.2 mile along the canyon floor before going underground. After several minutes of creekside companionship, you'll see the creek descending from its source about 100 feet up the canyon wall. The creekbed is generally dry above the point where the spring enters.

About 100 feet beyond where the creek reaches the canyon floor, you'll cross a bridge over the dry creekbed. This begins a series of steep switchbacks leading up the north slope of Malans Peak. Along the ascent, you'll see the spring as it emerges from the wall of the canyon.

Continue climbing the steep, shaded slope of Gambel oak sprinkled with spruce and fir. Along the way, and in the bottom of the canyon, you may see deer and the occasional raccoon or porcupine.

Malans Peak (via Taylor Canyon)

At the rocky crest of Malans Peak, the trees thin to reveal wide-angle views of the Great Salt Lake and peaks to the north and south. Looking back down the canyon slope, you've just ascended 1,400 vertical feet in about 1.2 miles, but the view makes every step worth it.

NEARBY ACTIVITIES

Ogden is a vibrant hub for year-round outdoor and indoor recreation. The **Salomon Center** (338 23rd St.; 801-399-5862, salomoncenter.com) is a high-adventure downtown sports complex with a vertical wind tunnel that simulates freefall skydiving, an indoor surf wave, and a huge climbing wall. The center also features 32 bowling lanes, billiards, a 55,000-square-foot gym, arcades, bumper cars, and restaurants.

• •

GPS TRAILHEAD COORDINATES N41° 12.644' W111° 55.917'

DIRECTIONS From the intersection of I-84 and I-15 north of Salt Lake City, drive north on I-15 for about 1.1 miles; then take Exit 341 for UT 79/31st Street. Turn right onto 31st Street, and drive 1.2 miles. Turn left onto US 89 North/Washington Boulevard, and drive 0.1 mile; then turn right onto 30th Street. Drive 1.3 miles; then turn left onto Tyler Avenue, and drive just 0.1 mile. Turn right onto 29th Street, and drive 0.7 mile; then turn right onto Buchanan Avenue into the trailhead parking lot. Look for the trailhead at the south end of the lot.

A creek runs alongside the trail for a brief but beautiful stretch.

The eponymous waterfall offers great spots to stop and relax.

A BEAUTIFUL HIKE, the Waterfall Canyon Trail follows a creek up a deep canyon to a breathtaking surprise. Area hikers love this steep, short trail, while trail runners and mountain bikers use the lower trail network, which connects the canyon with the Bonneville Shoreline Trail and other city trailheads.

DESCRIPTION

The dozens of canyons that flank the foothills of the Wasatch Front are full of surprises. Some are dry and some are wet, and you can't always be sure which is which from the valley below. As you walk along the dry bench trails above Ogden's eastern hillside, you'd never suspect a 200-foot waterfall to be spraying down a rock face just minutes up the trail.

The 29th Street trailhead provides the easiest access to Waterfall Canyon. This trailhead is also a popular access point for the Mount Ogden Exercise Trail, the Bonneville Shoreline Trail, Taylor Canyon, and Malans Peak (see previous hike).

From the 29th Street trailhead, follow the trail up the hillside to the east, with signs pointing to the Taylor Canyon South Trail. Upon reaching the Bonneville Shoreline Trail at 0.2 mile, take a sharp right and continue south along the wide trail. This portion of the trail is often shadeless and very hot in the summer.

DISTANCE & CONFIGURATION: 2.6-mile out-and-back

DIFFICULTY: Moderate

SCENERY: Spectacular waterfall in a deep canyon

EXPOSURE: Mostly shaded above bench trails

TRAIL TRAFFIC: Heavy on bench trails, moderate on upper trail

TRAIL SURFACE: Dirt and rock, becoming mostly rock near the waterfall

HIKING TIME: 1.5–2 hours

DRIVING DISTANCE: 36 miles from I-15/I-80 intersection

ELEVATION CHANGE: 4,780'–6,272'

ACCESS: Daily, sunrise–sunset; no fees or permits

WHEELCHAIR ACCESS: None

MAPS: USGS *Ogden*

FACILITIES: Restrooms and water available late spring–early fall

CONTACT: 801-625-5112, fs.usda.gov/uwcnf

LOCATION: Buchanan Avenue just south of 29th Street, Ogden, UT 84403

COMMENTS: Dogs allowed on leash. Can be combined with Malans Peak (see previous hike) to make a scenic loop. This hike passes through private property, so please obey posted signs and don't stray from the route.

Take care on this stretch of trail, which is winding and also popular with mountain bikers. While the most courteous of cyclists will often have a noisemaking device attached to their bikes (or will at least occasionally shout to warn hikers ahead), it's always a good idea to keep an eye out for approaching groups of bikers.

At 0.5 mile the path turns east into Waterfall Canyon and begins steeply ascending the northern slope of Malans Peak. After another 0.2 mile, you'll come to a bridge on the right. Cross the wooden bridge and take an immediate left, following the trail up the south side of the creek. Within another 100 feet, you'll pass a second bridge. The trail stays within 5–10 feet of the creek, so getting lost is never a problem.

After you cross the bridges, the trail becomes more rocky and may become a bit difficult for small children and less-agile hikers. Fortunately, the trail stays close to the creek and offers an abundance of rest spots for tired trekkers who need to take a quick break. The creekside is well shaded, and the boulders provide ample seating. This constant supply of miniature rest areas, along with the relative shortness of the route, makes the hike popular among families with small children.

The constantly increasing difficulty of the trail surface might discourage some adventurers, but just as the surface and grade become frustrating—especially for young hikers with shorter legs who may struggle to step over the large rocks—the waterfall appears and you'll immediately forget the steep climb.

A scramble up a talus slope leads to the base of the waterfall. Its height and the narrowness of the canyon make photographing the entire waterfall almost impossible. You'll be tempted to climb the rocks on the canyon wall opposite the falls to get the perfect picture, but these crags can be dangerous. Also keep in mind that as a guest on private property, you should stay on the trail and protect the canyon's natural beauty.

If you're full of energy, you can make a longer scenic loop hike by climbing the steep, rocky slope to the right of the waterfall. This drainage leads up to Malans

Waterfall Canyon

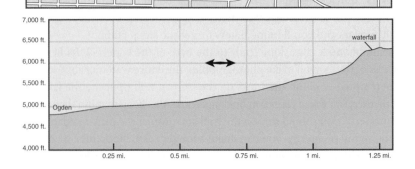

Basin, on to Malans Peak, and then down Taylor Canyon. If you decide to do this 5-mile loop, hike it counterclockwise: you can more safely ascend the rocky drainage above the waterfall than descend it.

NEARBY ACTIVITIES

Just a mile down the hillside from Waterfall Canyon, you'll find **Weber State University,** which you can see for much of the hike towards the mouth of Waterfall Canyon. The 12,000-seat Dee Events Center hosts Weber State sports, concerts, and other campus and community events. For tickets and event information, call 801-626-8500 or visit community.weber.edu/deeeventscenter.

• •

GPS TRAILHEAD COORDINATES N41° 12.644' W111° 55.917'

DIRECTIONS From the intersection of I-84 and I-15 north of Salt Lake City, drive north on I-15 for about 1.1 miles; then take Exit 341 for UT 79/31st Street. Turn right onto 31st Street, and drive 1.2 miles. Turn left onto US 89 North/Washington Boulevard, and drive 0.1 mile; then turn right onto 30th Street. Drive 1.3 miles; then turn left onto Tyler Avenue, and drive just 0.1 mile. Turn right onto 29th Street, and drive 0.7 mile; then turn right onto Buchanan Avenue into the trailhead parking lot. Look for the trailhead at the south end of the lot.

Runoff from the waterfall accompanies hikers for the last 0.75 mile.

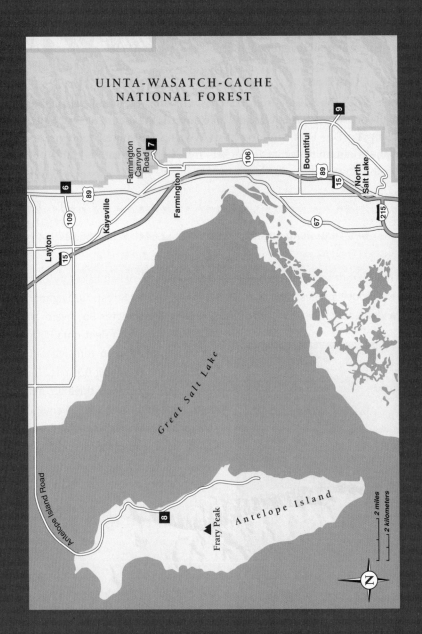

NORTH
(Davis County)

6 ADAMS CANYON

A waterfall flows in Adams Canyon.

Photo: Greg Witt

FROM THE VALLEY FLOOR, Adams Canyon appears no different from any other ordinary canyon along the Wasatch Front. But once inside, you'll find a paradise filled with white fir, a tumbling creek, and a stunning waterfall waiting at the end of the trail.

DESCRIPTION

Locals have done a good job of keeping Adams Canyon a secret. No signs at the trail-head indicate where you are or that you can even access this canyon. Its name differs from the name of the creek (North Fork Holmes Creek), which only makes it more anonymous. Even the spectacular waterfall at the end of the hike is nameless. Still, locals count this as a favorite hike, enjoying its deep-forest setting, vibrant mountain stream, and plunging waterfall.

From the northeast corner of the large parking area, take the trail leading along the fence through a thicket of Gambel oak. After 100 yards the path turns left up a steep slope and follows a series of switchbacks up the hillside. This part of the trail cuts through the sandy slopes of the Lake Bonneville shoreline and is particularly prone to erosion, so stay on the trail to avoid making the problem worse. At 0.2 mile you come to a quick overlook of the Great Salt Lake with views of mountains to the

DISTANCE & CONFIGURATION: 3.6-mile out-and-back

DIFFICULTY: Moderate

SCENERY: Valley views, deep-canyon stream, waterfall

EXPOSURE: Partially shaded initially, then mostly shaded in the canyon

TRAIL TRAFFIC: Moderate

TRAIL SURFACE: Dirt, rock

HIKING TIME: 2–3 hours

DRIVING DISTANCE: 25 miles from I-15/I-80 intersection

ELEVATION CHANGE: 4,832'–6,100'

ACCESS: Daily, sunrise–sunset; no fees or permits

MAPS: USGS *Kaysville* and *Peterson*

FACILITIES: None

WHEELCHAIR ACCESS: None

CONTACT: 801-625-5112, fs.usda.gov/uwcnf

LOCATION: Eastside Drive at Canyon Creek Circle just east of UT 89, Layton, UT 84040

COMMENTS: Dogs allowed on leash. Adams Canyon is especially beautiful in late spring as the creek swells with snowmelt.

north and south. This overlook demonstrates how much the view can change with just a few hundred feet of elevation gain.

Along the first part of the hike, you might well see a snake sunning itself on the trail. Frequent visitors include bull snakes, gopher snakes, and rattlers. Avoid surprising them at close range by watching the trail ahead; you can create a little noise to send them safely slithering into the underbrush. You might also glimpse deer, which often graze on the lower slopes, especially in winter.

At 0.5 mile the trail curves to the left and begins to enter the mouth of Adams Canyon. From the partially shaded slopes of oak on the north side of the canyon, you can see the towering conifers that cover its south side. Soon you become aware of the creek below on the canyon floor. At 0.7 mile another trail bends to the right and descends to a footbridge that crosses the creek. This is the Bonneville Shoreline Trail, which continues south. Stay on the trail straight ahead as it leads up Adams Canyon and along the bank of the north fork of Holmes Creek.

As you ascend the canyon, the trail steepens and becomes rockier. Holmes Creek is a fast-dropping stream with dozens of cascades and tumbles. The trail manages to parallel the creek's steep gradient as it winds around rocks and trees. White fir trees, most with trunks 2 feet in diameter, provide ample shade.

At 1.4 miles, the trail crosses from the north to the south side of the creek on a rickety wooden footbridge. Soon you pass several fire rings and primitive campsites. At one point, a huge slab of rock the size of a school bus blocks the trail as it meets the stream. Circumvent the rock most easily by climbing around on the right top side of the slab.

In the last 0.4 mile leading up to the waterfall, you'll find several steep sections of the creek with large cascades that could be appropriately considered waterfalls. In spring, abundant snowmelt easily triples the creek's flow, making these cascades particularly scenic. Beyond them, a bit of scrambling around rocks and tree trunks is required before arriving at the rock cliff that forms the backdrop for the waterfall.

Adams Canyon

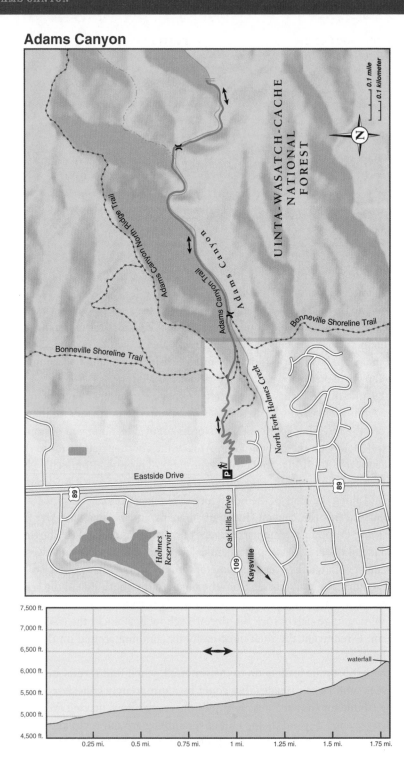

One last crossing of the creek will take you to the base of the falls, where you can enjoy the view and rest on a nearby rock or ledge. Throughout most of the year, you can easily cross the creek by stepping on large rocks, but in the surge of spring snow-melt, plan to get your feet wet.

NEARBY ACTIVITIES

Cherry Hill, a family recreation center, is off US 89 at 1325 S. Main in Kaysville, just 4 miles from the Adams Canyon trailhead. The resort features camping facilities, a water park, miniature golf, batting cages, a climbing wall, and other family-oriented activities. Call 801-451-5379 or visit cherry-hill.com for hours, prices, and camping reservations.

• •

GPS TRAILHEAD COORDINATES N41° 03.980' W111° 54.580'

DIRECTIONS From the southernmost intersection of I-80 and I-15 in Salt Lake City, drive north on I-15 for 19 miles. Take Exit 324 (South Ogden) to continue onto US 89 North, and drive 5.9 miles. When you see Oak Hills Drive on your left, continue on US 89 North for another 0.3 mile; then turn right onto a small frontage road and take an immediate right onto Eastside Drive. Drive 0.3 mile to the trailhead parking lot, on the left. The unmarked parking area lies at the northeast corner of Eastside Drive and Canyon Creek Circle.

Hikers cross Holmes Creek on a wooden footbridge.   *Photo: Greg Witt*

Farmington Creek supports a rich variety of plant life.

THE TRAIL FOLLOWS Farmington Creek, the largest watercourse in Davis County, up a broad canyon. A 40-foot waterfall near the top of the trail and expansive views make Farmington Canyon a rewarding destination, especially in spring and fall.

DESCRIPTION

Farmington Creek cuts through a wide canyon fed by several tributary creeks and springs. By the time it reaches the lower canyon, the water flow is substantial enough that it's probably no longer a mere creek. The Farmington Creek Trail ascends steadily along the south slope of the canyon, providing great views of the canyon and the creek below. Although the road above the trail receives year-round recreational use by ATVs, snowmobiles, and hunters, the trail below remains relatively quiet.

At the lower trailhead, take either of the steep trails at the north end of the small parking area. You won't find drinking water at the trailhead or along the trail, but there are small springs where you can draw and purify water. You can also access Farmington Creek at the trailhead and near the falls.

The hike follows the creek's gradient and stays 100–200 feet above the creek most of the way. The trail is on the north side of the creek, and with the exception of a few stands of oak, hikers are exposed to sunlight most of the way. Along the

DISTANCE & CONFIGURATION: 2.6-mile out-and-back

DIFFICULTY: Moderate

SCENERY: Canyon views, stream, waterfall

EXPOSURE: Mostly sunny

TRAIL TRAFFIC: Light

TRAIL SURFACE: Dirt, rock

HIKING TIME: 2.5–3 hours

DRIVING DISTANCE: 22 miles from I-15/I-80 intersection

ELEVATION CHANGE: 5,245'–6,423'

ACCESS: Daily, sunrise–sunset; no fees or permits

WHEELCHAIR ACCESS: None

MAPS: USGS *Bountiful Peak* and *Peterson*

FACILITIES: None

CONTACT: 801-733-2660, fs.usda.gov/uwcnf

LOCATION: Farmington Canyon Road, Morgan, UT 84050

COMMENTS: Dogs allowed on leash

1.6-mile trail, you'll cross at least four small creeks and springs as they descend into Farmington Creek. At times, the undergrowth and brush will make it seem as if the trail is all but nonexistent. For this reason—especially if your are hiking during the summer time—long pants can be a welcome barrier between your calves and the local flora.

During the spring, Farmington Creek gushes with water, and even though the trail is often hundreds of yards from the creek, you can always hear its roar below. In the fall, the flow is reduced, but the autumn colors and cooler air make for an equally pleasant hike.

Deer and foxes are frequently sighted in the canyon and along the trail. Also watch for two old cars—one on the north side of the trail, another on the south side— that plunged over the cliff from the road above nearly 50 years ago and have made the thick underbrush near the trail their final rusting place. For any hiker, but especially those traveling with children, this provides an ideal location to stop for a quick break. There is enough shade to keep weary adventurers cool, and the rusted-out cars provide a great visual and mental distraction for kids of all ages.

At 1.3 miles the trail comes within 50 feet of the creek, near the base of a broad waterfall. This is your turnaround point. The trail continues 0.3 mile farther up steep switchbacks to Sunset Campground, which closed in late 2018 due to environmental concerns.

If you want to do more exploring before you head back the way you came, a steep spur trail enables sure-footed hikers to access the creek below the 40-foot waterfall. Be careful, though, and don't be shy about using the rope to steady yourself. Even though the stretch of trail is short, it won't feel that way when you're sliding downhill on your backside.

NEARBY ACTIVITIES

Lagoon, just off I-15 in Farmington, is the largest amusement park in Utah, with 50 rides, a water park, a replica of a 19th-century pioneer village, live entertainment,

Farmington Creek Trail

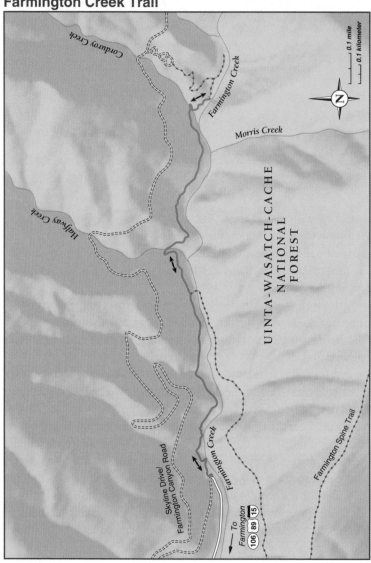

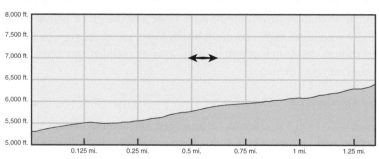

shops, games, and restaurants. For a schedule of events, call 801-451-8000 or visit lagoonpark.com.

• •

GPS TRAILHEAD COORDINATES N41° 00.018' W111° 51.983'

DIRECTIONS From the southernmost intersection of I-80 and I-15 in Salt Lake City, drive north on I-15 or 19 miles. Take Exit 324 (South Ogden) to continue onto US 89 North, and drive 0.3 mile; then take Exit 395 for UT 225 East/Park Lane. Turn right onto UT 225 East, and drive 0.3 mile. Turn right onto Main Street and drive 0.3 mile; then, in 0.1 mile, turn left onto 600 North Drive, and then turn left onto 100 East/Farmington Canyon Road, and drive 1.6 miles. Look for a dirt parking area on the right, at the point where the pavement ends.

Decades-old junk cars and tires lend unique decorative touches around the creek.

8 FRARY PEAK

Huge herds of buffalo wander the grassy expanses beneath Frary Peak.

ASCEND TO THE SUMMIT of the largest island in the Great Salt Lake. You'll find spectacular vistas and excellent wildlife-viewing in a surprisingly distinctive geologic zone and natural habitat. This hike offers the best chance in Utah of spotting bighorn sheep.

DESCRIPTION

At just 6,596 feet in elevation, Frary Peak really isn't that remarkable by Utah standards, but it may be the most unusually located summit in the state. On Antelope Island in the Great Salt Lake, the peak rises 2,400 feet above the surrounding lake. Its location was intriguing enough that Kit Carson and John C. Fremont made the first Anglo exploration of the island in 1845. The entire island is a high-desert grassland that provides a hospitable habitat for migrating birds, bighorn sheep, pronghorn antelope, and a herd of more than 500 bison.

You'll find the trail consistently well marked and easy to follow. From the trailhead it winds its way quickly up the island's grassy eastern slopes. Don't be intimidated by the first mile's steep terrain, because the trail climbs more gradually once you hit the ridgeline. At 0.7 mile you'll pass the Dooley Knob Trail junction and arrive at the island ridgeline for first views to the west.

DISTANCE & CONFIGURATION: 6.6-mile out-and-back

DIFFICULTY: Moderate

SCENERY: Superb 360° summit views of Great Salt Lake, valley, and surrounding peaks

EXPOSURE: No shade

TRAIL TRAFFIC: Moderate

TRAIL SURFACE: Dirt, rock

HIKING TIME: 3.5–6 hours

DRIVING DISTANCE: 48 miles from I-15/I-80 intersection

ELEVATION CHANGE: 4,528'–6,596'

ACCESS: Daily, 6 a.m.–6 p.m. (closed Thanksgiving and December 25). Pay entrance fee of

$10/vehicle at the state-park gate before crossing the causeway.

MAPS: USGS *Antelope Island* and *Antelope Island North*

FACILITIES: None at trailhead; restrooms at nearby Mountain View trailhead

WHEELCHAIR ACCESS: None on the trail. Other parts of the park, including the visitor center, are wheelchair accessible.

CONTACT: 801-725-9263, stateparks.utah.gov /parks/antelope-island

LOCATION: Antelope Island State Park, 4500 W. 1700 S., Syracuse, UT 84075

COMMENTS: Dogs allowed on leash

From this lower ridgeline, the trail crosses to the island's western side and follows a fairly gentle contour along the western slopes for most of the way to the summit. As the trail begins to descend the slope and move toward the prominent Elephant Head knoll on the western shore, you might even begin to wonder if you're on the right trail. Soon, at 1.2 miles, you'll see a set of wooden steps that lead up and to the east through the rocky escarpment. These steps quickly bring you back to the ridgeline and some expansive views to both the east and west. The trail continues through grassy meadows to cross the rounded slopes of Stringham Peak (elevation 6,374'), capped by a large communications tower.

From Stringham Peak you have a clear view of the craggy Frary Peak summit, just 0.6 mile and about 15 minutes ahead to the south. At this point you might be tempted to follow the faint trail along the ridgeline straight ahead, but you're really much better off staying on the main trail as it descends to the right along the western slopes, losing about 150 feet of elevation. You'll soon regain the elevation loss by following a well-cleared trail that leads back up to the ridge.

The higher slopes are blanketed with big sagebrush and an occasional juniper tree, not large enough to create much shade. A short scramble up a steep slope soon brings you to the rocky, beige outcrop that is Frary Peak. The summit's flat rock provides an ideal place to sit down, enjoy lunch, and take in the views in all directions. Directly to the east, Bountiful Peak and the Wasatch Range are reflected in the Great Salt Lake. Forty miles to the southwest, you'll spot the easily recognizable Deseret Peak (11,031'). On a clear day, you can even see Ibapah Peak (12,087') nearly 120 miles to the southwest.

The rocky slopes near the summit also provide a good place to watch for bighorn sheep. The Utah Department of Wildlife introduced a herd of 22 bighorn to

Frary Peak

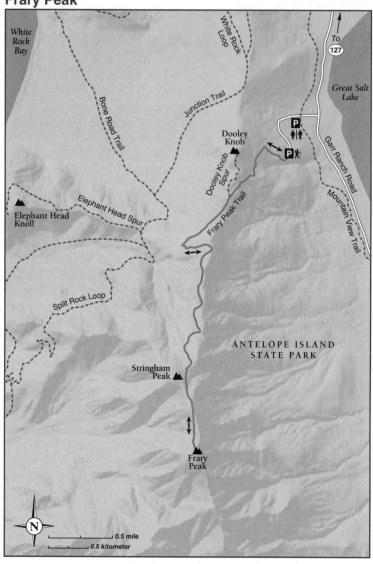

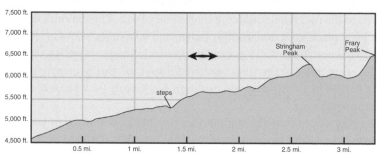

the island in 1996 as a nursery herd that could supply animals to other areas of the state. With few natural predators, the bighorn population on the island has grown to 160, and portions of the herd are frequently exported. If you don't happen to see a bighorn, you'll certainly see their clumps of wool along the trail.

Nearly 200 pronghorn antelope and 350 deer graze the island's slopes and range-lands. But Antelope Island's most famous residents are the bison, often found grazing along the trail. The 12 animals introduced in 1893 as part of a private ranch and hunting preserve formed the foundation for today's free-roaming herd of 500–700.

Antelope Island plays host to millions of migratory birds each year. The Great Salt Lake's brine flies and brine shrimp provide a primary food source for many of the area's 250 bird species.

Along the trail you'll often spot western meadowlarks, yellow-headed black-birds, and various raptors. Chukars nest year-round on the island, concealed in rocks or in the brush near the trail.

Although you'll find no water on the trail, Antelope Island's 40 major freshwater springs, primarily on the eastern slopes, produce 36 million gallons of water annually and support much of the island's wildlife and vegetation. The island's geology exposes some of the oldest rocks on Earth in the 2.7-billion-year-old Farmington Canyon complex. Along the trail you'll also see granite, limestone outcrops, and shale.

Range grasses such as purple threeawn cover most of the lower meadows and slopes. Common wildflowers along the trail include fiddleneck, a bristly annual with yellow flowers, and the vernal daisy.

Frary Peak is an ideal hike in the early spring when most of the higher mountain trails are still covered in snow. Summer can be grueling on the shadeless trail, so bring plenty of water. Fall brings more pleasant hiking conditions, along with migrating raptors, pronghorn harems, and more-frequent buck deer sightings. Throughout the year, Frary Peak offers exceptional views surrounded by a surprising and continually varying array of wildlife.

NEARBY ACTIVITIES

The **Antelope Island State Park Visitor Center,** at the island's north end, is open year-round (801-725-9263). Here you'll find exhibits, a bookstore, restrooms, and a video presentation on the island's natural and human history. Knowledgeable rangers provide interpretive assistance and suggestions on wildlife-viewing. Popular events offered throughout the year center around bird migrations and the annual bison roundup. Look for the day-use facility and primitive campgrounds on the north side of the island. The day-use area offers covered picnic tables, drinking water, restrooms, and showers for those wanting to take a dip in the Great Salt Lake's buoyant water.

• •

GPS TRAILHEAD COORDINATES N40° 59.623' W112° 12.152'

DIRECTIONS From the southernmost intersection of I-80 and I-15 in Salt Lake City, drive north on I-15 for 27.5 miles. Take Exit 332 and turn left onto Antelope Drive/UT 108 West. Drive 14.4 miles, during which Antelope Drive becomes a causeway called Antelope Island Drive. Turn left when you see the RANCH sign, and drive 5.2 miles south and east along the east side of the island. Turn right at the sign for Frary Trailhead, and then drive 0.5 mile up to the large dirt parking area. The trailhead is at the parking lot's southwest corner.

Hikers descend the northern ridge of Frary Peak.

Autumn blankets Mueller Park in vibrant reds and yellows.

THIS STEEP TRAIL follows three separate mountain springs through deep woods and open meadows, finally arriving at a 100-year-old miner's cabin. The trail is as popular with deer and moose as it is with humans.

DESCRIPTION

Some trails switchback or wind their way up the side of a mountain to mitigate the steep ascent, but not the Kenney Creek Trail. The miners who worked this area 100 years ago found the most direct means possible to reach their lode, and the Kenney Creek Trail is it. In less than 2.2 miles you gain more than 2,200 feet without ever having to scramble or use your hands.

The Kenney Creek Trail starts on the north side of the road, across from the parking area and restrooms in Bountiful's Mueller Park. On weekends, the small parking area can quickly fill up, but don't be discouraged, as most of the people in the park will be hiking or biking one of the easier, more popular trails (namely Big Rock via the Elephant Rock Trail, a wonderful but crowded option). If the parking area is full, you can easily park outside the entrance gate and quickly walk to the trailhead.

While Mueller Park is a popular mountain biking destination, most cyclists find the Kenney Creek Trail too steep and narrow.

DISTANCE & CONFIGURATION: 4.5-mile out-and-back

DIFFICULTY: Moderate

SCENERY: Valley views, creeks, spring-fed mountain meadows

EXPOSURE: Mostly shaded

TRAIL TRAFFIC: Light

TRAIL SURFACE: Dirt

HIKING TIME: 2.5–3.5 hours

DRIVING DISTANCE: 14 miles from I-15/I-80 intersection

ELEVATION CHANGE: 5,247'–7,464'

ACCESS: Daily, 7 a.m.–10 p.m.; $9 fee payable at Mueller Park entrance

MAPS: USGS *Fort Douglas*

FACILITIES: Restrooms and water at trailhead parking area

WHEELCHAIR ACCESS: None

CONTACT: 801-733-2660, fs.usda.gov/uwcnf; 801-298-6178, daviscounty.gov/healthresource locator (click "Trails")

LOCATION: 2067 Mueller Park Rd., Bountiful UT 84010

COMMENTS: Dogs allowed on leash. This is a narrow trail with thick underbrush, so you'll want to wear long pants on this hike.

From Mueller Park Road, the trail ascends through dense woods along the western bank of Kenney Creek. Even during spring runoff, Kenney Creek is only a few feet wide and can easily be stepped across without getting your feet wet. After the trail crosses Kenney Creek at 0.2 mile, you won't see it again until your return.

After leaving the creek, the trail ascends quickly through a ground cover of grasses, forbs, and mountain shrubs under the shade of oak and maple. The trail is narrow, and the thick chaparral will scrape unprotected legs to pieces, so wear long pants.

At 0.9 mile, the trail leaves Mueller Park and enters Uinta-Wasatch-Cache National Forest. The forest canopy opens briefly to display views of the Great Salt Lake, Antelope Island, and mountains to the west. But even at this overlook, you'll notice hillside homes across the canyon at the same elevation—it will take more climbing to escape the rapidly encroaching development.

As the trail rises above the meadow, you encounter a large thicket of Gambel oak. You'll swear you're bushwhacking, but a trail actually exists under the brush. It's maintained but intentionally preserved as an unimproved wilderness trail.

The path crosses perennial streams and meadows between stands of oak and maple. At higher elevations, above 7,300 feet, clusters of quaking aspen dot the hillside. Moose and deer inhabit these higher slopes year-round and use the trail regularly. Watch for their tracks on the wet trail, along with those of mountain lions. In the trees, spotted towhees and mountain chickadees make their nests.

After 2.2 miles of heart-pounding ascent, you'll come to an old miner's cabin in a clearing: a great place to take a rest and consider your options. Most hikers make the cabin their destination and turnaround point, but you can also climb the higher ridge in the Sessions Mountains to the northeast and access the Great Western Trail (see Hike 33, page 155), or you can head southeast along a faint and sometimes nonexistent trail to Willey Hollow. If you choose to turn around at the cabin, you've given your legs and your heart a great workout and you'll enjoy the speedy descent.

Kenney Creek Trail

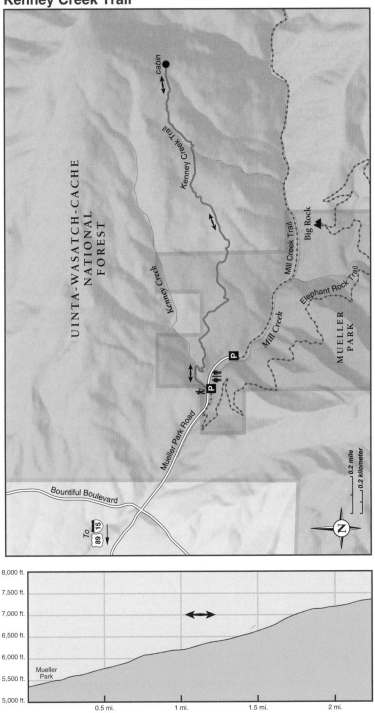

Because Mueller Park charges an entrance fee, be sure to get the most out of your admission by exploring other trails in the area. While few of these trails offer the isolation or even the physical challenge that Kenney Creek does, you'll quickly learn why this protected area has become an important refuge to the burgeoning suburban community that it nestles against.

NEARBY ACTIVITIES

Mueller Park is within minutes of Bountiful neighborhoods and shopping areas. For mountain bikers, the Mueller Park Trail is a great lower-altitude alpine ride that can be done as a 7-mile route to Big Rock or a 13-mile out-and-back to Rudy's Flat. Restrooms, water, and picnic facilities are available.

• •

GPS TRAILHEAD COORDINATES N40° 51.846' W111° 50.202'

DIRECTIONS From the southernmost intersection of I-80 and I-15 in Salt Lake City, drive north on I-15 for about 10.5 miles. Take Exit 315 in Bountiful, and turn right onto West 2600 South. Drive 1.7 miles, during which 2600 South becomes Orchard Drive. Turn right onto West 1800 South, and drive 2.4 miles. Enter the first parking area on the right after the Mueller Park entrance. You'll find the trailhead across the street.

OPPOSITE: The well-marked Kenney Creek Trail winds back toward the canyon floor.

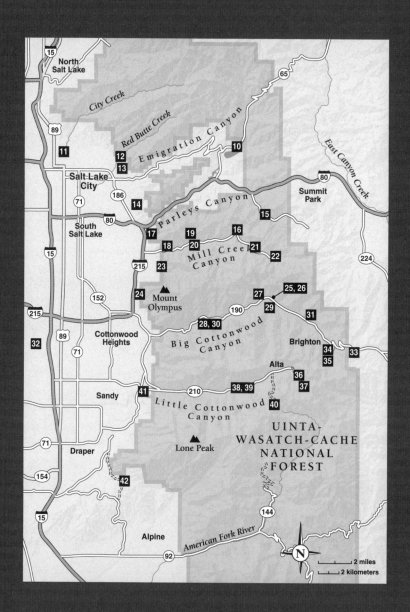

CENTRAL
(Salt Lake County)

The trail is surrounded by stunning Wasatch views in every direction.

THE DONNER PARTY blazed this historic trail in 1846, followed by 70,000 Mormon pioneers from 1847 to 1868; the trail also served as a leg of the Pony Express route. Still, for all its history, this section of the trail remains an inviting, tranquil, and exceptionally beautiful path through the woods of a gentle canyon. It's most alluring in late spring and early fall.

If you prefer to do a shorter section of the hike, either one-way or round-trip, choose the quieter, more remote 4-mile section between Mormon Flat and Big Mountain, where your chances of sharing the trail with wildlife are increased.

DESCRIPTION

As the Mormon pioneers began their epic 1,300-mile trek from Nauvoo, Illinois, to the Salt Lake Valley, they didn't know that the steepest and longest sustained ascent—and the highest elevation of the entire journey—would occur at the end of the trail, on the day they first glimpsed their destination. This section of the Mormon Pioneer National Historic Trail captures that last full day of the trip and gives modern hikers some sense of what it might have been like to be a pioneer on a westward journey.

The 9.1-mile section of the trail was originally blazed by the ill-fated Donner Party in 1846, a year before the Mormon pioneers came along. It took the group's 87 members more than a week to cut a path through the underbrush that you will hike

DISTANCE & CONFIGURATION: 9.1-mile point-to-point, with shorter out-and-back/point-to-point options

DIFFICULTY: Moderate

SCENERY: Canyon drainage, mountain views, view of Salt Lake Valley

EXPOSURE: Mostly shaded

TRAIL TRAFFIC: Moderate

TRAIL SURFACE: Dirt, some rocks

HIKING TIME: 4–5 hours

DRIVING DISTANCE: 31 miles from I-15/I-80 intersection

ELEVATION CHANGE: 6,039'–7,403'

ACCESS: Daily, sunrise–sunset, but road access is limited early fall–late spring, when UT 65 is closed; gate to Little Dell Recreation Area opens at 8 a.m. in season. A $5 parking fee is charged at Little Dell in season; no fees or permits at Mormon Flat and Big Mountain trailheads.

MAPS: USGS *Mountain Dell*

FACILITIES: Restrooms at Mormon Flat, Little Dell, Big Mountain, and Affleck Park; no drinking water at Mormon Flat or Little Dell

CONTACT: 801-733-2660, fs.usda.gov/uwcnf; 801-483-6705, slc.gov/utilities

WHEELCHAIR ACCESS: None

LOCATION: Jeremy Ranch Road, Summit Park, UT 84098 (Mormon Flat trailhead); Little Dell Recreation Area just south of UT 65, Emigration Canyon, UT 84108 (Little Dell trailhead); UT 65, Emigration Canyon, UT 84108 (Big Mountain trailhead)

COMMENTS: Despite the seasonal road closure, this hike is popular with snowshoers and backcountry skiers because of its negligible avalanche hazard. Dogs prohibited in Mountain Dell Canyon, a protected watershed.

in 5 hours or less. That delay would prove disastrous, as the party got caught in a winter storm in the Sierra Nevada less than three months later.

California gold-seekers and the Overland Stage used the trail in the 1850s. In 1860 and 1861, the trail served as the Pony Express route through the Wasatch Mountains. Riders would leave Bauchmann's Station (now covered by East Canyon Reservoir) on East Canyon Creek and arrive at the Mountain Dell Station within several hours.

The Mormon Pioneer Trail is best enjoyed as a one-way hike that re-creates the arrival of the pioneers as they traveled from Mormon Flat up to Big Mountain Pass, where they first saw the Salt Lake Valley, and then down into Mountain Dell Canyon. The hike can also be done in shorter round-trip or one-way segments, using Big Mountain Pass as a stopping or turnaround point.

To recapture the lore and scenic appeal of this historic trail, leave a shuttle vehicle at Little Dell Reservoir (the trail's end) and then drive on to Mormon Flat on East Canyon Creek. Cross the creek through a meadow of low-lying willow, and follow the trail as it enters the mouth of Little Emigration Canyon—you're immediately transported back more than 150 years.

Within 0.5 mile after entering the canyon, the trail hugs a cottonwood-lined creek. The trail gradually ascends the wide canyon floor, which is marked with aspen and spruce. Pioneers would have welcomed the shade of the wooded slopes, having just spent much of their journey on the open plains of Nebraska and Wyoming. Like you, they may have seen their first moose or beaver dam while walking through this lush drainage. They also may have spotted a cougar or been lucky enough to augment their diminishing rations with some venison.

Mormon Pioneer Trail

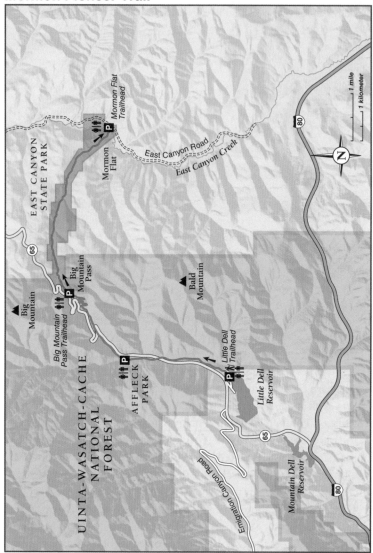

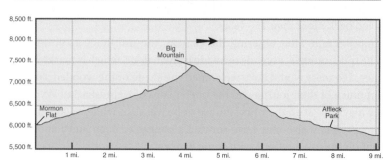

At 3.5 miles the trail steepens as it approaches Big Mountain Pass, gaining about 400 feet of elevation in the final 0.5 mile. When you arrive at the pass—now a parking lot with restrooms and a historical marker—take a moment to gaze to the west and imagine what it would have been like to have walked more than 1,300 miles and suddenly see your ultimate destination laid out below. On July 23, 1847, Brigham Young arrived at this pass, gazed out over the Salt Lake Valley, and said, "This is the place. Drive on." Three days earlier, Orson Pratt, one of the church leaders who helped Young plan and lead the trip west, had arrived at Big Mountain Pass and measured the elevation at 7,245 feet above sea level. Although the actual elevation is 7,403 feet, his calculation was amazingly accurate given the simple handheld instruments of the day.

From Big Mountain Pass, the party locked their wagon wheels with chains, attached a drag shoe, and essentially slid down the slope into Mountain Dell Canyon, arriving near what is now Affleck Park, where they camped for the night. Your Big Mountain descent will be less treacherous on a singletrack trail that switchbacks down the head of the canyon through groves of aspen, bigtooth maple, and fir. Within 1.3 miles of the pass, the trail joins Mountain Dell Creek, which continues near the trail until it enters Little Dell Reservoir. Along the way, the trail crosses the road twice and passes through Affleck Park at 2.5 miles from Big Mountain Pass, with restrooms, campsites, and picnic sites under the shade of towering cottonwoods.

Just down the trail from Affleck Park, you'll notice a small, rounded peak to the west known as Little Mountain. The pioneers camped at the base of Little Mountain before crossing into Emigration Canyon to the west and entering the Salt Lake Valley the next day. A good trail leads over to Emigration Canyon from Affleck Park, but the Mormon Pioneer National Historic Trail follows the creek another 1.6 miles into Little Dell Recreation Area, where your shuttle vehicle awaits (in season).

NEARBY ACTIVITIES

To complete your experience on the Mormon Pioneer Trail, visit **This Is The Place Heritage Park** (2601 E. Sunnyside Ave.; 801-582-1847, thisistheplace.org), an outdoor living-history attraction that presents the story of everyday life in a typical Utah settlement from 1847 to 1897. Located at the mouth of Emigration Canyon, the park includes more than 40 re-created and original buildings from settlements throughout Utah. Staff in period attire demonstrate life as it would have been for 19th-century Utahns.

• •

GPS TRAILHEAD COORDINATES
Little Dell Reservoir: N40° 46.620' W111° 41.318'
Mormon Flat: N40° 48.930' W111° 35.090'
Big Mountain Pass: N40° 49.680' W111° 39.218'

DIRECTIONS *Little Dell Reservoir (ending trailhead):* From the eastern intersection of I-80 and I-215, head east on I-80 for about 4.7 miles; then take Exit 134 for UT 65 North/East Canyon. Turn left onto UT 65 North, and drive 2.9 miles. The entrance road to Little Dell Recreation Area will be on your right—make a sharp right and, in 0.3 mile, make a sharp left to reach the parking area, 0.2 mile ahead. The trail is accessed from the east end of the parking area, near the reservoir's shore.

Mormon Flat (starting trailhead): After leaving a shuttle at the Little Dell Recreation Area parking lot, return to UT 65 North, turn right, and drive 10.8 miles; then make a sharp right onto Jeremy Ranch Road. In 3.2 miles make another right to reach the trailhead parking area. Cross the footbridge over East Canyon Creek to reach the well-marked trailhead.

Big Mountain Pass (hike midpoint/alternative trailhead): From Exit 134 off I-80 East, turn left onto UT 65 North and drive 8.4 miles to the large Big Mountain Pass parking area, on the right. The trail to Mormon Flat departs down the slope on the lot's east side, while the trail to Little Dell begins from the lot's southwest side. To shuttle between Big Mountain and Mormon Flat or Little Dell, use the GPS coordinates to plot your trip.

Note: From early fall to late spring, UT 65 (known locally as the Big Mountain Highway) is closed to cars in the area covered by this hike, but in winter the highway is groomed periodically by **The Utah Nordic Alliance** for hikers, runners, cyclists, snowshoers, cross-country skiers, and snowmobilers. Visit utahnordic.com/skiing/locations/sr65 for the latest information.

City Creek Canyon Road is fully paved but driven on only by the rare government vehicle.

WITH THE 28-STORY LDS Church office building to your back and the Utah state capitol in front of you, follow a creek through a city park, quickly leaving the city behind. Within 2 miles you'll be walking in a national forest and nature preserve shared with elk, moose, and mountain lions.

DESCRIPTION

City Creek has served as Salt Lake City's primary water source since 1847, when Mormon pioneers first arrived in the valley. No other hike in the United States allows you to be in an urban center, within a block of the state capitol, and then so quickly find yourself following a tumbling creek through the depths of a protected canyon filled with undisturbed wildlife and dense vegetation.

If the hardest part of this hike is finding parking, then the most dangerous part is crossing the pedestrian crosswalk on State Street to access the "trailhead." Starting at the northeast corner of State Street and North Temple, walk one-half block to the east along the decorative sidewalk, and continue as the sidewalk curves north onto Canyon Road, away from downtown and into a quiet residential area. Tiles embedded in the concrete identify native animals and birds by their footprints, preparing you for what you're likely to find upcanyon.

DISTANCE & CONFIGURATION: 3- to 12-mile out-and-back

DIFFICULTY: Easy

SCENERY: Riparian canyon with brushy slopes; good bird-watching

EXPOSURE: Partially shaded

TRAIL TRAFFIC: Moderate–heavy

TRAIL SURFACE: Paved or dirt, depending on options chosen

HIKING TIME: 1–4 hours

DRIVING DISTANCE: 5 miles from I-15/I-80 intersection

ELEVATION CHANGE: 4,370'–5,005'

ACCESS: Daily, 8:30 a.m.–10 p.m.; no fees or permits

MAPS: USGS *Salt Lake City North*

FACILITIES: Restrooms near trailhead and at numerous points along the route

WHEELCHAIR ACCESS: Yes

CONTACT: 801-535-7800, slc.gov/parks

LOCATION: Northeast corner of State Street and North Temple, Salt Lake City, UT 84103 (main trailhead); City Creek Canyon Road 0.1 mile north of East Bonneville Boulevard, Salt Lake City, UT 84103 (alternative trailhead)

COMMENTS: Dogs allowed on leash for the first 2.5 miles

On July 21, 1847, near the location of the trailhead, Orson Pratt and Erastus Snow, along with other members of the vanguard party that led the Mormon emigration from Illinois, arrived in the Salt Lake Valley and set up camp. They quickly diverted water from City Creek to soften the soil. By the time Brigham Young arrived three days later, they had already planted 5 acres of potatoes. Within a matter of weeks, a gristmill had been built on City Creek. During the early years of Salt Lake City, energy harnessed from the creek powered many essential industries, such as blacksmith shops, furniture makers, and clothing mills. Water from City Creek still supplies drinking water for much of downtown Salt Lake City and the adjacent Avenues neighborhood.

After walking through two residential blocks, pass through the gate at the entrance of Memory Grove Park. As you enter the park, the rising canyon walls have already blocked the view of the city—it's easy to forget that the capitol building is just 400 feet to your left but completely out of sight.

Once within the park, walk along the main paved road or on any of the pathways that pass the various monuments and benches placed throughout. Several footbridges cross the creek and allow you to use the dirt trail on the creek's east side. This trail hugs the creek and provides more shade, solitude, and varied terrain than the paved parkway. It normally delivers a sure footing but can be slick during snowmelt or after a heavy rain.

Follow the creek up Memory Grove Park and through a second gate. After 1.5 miles, the paved parkway curves to the right and crosses City Creek to join Bonneville Boulevard; take the narrower paved trail that rises to the left, passing the retention pond on your right, which is often home to ducks and geese. This area provides a convenient turnaround point for a 3-mile round-trip hike, or you can cross Bonneville Boulevard and enter City Creek Natural Area, straight ahead.

City Creek Canyon

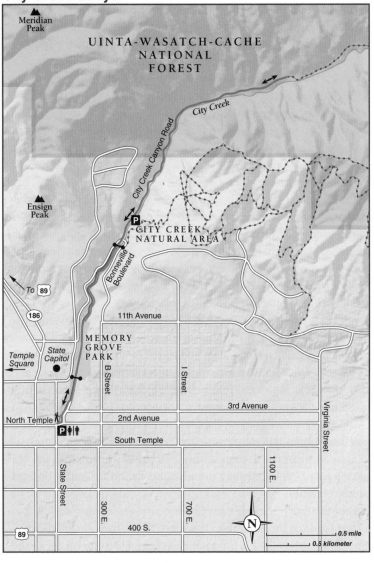

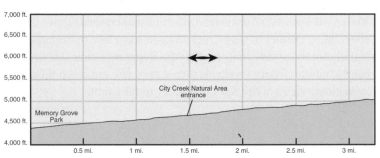

After crossing Bonneville Boulevard, walk 0.1 mile to a small parking area with an entrance station, water fountain, and restrooms. You can use this area as an alternate trailhead, allowing you to bypass the hassle of downtown parking and begin your hike in more of a wilderness setting. The road, which continues up the canyon, closes to vehicle traffic October 30–May 25, and even when it's open, cars are allowed only on even-numbered days. The city manages the area beyond the entrance station as a protected watershed and wildlife refuge.

As you walk up the paved parkway, remember that you're sharing the road with cyclists, who often come down the canyon at high speeds. Hikers should stay on the side of the road nearest the creek.

About 800 feet past the entrance station, a trail (marked by a sign) heads uphill to the left. This trail, which parallels the creek and the parkway up the canyon, provides a quieter, more natural alternative to the parkway. It follows the gentle slope of the canyon hillside, which is covered by grasses, dense brush, and Gambel oaks. Expect both less shade and less traffic on the trail, which still provides easy access to the frequent restrooms and drinking fountains along the parkway. To the right of the parkway, City Creek descends the canyon in a series of meandering stretches punctuated by dozens of small waterfalls.

The canyon is a year-round home to deer, coyote, and elusive mountain lions. In winter you may well spot elk and moose, even in the lower elevations below the reservoir. Bird-watchers enjoy the abundant and varied raptor populations throughout the year. Hawks, eagles, falcons, and owls find small rodents on the canyon's grassy slopes to be easy pickings. Grouse, quail, chukar, and pheasants are plentiful in the brush.

Along both the creek and parkway, cottonwoods offer ample shade. About 2 miles from the entrance station, the higher elevation and north-facing slope provide a hospitable environment for stands of balsam and spruce. Scattered along the parkway are convenient rest areas with picnic tables, restrooms, and water fountains, making City Creek Canyon a popular destination for family outings, picnics, and outdoor relaxation.

From the entrance station, City Creek continues up the canyon for 13 miles, and the road is paved for 5.8 miles. The creek is fed by snowmelt, natural springs at the top of the canyon, and many smaller springs along the course of the creek. A reservoir, 3 miles from the entrance station, makes a convenient turnaround point. Because the area is a protected watershed, no dogs are permitted above the reservoir.

Although most visitors to City Creek Canyon stay close to the parkway, creek, and main trail, dozens of side trails lead up the slopes on either side of the canyon. In less than 15 minutes from a creekside picnic area, you can reach the ridge, which offers commanding views of the Salt Lake Valley to the south.

NEARBY ACTIVITIES

Because this hike originates in downtown Salt Lake City, you'll find lots of shopping, dining, and recreational/cultural options close by. Historic **Temple Square** is just a block to the west, and the **Utah State Capitol** is two blocks to the north. Before starting the hike, you may want to walk through **Brigham Young Historic Park,** on the southeast corner of State Street and North Temple. A waterwheel, mill, and other displays depict the role of City Creek in Salt Lake City history.

• •

GPS TRAILHEAD COORDINATES
Main trailhead: N40° 46.300' W111° 53.280'
Alternative trailhead: N40° 47.494' W111° 52.714'

DIRECTIONS It may seem strange to refer to one of the busiest intersections in downtown Salt Lake City as a trailhead, but the hike starts at the northeast corner of State Street (US 89) and North Temple, just a block from Temple Square and convenient to downtown dining and shopping. The most difficult part of getting to the trailhead will be finding a place to park. Use one of the public or commercial lots nearby—most street parking in the vicinity is limited to 2 hours.

You can also start your hike farther up the canyon by driving to the City Creek Natural Area entrance. From State Street and North Temple/Second Avenue, head east on Second Avenue; in 0.3 mile, turn left on B Street/250 East, and continue north 0.7 mile through the Avenues neighborhood. At the corner of B Street and 11th Avenue, B Street becomes East Bonneville Boulevard; continue north 0.6 mile on East Bonneville Boulevard along the east rim of City Creek Canyon. As East Bonneville makes a hairpin turn left, turn right onto City Creek Canyon Road/350 East, the narrow paved road leading into City Creek Natural Area, marked by a large CITY CREEK CANYON sign on the left. Drive 0.1 mile to the small parking area on the right.

This waterfall and pond are among Red Butte Garden's many natural attractions.

Photo: Greg Witt

JUST MINUTES BY FOOT from the University of Utah, formal gardens give way to natural-area trails in a peaceful setting of beauty and historical significance that also provides education and fun. At Red Butte Garden, there's something for everyone at any time of year.

DESCRIPTION

It would be easy to visit Red Butte Garden and spend the better part of a day enjoying the colorful floral gardens, ponds, and waterfalls without ever venturing into the more-remote natural area. Indeed, most visitors find sufficient variety and entertainment in the 18 acres of landscaped gardens that they never leave the paved trails for the nearly 100 acres of grassy hillsides, wildflower meadows, and rocky outcrops that lie to the east of the formal gardens. But those who come prepared with basic trail shoes and water can enjoy a network of more than 4 miles of hill trails, offering gentle ascents that lead to sweeping views of the Salt Lake Valley.

Beginning in the late 1800s, the U.S. Army used the strategically important hillside as a camp, firing range, and fort. The red-sandstone crags that form the hill's main ridge served as a quarry that was actively worked until about 1934, producing the redstone blocks still seen in many of the prominent homes and buildings throughout the Salt Lake Valley.

DISTANCE & CONFIGURATION: 2–4 miles of loops with various side trails and extensions

DIFFICULTY: Easy

SCENERY: Foothills, outcrops of red sandstone, riparian corridor, valley views

EXPOSURE: Full sun, partial shade

TRAIL TRAFFIC: High in formal gardens, low in natural area

TRAIL SURFACE: Paved in formal gardens, dirt trails in natural area

HIKING TIME: 1–2 hours

DRIVING DISTANCE: 7 miles from I-15/ I-80 intersection

ELEVATION CHANGE: 5,065'–5,475'

ACCESS: Varies; check redbuttegarden.org /general-info for hours and entrance fees

MAPS: USGS *Sugar House;* redbuttegarden.org /garden-maps

FACILITIES: Restrooms, water, phone, snacks, gift shop at visitor center

WHEELCHAIR ACCESS: Yes

CONTACT: 801-585-0556, redbuttegarden.org

LOCATION: 300 Wakara Way, Salt Lake City, UT 84108

COMMENTS: Dogs prohibited

At the visitor center you'll receive a useful guide and map that identify many of the garden highlights, such as the Courtyard Garden, the Herb Garden, the Water Pavilion, and the Children's Garden. The guide also features a map of the natural-area trails, showing four different trailheads that access the natural area from the formal gardens.

One popular trail loop follows the perimeter of the Red Butte Garden property and offers a surprising variety of terrain, foliage, and scenery in a 2-mile hike. Beginning at the Courtyard Garden, just outside the visitor center, take the trail for 200 feet along the south side of the Four Seasons Garden. Leaving the formal area, continue to the right along a wide bark path, cross Quarry Road, and continue up the Seepy Hollow Trail for 0.2 mile to another Quarry Road crossing. Seepy Hollow follows the course of a natural spring seepage, so in wet conditions you might want to take the longer Quarry Road. A short 0.1-mile walk up Quarry Road brings you to a sign marking the junction with the Zeke's Mountain Trail loop, to the left.

From this junction you can take a 0.1-mile spur trail to the end of Quarry Road and visit the historic Quarry House. This fascinating sandstone structure, dating to the late 1800s, was built to store equipment and house the quarry superintendent. Although the roof is gone and some of the walls have been vandalized, the house's stonework shows the masons' enduring craftsmanship. The centerpiece of the Quarry House is a large double-sided fireplace.

Returning to Zeke's Mountain Trail, you'll wind through a thicket of Gambel oak up the craggy hillside to the Bennett Vista Trail, which leads to the hill's crest and offers commanding views of the Salt Lake Valley. From the hilltop, continue east on Zeke's Mountain Trail, generally following the property's fenced perimeter. At the far east side of the property, the trail meets the fence. Here, a one-way gate allows unwelcome deer to leave the property so they can forage on adjoining U.S. Forest Service land rather than eat the cultivated flowers in Red Butte Garden.

Red Butte Garden

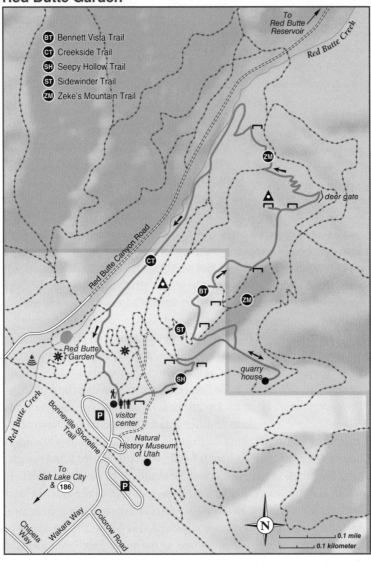

Bennett Vista Trail
Creekside Trail
Seepy Hollow Trail
Sidewinder Trail
Zeke's Mountain Trail

To Red Butte Reservoir

Red Butte Creek

deer gate

Red Butte Canyon Road

quarry house

Red Butte Garden

visitor center

Natural History Museum of Utah

Red Butte Creek

Bonneville Shoreline Trail

To Salt Lake City & 186

Chipeta Way Wakara Way Colorow Road

N

0.1 mile
0.1 kilometer

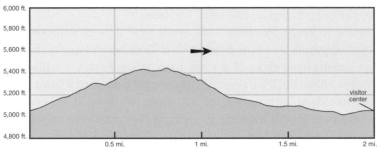

6,000 ft.
5,800 ft.
5,600 ft.
5,400 ft.
5,200 ft.
5,000 ft.
4,800 ft.

visitor center

0.5 mi.   1 mi.   1.5 mi.   2 mi.

The trail descends along the fence line to the creek, which forms the northern boundary of the garden. Along the Creekside Trail, you'll enjoy the shade of oaks and bigtooth maples. Continue on this trail 0.4 mile before returning to the formal gardens.

Throughout the natural-area trails, you'll find more than 130 native plants and trees. In spring, when the garden is especially colorful, yellow blooms of arrowleaf balsamroot and speckles of blue Wasatch penstemon dot the green hillside. You might see a Great Basin rattlesnake sunning itself on the trail or spot rodents, rabbits, or even evidence of an occasional bobcat.

Red Butte Garden's natural-area trails are well marked with signs at all trailheads. While the signs become more scarce in the outlying areas, getting lost is never much of a concern—the property is fenced on all sides, and you can visually orient yourself along most of the trails: if you're ever in doubt, just follow any trail downhill and to the west, and you'll soon find yourself back within the formal gardens.

The natural-area trails offer plenty of options in the way of short loops, spurs, and side trails. After exploring the foothills and creekside in the natural area, you can return to the wide, paved trails of the formal gardens and easily spend an additional hour or more enjoying the year-round beauty in this community treasure.

NEARBY ACTIVITIES

Red Butte Garden offers a year-round program of classes, workshops, activities, tours, and community programs. The Outdoor Concert Series features world-renowned performing artists on the garden's amphitheater stage during June, July, and August; call 801-585-0556 or visit redbuttegarden.org for schedules and ticket information.

Adjacent to the garden, the **University of Utah** (810-581-7200, utah.edu) plays host to many concerts, sporting events, and campus activities.

• •

GPS TRAILHEAD COORDINATES N40° 45.929' W111° 49.422'

DIRECTIONS From east- or westbound I-80 between I-15 and I-215 in Salt Lake City, take Exit 129 for UT 186 West/Foothill Drive, or from I-215 North just west of the I-215/I-80 interchange, take Exit 1 for UT 186 West/Foothill Drive. Merge northwest onto Foothill Drive, and drive 3.3 miles. Turn right onto Wakara Way, and drive 0.9 mile to the Red Butte Garden entrance; parking is 0.1 mile ahead on the left. Enter the garden and trail system through the visitor center.

13 THE LIVING ROOM
(with Red Butte Extension)

Dogs and people alike can enjoy the rocky furniture of the Living Room.

THE LIVING ROOM is the best room in the house for an in-town overview of the Salt Lake Valley. It's furnished with charming sandstone chairs, armrests, and even coffee tables you can put your feet on. The hike leads through foothill vegetation and offers an onward scramble to a higher sandstone outcrop on a ridge above Red Butte Canyon.

DESCRIPTION

Red Butte Canyon, the smallest of seven canyons streaming down the Wasatch ridges east of Salt Lake City, lies directly east of downtown Salt Lake City and above Fort Douglas and the University of Utah campus. A hike to the popular Living Room overlook will take you through foothill vegetation to Red Butte Ridge, which forms the south side of Red Butte Canyon.

The historical significance of the area was first tied to its use as a sandstone quarry and later to water rights. In 1862, U.S. troops established Fort Douglas and used the spring water of Red Butte Creek for domestic and irrigation purposes, affecting the 3,000 local residents who relied on the creek for their water supply. Today the canyon is managed as a protected Natural Research Area under the control of the U.S. Forest Service and is recognized as the most pristine watershed along the Wasatch Front.

DISTANCE & CONFIGURATION: 2.3-mile out-and-back to Living Room, 2.7-mile out-and-back with Red Butte extension

DIFFICULTY: Easy

SCENERY: Foothills, valley views

EXPOSURE: Partial shade to Living Room, unshaded from Living Room to Red Butte extension

TRAIL TRAFFIC: Moderate

TRAIL SURFACE: Dirt and gravel to Living Room, rock to Red Butte extension

HIKING TIME: 1.5–2 hours round-trip to Living Room, 2–3 hours round-trip with Red Butte extension

DRIVING DISTANCE: 7 miles from I-15/I-80 intersection

ELEVATION CHANGE: 5,000'–6,340'

ACCESS: Daily, sunrise–sunset; no fees or permits

MAPS: USGS *Fort Douglas*

FACILITIES: None

WHEELCHAIR ACCESS: None

CONTACT: 801-733-2660, fs.usda.gov/uwcnf

LOCATION: East side of Colorow Road just north of Huntsman Way, Salt Lake City, UT 84108

COMMENTS: Dogs allowed on leash

Within 100 yards of the marked trailhead on the east side of Colorow Drive, you come to a small spring-fed creek. The trail crosses the creek at the base of a large, mature Russian olive tree, one of several in the riparian corridor. The path continues up the slope for another 0.1 mile before arriving at the wide Bonneville Shoreline Trail. Here you take a jog to the right for 50 feet before continuing up and to the left along a gravel trail. You'll enter a dense cover of Gambel oak and bigtooth maple near the mouth of a small ravine known as Georges Hollow.

At 0.7 mile from the trailhead, the route breaks out onto a ridgeline that you'll follow up and to the east along the south slope of a ravine. At 1.1 miles, you come to a trail junction at the top of the ravine. Continuing straight ahead leads up to the 6,472-foot Red Butte peak—for this hike take the trail that crosses the ravine and curves to the left. This path to the Living Room now ascends westward along the north side of the ravine. Upon crossing to the north side of the ravine, the rocks change from gray limestone to peach-colored sandstone. After walking just 0.1 mile from the junction along the sandstone-studded slope, you arrive at the Living Room.

The Living Room invites a relaxing stay. A man-made arrangement of angular sandstone slabs provides a comfortable observation point complete with several chairs, armrests, ottomans, and coffee tables. There's no better place to sit and watch a sunset, take in the spring wildflowers or fall colors, or just relax and enjoy a snack. The Living Room overlooks the University of Utah and Fort Douglas, where athletes were housed during the 2002 Winter Olympics. The extended views stretch from the Great Salt Lake to the north to the Oquirrh Mountains in the west, and down to the southern end of the Salt Lake Valley, clear to the Point of the Mountain.

While the Living Room is the final destination for most hikers, you can undertake an easy scramble to a higher overlook if you have a little extra energy. Behind the Living Room, a faint and noticeably steeper trail leads up the sandstone crags to the east along a ridgeline to a clearly visible viewpoint. In about 15 minutes, you'll

The Living Room (with Red Butte Extension)

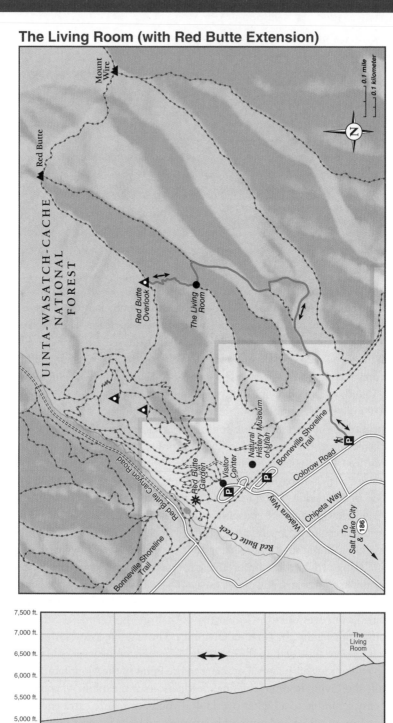

find yourself on a shelf of large sandstone slabs with views down into Red Butte Canyon and the Red Butte Reservoir to the north. The extension to this overlook adds about 0.4 mile round-trip beyond the Living Room.

NEARBY ACTIVITIES

Ensign Peak is a popular Salt Lake overlook with a well-maintained trail and a round-trip distance of less than 1 mile. From downtown take State Street to the east of the State Capitol Building on East Capitol Boulevard. Continue up to Edgecombe Drive, turn left, and continue 0.4 mile to the trailhead, on the left at Ensign Peak Nature Park.

• •

GPS TRAILHEAD COORDINATES N40° 45.557' W111° 49.277'

DIRECTIONS From east- or westbound I-80 between I-15 and I-215 in Salt Lake City, take Exit 129 for UT 186 West/Foothill Drive. Or from I-215 North just west of the I-215/I-80 interchange, take Exit 1 for UT 186 West/Foothill Drive. Merge northwest onto Foothill Drive, and drive 3.3 miles. Turn right on Wakara Way; then, in 0.6 mile, just before you reach the entrance to Red Butte Garden, turn right onto Colorow Road. Continue 0.2 mile to the trailhead, on the left side of the street.

Unique flora dot the path as you ascend from the Bonneville Shoreline Trail. *Photo: Greg Witt*

Hikers on Jack's Mountain have constant views of the valley below.

THIS SHORT BUT moderately strenuous hike rewards those who endure the steep climb out of the valley with not only impressive views of the city but also a uniquely touching tribute to a local boy who died from leukemia. The memorial and the views combine to make this a wonderful afternoon or winter hike.

DESCRIPTION

Many of Utah's mountains, rivers, and canyons were named in the 19th century for contemporary bigwigs. Jack's Mountain, a far more recent addition to Salt Lake Valley's named peaks, commemorates Jack Edwards, a toddler who passed away from leukemia in 1995, just shy of his second birthday. His parents scattered his ashes from the summit, which overlooks the Salt Lake Valley to the west. The mountain, also known locally as Jack's Mailbox Peak, now serves not only as a loving tribute to Jack and the Edwards family but as a quick escape from Salt Lake's historic-but-hectic Sugar House neighborhood.

As is the case with a number of other hikes covered in this book, the trail leading up Jack's Mountain begins from a residential area. Because you'll be parking on a street that several families call home, please take care not to block their driveways or the gate at the end of the road. Given the limited parking, you'd be best served to do this hike on a weekday or in the early morning.

DISTANCE & CONFIGURATION: 2.6-mile out-and-back

DIFFICULTY: Moderate

SCENERY: Valley and ravine views, and a unique memorial at the summit

EXPOSURE: No shade

TRAIL TRAFFIC: Light

TRAIL SURFACE: Dirt, rock

HIKING TIME: 1.5–2 hours

DRIVING DISTANCE: 7 miles from I-15/I-80 intersection

ELEVATION CHANGE: 5,210'–6,465'

ACCESS: Daily, sunrise–sunset; no fees or permits, but parking is limited at the trailhead. Best accessed weekdays and mornings.

MAPS: USGS *Sugar House*

FACILITIES: None

WHEELCHAIR ACCESS: None

CONTACT: 385-468-7275, slco.org/parks/trails

LOCATION: Northern end of Lakeline Drive, 0.3 mile north of Hyland Hills Road, Salt Lake City, UT 84109

COMMENTS: The low elevation and well-worn path make this a great winter destination. Dogs allowed on leash. The trailhead is at the end of a residential street, so please be considerate of nearby homeowners.

Two popular routes lead up to Jack's Mountain. The route described here is marginally shorter (and thus steeper) than the other one, but it's also markedly easier to follow—on your way back from the summit, it's not difficult to identify the alternative route back to trailhead, but the shorter route remains the most obvious and most heavily trafficked.

Regardless of the route you take, the trailhead is the same: it's at the end of Lakeline Drive, at the northeast corner of the cul-de-sac. The first 60 feet of the hike are paved, but the trail's true beginning is marked by a pair of painted benches located to the left of the concrete path.

As you walk past the benches, you drop quickly onto the summit trail. The trail initially points northeast, paralleling a private road that leads through a nearby gated community. As you hike east, you'll arrive at an unmissably large sign warning you that to continue east will put you on the property of the local homeowners' association. At this point, the trail doubles back on itself, now pointing west, back toward the Salt Lake Valley.

Less than 200 feet after the HOA sign, just before the trail begins to lose elevation, turn right and follow the trail up the south face of the hill. This stretch, like much of the trail leading up to the summit, is lacking in switchbacks, but the rapid gains in elevation are accompanied by similarly rapid gains in views. Vistas into Carrigan Canyon, and later Spring Canyon, become more breathtaking the higher you climb.

As you ascend, you'll quickly notice that the trail heads toward a barely camouflaged communications tower. While not particularly interesting in itself, it's a great place to catch your breath or take some photos. Immediately after you reach the tower, the trail descends more than 100 feet before bending back uphill for the final approach to the summit.

Jack's Mountain

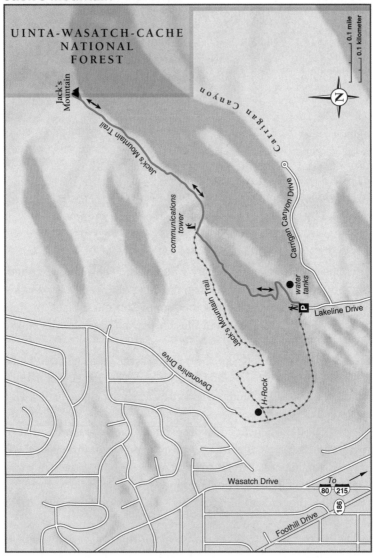

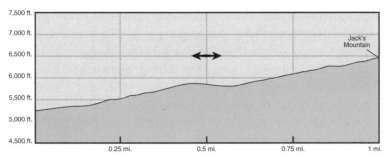

Because the remainder of the clearly visible trail follows the ridgeline, you have few opportunities to get lost between the tower and the summit. The lichenous rock outcrops impart the landscape with a visually arresting texture, and the views—both north and south—continuously expand as you ascend above the neighboring ridges and peaks. In the springtime, small clutches of wildflowers grow around the summit; the level of exposure on the south face of Jack's Mountain, however, makes their season short-lived.

After reaching the summit, descend a few feet to the north to find the well-marked memorial. Tucked into the rocks are two mailboxes containing notebooks, along with an invitation to leave a note. Take some time here to read the messages of support, hope, and encouragement left by hikers over the years. Many of the journal entries are notes to the family, while others are notes to other hikers. All offer an uplifting and wholesome message that can be appreciated in a serene and stunning environment.

When you're ready to return, simply follow the trail back down the ridgeline to the communications tower and bear left at the junction. For an alternative route back to the trailhead, continue to follow the ridgeline to the right (west) until it descends past H-Rock, a large, rocky outcrop that students at nearby Highland High School have marked as their own. As you descend the ridge, you'll be dropped onto the famous and broad Bonneville Shoreline Trail. Turn left and follow this trail until it wanders past the cul-de-sac in which you parked.

Because of the low elevation, this hike is a good one to do in winter using either spikes or snowshoes (depending on the amount of snow). It's also particularly impressive when the wildflowers bloom in the spring.

NEARBY ACTIVITIES

Sugar House Park is one of the largest parks in the city, made up of more than 100 acres of lush green space. It not only offers ample room to relax and picnic but also provides runners, walkers, and cyclists with almost 2 miles of paved trails along the perimeter of the park. For more information, call 385-468-7275 or visit sugarhousepark.org.

• •

GPS TRAILHEAD COORDINATES N40° 43.738' W111° 48.372'

DIRECTIONS From east- or westbound I-80 between I-15 and I-215 in Salt Lake City, take Exit 129 for UT 186 West/Foothill Drive, or from I-215 North just west of the I-215/I-80 interchange, take Exit 1 for UT 186 West/Foothill Drive. Take Foothill Drive north for 1 mile; then turn right onto 2100 South and follow it 0.5 mile, during which 2100 South becomes Hyland Hills Road. Turn left onto Lakeline Drive, and follow it 0.3 mile until it dead-ends at a cul-de-sac.

15 LAMBS CANYON

Aspens, firs, and thick undergrowth envelop the Lambs Canyon Trail.

OLD-GROWTH FORESTS of spruce and fir, shared with quaking aspen, line a canyon fed by several springs. A steep trail to an 8,100-foot pass offers views into the valley before leading down Elbow Fork and into Mill Creek Canyon. It's a symphony of woods, wildflowers, berries, creeks, and views. This is a great snowshoe trail in the depths of winter, easily accessed on cross-country skis along Mill Creek Canyon.

DESCRIPTION

In the 1860s, Abel Lamb recognized the value of the timber in the canyon that now bears his name. He built a cabin in the canyon, and his son, Horace, built a sawmill. To meet the construction demands in the growing Salt Lake Valley, the sawmill hauled lumber down the new Golden Pass Toll Road (now I-80), which was constructed by Parley P. Pratt through Big Canyon (now known as Parleys Canyon). But Lamb's sawmill couldn't make a dent in the thousands of acres of timber that still cover Lambs Canyon today.

You can explore Lambs Canyon in a variety of ways, and the one-way canyon-to-canyon route described here requires shuttle vehicles left at both end. The hike leads from Lambs Canyon to Mill Creek Canyon via the Great Western Trail and Elbow Fork, but you can just as easily undertake this hike as a 4-mile out-and-back

DISTANCE & CONFIGURATION: 6-mile point-to-point or 8-mile out-and-back

DIFFICULTY: Moderate

SCENERY: Abundant plant life in two deep canyons, views of Salt Lake Valley and surrounding peaks from pass

EXPOSURE: Mostly shaded

TRAIL TRAFFIC: Light

TRAIL SURFACE: Dirt

HIKING TIME: 2.5–3.5 hours

DRIVING DISTANCE: 16 miles from I-15/ I-80 intersection

ELEVATION CHANGE: 6,615'–8,133'

ACCESS: Daily, sunrise–sunset, but road access is limited seasonally: the Maple Grove gate across Mill Creek Canyon Road is locked November 1– July 1, and Lambs Canyon Road is closed November 1–June 1 (see Description for details). Current use fees for Mill Creek Canyon are $3/car (collected as you leave the canyon) or $40/year.

MAPS: USGS *Mount Aire;* Trails Illustrated *Wasatch Front* (709)

FACILITIES: Vault toilets at trailheads but no water

WHEELCHAIR ACCESS: None

CONTACT: 801-466-6411, fs.usda.gov/uwcnf; 385-468-7275, slco.org/parks/millcreek-canyon

LOCATION: Lambs Canyon Road 2 miles south of I-80, Summit Park, UT 84098 (Lambs Canyon trailhead); Mill Creek Canyon Road, Salt Lake City, UT 84109 (Elbow Fork trailhead)

COMMENTS: Dogs prohibited in Lambs Canyon, a protected watershed. Hiking from the Lambs Canyon trailhead to the saddle and back avoids the Mill Creek Canyon use fee.

within Lambs Canyon. Simply park at the Lambs Canyon trailhead, hike to the pass for views into the valley, and then return back down the trail to your car. The out-and-back option also avoids the access fee for Mill Creek Canyon.

The Lambs Canyon Trail also serves as a section of the Great Western Trail, which when completed will stretch continuously from Mexico to Canada and traverse some of the most spectacular scenery in the West. The Lambs Canyon section, from I-80 to Mill Creek, is one of the most beautifully wooded and shaded sections of the trail. (For another hike on the Great Western Trail, see Hike 33, page 155.)

Note: Access to both trailheads is affected by two seasonal road closures. When the gate across upper Mill Creek Canyon Road is closed (November 1–July 1), you must park at the Maple Grove picnic area, located just before the gate on the right, 1.5 miles west of the Elbow Fork trailhead. Lambs Canyon Road was formerly maintained in winter but is now closed to motorized vehicles (including snowmobiles, except for residents of homes along the road) November 1–June 1, where the road meets I-80 at Exit 137, 1.7 miles north of the trailhead. When these roads are closed, you'll need to hike, bike, ski, or snowshoe to/from the trailheads.

From the Lambs Canyon trailhead parking area, cross Lambs Canyon Road and immediately cross a bridge over a stream lined with willows. Immediately, you're engulfed in a forest of aspen, fir, and spruce—but don't ignore the foliage at your feet. Wild strawberries, raspberries, grapes, and mint line the trail. In spring, wyethia, larkspur, and harebell brighten the trail—and as long as they're not on your lawn, even dandelions are a welcome wildflower in the woods. Diverse shrubbery also lines the narrow trail and makes long pants preferable. The soil is dark and well packed, sprinkled with fir needles and ribboned with roots of trees.

Lambs Canyon

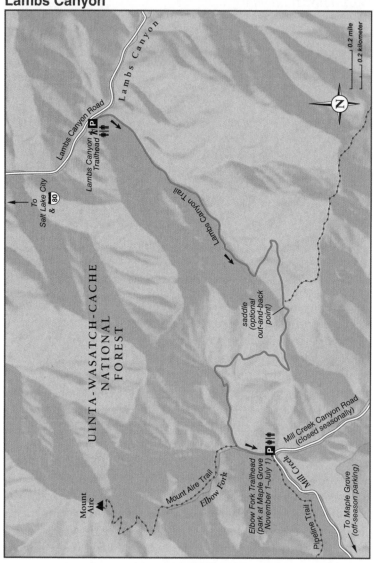

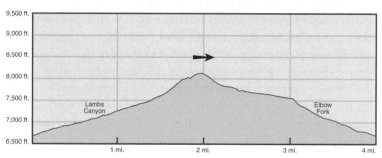

Moose and deer find Lambs Canyon a welcoming habitat. Watch for the burrows of ground squirrels near the trail, and look out for wrens, varied thrushes, hummingbirds, and sparrows.

At about 1.5 miles up the canyon, the trail departs the spring and enters a series of wide, steep switchbacks through stands of aspen as you approach the pass. At the saddle elevation of 8,133 feet, the woods open to views of Gobblers Knob and Mount Raymond to the south and Grandeur Peak to the west. To the left of Grandeur Peak, you can also see a slice of the Salt Lake Valley.

From the saddle at the top of the pass, you have a choice based on where your car is waiting: you can return to Lambs Canyon for an out-and-back hike, or you can continue on down Elbow Fork into Mill Creek Canyon for a one-way hike with all-new territory.

The trail from the pass down to Mill Creek is slightly less shaded than the trail leading up from Lambs Canyon. Still, within minutes you drop into the canyon along a gathering creek and soon find yourself back in the shade. The trail through Elbow Fork lacks the diversity of foliage found in Lambs Canyon but offers some fine views of the surrounding canyon and occasional glimpses of the sandstone crags on Mount Aire to the north.

At 1.8 miles from the pass and less than 0.2 mile from the Elbow Fork trailhead, you come to a trail junction. The fork to the right leads up the main branch of Elbow Fork on the Mount Aire Trail—take the fork to the left to reach the Elbow Fork trailhead and Mill Creek Canyon Road.

As noted earlier, the gate to the upper canyon, at Maple Grove, is open only seasonally, so if you've left a shuttle November 1–July 1, you'll need to walk west on Mill Creek Canyon Road from Elbow Fork back to the Maple Grove picnic area. But a shaded walk on a car-free road with Mill Creek at your side can be enchanting.

NEARBY ACTIVITIES

The **Mill Creek Canyon Fishing Dock and Boardwalk** is at the Terraces, 1.7 miles west of the Elbow Fork trailhead on the south side of Mill Creek Canyon Road. A short 0.1-mile walk leads to fishing fun for young and old.

• •

GPS TRAILHEAD COORDINATES
Elbow Fork: N40° 42.397' W111° 41.408'
Maple Grove: N40° 41.995' W111° 42.804'
Lambs Canyon: N40° 43.277' W111° 39.490'

DIRECTIONS *Elbow Fork (ending trailhead):* From the eastern intersection of I-80 and I-215, take I-215 South and drive 1.2 miles; then take Exit 4 for 3900 South. Turn left onto 3900 South, and drive 0.1 mile; then turn left onto Wasatch Boulevard, and drive another 0.1 mile. Turn right onto Mill Creek Canyon Road, and drive 6.1 miles, passing a fee booth at 0.7 mile (you'll pay the canyon use fee here later on your way out). The trailhead will be on the left where Mill Creek and the road turn sharply to the right. Roadside parking is available at the trailhead (see earlier notes about off-season parking at Maple Grove).

Lambs Canyon (starting trailhead): After leaving a shuttle at Elbow Fork, backtrack 6.1 miles west on Mill Creek Canyon Road. Immediately after crossing Wasatch Boulevard, turn right to merge onto I-215 North. In 1.1 miles take Exit 2 off I-215 to merge onto I-80 East. In 7.9 miles take Exit 137 for Lambs Canyon, and turn right onto Lambs Canyon Road. Drive 1.7 miles up the canyon to the trailhead parking area, on the left. The trailhead is across the street, on the west side of the road.

Note: Lambs Canyon Road is closed to motorized vehicles (including snowmobiles for trail users who do not live along the road) November 1–June 1. A small dirt parking pullout is located on the left side of the road just past the two I-80 exit ramps, 1.7 miles north of the trailhead.

Runners enjoy Lambs Canyon for its beauty and easily accessed views.

Due to the trail's quick ascent from the canyon floor, sprawling views are an immediate reward.

TUCKED AWAY ON the ridge behind Grandeur Peak, Mount Aire is hidden from most of Salt Lake City. Still, it offers excellent views to the east and of surrounding peaks. The Mount Aire Trail connects with many other Mill Creek trails and the Great Western Trail.

DESCRIPTION

Mount Aire is a bite-size challenge. If you're in great shape, you can drive to the trailhead after work, bag the summit, and be back to your car in 2.5 hours. If you're looking to build speed and endurance, Mount Aire offers a steep and steady incline for nearly 2 miles that will let you know if you're ready for a more demanding adventure. It's also an ideal snowshoe ascent in winter that offers a real challenge, rewarding you with great views of snow-covered peaks and hills in all directions.

During the summer and fall, you can drive directly to the Elbow Fork trailhead and go straight to the summit in just 1.9 miles. But from November 1 to July 1 (with some variation based on weather), the gate at Maple Grove is closed to motor vehicles, so you'll have to walk, ski, or snowshoe the 1.5 miles from Maple Grove up to the Elbow Fork trailhead. Walking along the shaded road as it follows Mill Creek up the canyon is really quite enjoyable, even if it adds 3 miles to the round-trip.

DISTANCE & CONFIGURATION: 3.8-mile out-and-back

DIFFICULTY: Moderate

SCENERY: Wooded canyon leading to a summit with panoramic views

EXPOSURE: Mostly shaded the first mile up to ridgeline saddle; partially shaded to summit

TRAIL TRAFFIC: Light

TRAIL SURFACE: Dirt, rock

HIKING TIME: 2.5–4 hours

DRIVING DISTANCE: 14 miles from I-15/I-80 intersection

ELEVATION CHANGE: 6,686'–8,673'

ACCESS: Daily, sunrise–sunset, but the Maple Grove gate across Mill Creek Canyon Road is closed November 1–July 1. During this time, you must park at the Maple Grove picnic area and then hike/ski/snowshoe 1.5 miles east to the Elbow Fork trailhead. Current use fees for Mill Creek Canyon are $3/car (collected as you leave the canyon) or $40/year.

MAPS: USGS *Mount Aire;* Trails Illustrated *Wasatch Front* (709)

FACILITIES: Vault toilet at trailhead but no drinking water. Creek water should be purified.

WHEELCHAIR ACCESS: None

CONTACT: 801-466-6411, fs.usda.gov/uwcnf; 385-468-7275, slco.org/parks/millcreek-canyon

LOCATION: Mill Creek Canyon Road, Salt Lake City, UT 84109

COMMENTS: Dogs must be leashed on even-numbered days; can be unleashed on odd-numbered days

The Elbow Fork trailhead lies at the point where Mill Creek and the road make a sharp 90-degree turn to the south. This trailhead also provides access to the Lambs Canyon Trail (see previous hike), the Pipeline Trail (see Hike 18, page 95), and the Great Western Trail (see Hike 33, page 155). Within 0.2 mile of the trailhead, you come to a well-marked fork in the trail, with the Mount Aire Trail taking off to the left. It quickly crosses a footbridge over the small creek and follows the creek up a deep, shaded canyon filled with Douglas-fir, maple, and quaking aspen at the higher elevations.

Continue following the trail along Elbow Fork, a tributary of Mill Creek, for 0.8 mile to the point where the creek is just a trickle. At this point the trail ascends a series of short, steep switchbacks, and within less than a minute you're high above the creek on the east slope of the side canyon. Within another 0.2 mile you emerge from the canyon's shade to arrive at the ridgeline saddle, which offers views down Parleys Canyon to the north. A faint, unmaintained trail follows the ridgeline to the west. With some advance planning you could take this trail to Grandeur Peak (see next hike and Hike 19, page 99) and descend to Mill Creek through Church Fork. But for now, keep to the right and set your sights on Mount Aire to the east.

Leaving the saddle, the trail winds through the sandstone along Mount Aire's western and southern slopes. This sandstone formation, while unusual for the Wasatch, is the same formation you see on Grandeur Peak and along the entire ridge. Although the climb along the upper slope is largely shadeless, it is fragrant with sage and arrowleaf balsamroot. While the trail is easy to follow during most of the year, hiking it in the winter could pose some route-finding challenges when you factor in a foot or more of snow.

Mount Aire

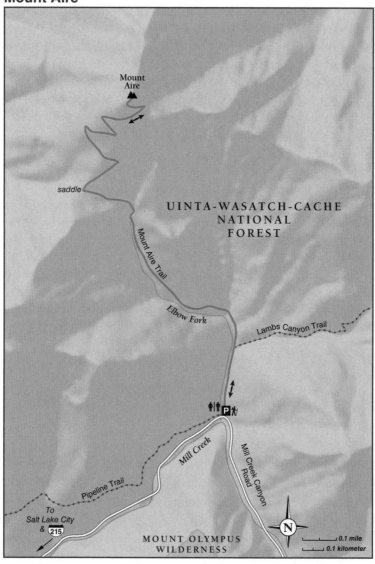

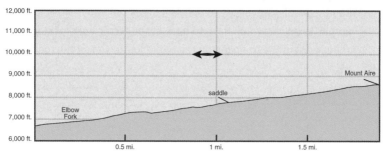

Nearing the summit, you come to an overlook with impressive views of the densely wooded slopes of upper Mill Creek Canyon and Gobblers Knob to the south. From this overlook, a sharp turn to the north leads to the summit just 100 yards ahead. Although the summit ridge extends to the north for more than 200 yards, the true summit is the rocky sandstone outcrop first reached from the south. From this spot you can frequently watch eagles soaring high above the canyon. Below and to the east, you'll see I-80 leading toward Park City. The Salt Lake Valley views to the west are limited, but the panoramic views of mountains in all directions go on forever.

NEARBY ACTIVITIES

Most visitors to Mill Creek Canyon find so much to keep them busy—picnicking, hiking, bicycling, mountain biking, snowshoeing, and cross-country skiing—that they never seem to have much need for add-ons. But if you have an extra 30 minutes at the end of your hike, consider driving another 3.5 miles up to the top of the canyon to scout your next adventure. When the pavement ends at the Big Water trailhead, you're at an elevation of more than 8,000 feet. From this point you can access the **Great Western Trail** (see Hike 33, page 155) or the **Desolation Trail** (see Hike 20, page 103) into Big Cottonwood Canyon, opening the door to hundreds of miles of hiking and biking trails.

* *

GPS TRAILHEAD COORDINATES
Elbow Fork: N40° 42.397' W111° 41.408'
Maple Grove: N40° 41.995' W111° 42.804'

DIRECTIONS From the eastern intersection of I-80 and I-215, take I-215 South and drive 1.2 miles, and then take Exit 4 for 3900 South. Turn left onto 3900 South, and drive 0.1 mile; then turn left onto Wasatch Boulevard, and drive another 0.1 mile. Turn right onto Mill Creek Canyon Road, and drive 6.1 miles, passing a fee booth at 0.7 mile (you'll pay the canyon use fee here later on your way out). The trailhead will be on the left where Mill Creek and the road turn sharply to the right. Roadside parking is available at the trailhead.

Note: When the Maple Grove gate across Mill Creek Canyon Road is locked for the season (November 1–July 1), you'll have to park at the picnic area located just before the gate, 1.7 miles west of the trailhead on the right (south) side of the road.

Big Cottonwood Canyon comes into view as you ascend the western slope.

STARTING FROM A SALT LAKE CITY residential area, this hike not only is rapidly accessible from the city but it ascends rapidly, putting committed hikers atop one of the valley's most famous peaks in just over 2 miles. Hikers who can take the physical challenge of this summit are rewarded with constant valley views, as well as sprawling views of the Wasatch from the summit.

DESCRIPTION

Grandeur Peak is a beautiful summit, affording fantastic views of the Salt Lake Valley as well as breathtaking peaks to the south and east. This beauty, however, comes at the expense of popularity. Hikers who approach the summit from Mill Creek Canyon (see Hike 19, page 99) are often frustrated by the congestion on the eastern trail. By contrast, approaching the summit from the west offers hikers a physical challenge wholly different from the Mill Creek route—but with hardly any crowds at all.

From the parking area, find the trail at the northeast corner of the lot. Don't be put off by the sound of traffic on nearby I-80 and I-215. The trail ascends from the valley so quickly that this noise soon gives way to the dull roar of the wind whipping over the ridgeline. During the early stages of the hike, when the sound of traffic is most pronounced, let it serve as a reminder of just how quickly you can get away

DISTANCE & CONFIGURATION: 4.4-mile out-and-back

DIFFICULTY: Strenuous

SCENERY: Canyon, mountain, and city views

EXPOSURE: Little to no shade

TRAIL TRAFFIC: Light

TRAIL SURFACE: Dirt, rock

HIKING TIME: 2.5–3.5 hours

DRIVING DISTANCE: 7 miles from I-15/I-80 intersection

ELEVATION CHANGE: 4,964'–8,299'

ACCESS: Daily, sunrise–sunset; no fees or permits

MAPS: USGS *Sugar House*

FACILITIES: Water at the trailhead

WHEELCHAIR ACCESS: None

CONTACT: 801-733-2660, fs.usda.gov/uwcnf

LOCATION: Northern end of Wasatch Boulevard just east of I-215, Salt Lake City, UT 84109

COMMENTS: This hike is very steep, so good shoes and trekking poles are recommended. Dogs are allowed on leash.

from the commotion of the city to the isolation of the mountains. This hike represents one of the most stark collisions between these two worlds.

Begin your journey by heading east on the well-defined trail. After just a few hundred yards, you will come to a three-way junction. The simplest route is to go right (south), although the maze of intersecting and intertwining trails in the area offers lots to explore and all of the trails quickly reconnect with one another.

A quarter mile after the first junction, you'll come to the second and final junction of the hike, which presents you with three options. The simplest—but steepest—route is the middle trail, which immediately rises onto the western ridge of Grandeur Peak. Some hikers may want to take the leftmost trail, which ascends more slowly but adds a not-insignificant amount of distance. (The trail to the far right does not ascend to the peak but rather follows the historic Lake Bonneville Shoreline.)

At this point in the hike, the true physical challenge begins. The trailsmiths who designed this route to Grandeur Peak didn't waste any time building switchbacks. From the ridgeline the route to the summit is suddenly very clear, and the path to the summit rarely deviates from the ridge.

The steep and exposed route features plant cover that is unlike that of many other nearby hikes, including the eastern side of this very same mountain. The windy ridge is host primarily to low grasses and tiny, colorful wildflowers. These robust survivors have to endure the same blustery conditions you do.

The level of sun exposure represents a challenge, no doubt. But the reward for the lack of shade is constantly evolving, unobstructed views. The way the views unfold is unique in the region: as you climb east, rapidly gaining altitude, the nearby canyons reveal themselves almost like pictures in a children's pop-up book.

With each exhausting step you take up the ridge, you can see deeper into the neighboring canyons and gullies. First, the unnamed valleys reveal themselves. Then Parleys Canyon slowly emerges into view, followed by Rattlesnake Gulch and then Mill Creek Canyon.

Grandeur Peak (via the Western Ridge)

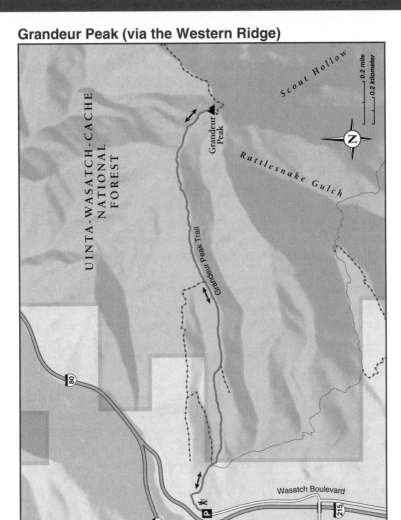

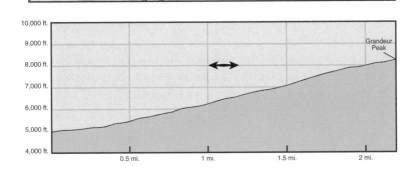

The largest mark of progress on the hike is the appearance of Mount Olympus, just beyond the southern ridge of Mill Creek Canyon. Olympus is likely the best-known feature of Salt Lake Valley's Wasatch ridgeline. As this rocky peak begins to poke its head over the other mountains, you should feel proud of your progress, as the summit is now less than 0.5 mile away.

As you get closer to the final ascent, the ridgeline curves slowly to the south, and the tree cover increases dramatically.

The steepness of the trail suddenly abates just as the views of the mountains east of Grandeur open up. After hours of valley and canyon vistas, the view suddenly shifts to the broad, mountainous expanses of the Wasatch, including Mount Aire (see previous hike) and Lambs Canyon (see Hike 15, page 82).

Upon arriving at the summit, you'll likely be asked how you got there by hikers unaware of this option. Despite the mountain's perennial popularity, the western ridge remains a hidden gem.

Be sure to take your time on the trip down. Many hikers expect to make up a great deal of time on the descent, only to quickly realize that the trail is simply too steep to blithely gallop down. Instead of getting tripped up by your own need for speed, keep your pace to a calm walk, and save your knees and thighs the unnecessary punishment.

NEARBY ACTIVITIES

Whether or not you've brought a dog on the trail, **Tanner Park,** on the other side of I-215, offers 10 acres of carefully kept green space. It's the perfect place to play fetch with your pup while you bask in the views of Grandeur Peak and Mill Creek Canyon. Open daily, sunrise–sunset, the park is located at 2695 E. Heritage Way. For more information, call 385-468-7275 or visit slco.org/parks/tanner-park.

* *

GPS TRAILHEAD COORDINATES N40° 42.453' W111° 47.752'

DIRECTIONS From I-215 North on Salt Lake City's east side, take Exit 4 for 3900 South/3300 South. Turn left onto Wasatch Boulevard, and drive 1.2 miles. Turn right onto 3300 South/Wasatch Boulevard, and drive 0.6 miles to the trailhead parking lot, where the road dead-ends.

From 1-80 East on Salt Lake City's east side, take Exit 128 for I-215 South. Drive 0.5 mile on I-215; then take Exit 3 for UT 171 East/3300 South. Turn left onto 3300 South/Wasatch Boulevard, and drive 0.6 mile to the trailhead parking lot.

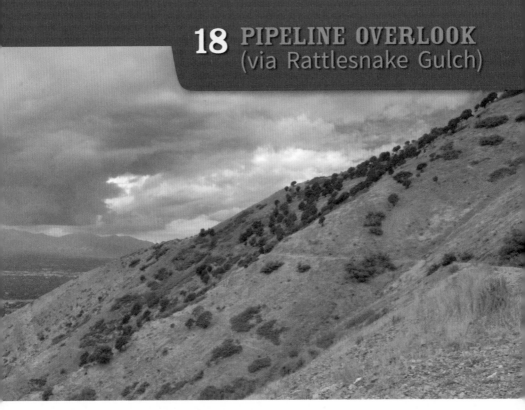

After the initial steep ascent, the trail is largely flat.

THIS HIKE GETS off to a challenging start, but hikers who persevere are rewarded with a calm stroll along a hillside trail with sweeping views of the valley and nearby canyons.

DESCRIPTION

With most hikes, there's a constant tradeoff between views and shade. A thick canopy of trees might be wonderful for your skin, for example, but you lose the panoramic sights. By taking Rattlesnake Gulch to the Pipeline Overlook, you get a healthy dose of both—and in digestible portions.

The hike begins at the Rattlesnake Gulch trailhead, on the left side of the road as you head east up Mill Creek Canyon. The clearly marked trailhead lies at the south-facing mouth of Rattlesnake Gulch. As soon as you set foot on the trail, you immediately and quickly begin to gain elevation.

The first 0.7 mile is distinctly steep, but this is certainly not the defining feature of the segment. The most notable aspect of the walk up the gulch is just how surrounded you are by trees. Gambel oaks and maples seem to lean over the rocky trail, giving the whole ascent a tunnel-like feel that's as cozy as it is lush. During this portion, you will gain almost 600 feet in elevation; fortunately, this is almost all of the elevation change that you'll experience on the hike.

DISTANCE & CONFIGURATION: 3.3-mile out-and-back

DIFFICULTY: Easy

SCENERY: Canyon, mountain, and city views

EXPOSURE: Shaded for first 0.7 mile, unshaded for remainder

TRAIL TRAFFIC: Heavy

TRAIL SURFACE: Dirt, rock

HIKING TIME: 1.5–2 hours

DRIVING DISTANCE: 9 miles from I-15/I-80 intersection

ELEVATION CHANGE: 5,337'–6,012'

ACCESS: Daily, sunrise–sunset. Current use fees for Mill Creek Canyon are $3/car (collected as you leave the canyon) or $40/year.

MAPS: USGS *Sugar House*

FACILITIES: None

WHEELCHAIR ACCESS: None

CONTACT: 801-466-6411, fs.usda.gov/uwcnf; 385-468-7275, slco.org/parks/millcreek-canyon

LOCATION: Mill Creek Canyon Road, Salt Lake City, UT 84109

COMMENTS: The last mile of this hike is part of the Pipeline Trail, a route popular with mountain bikers. Stay especially alert in this section.

During the fall months, as the leaves change, the visual effect on this hike is a textural, multicolored experience. The maples add shocking pops of red that will give you a wonderful reason to stop aside from just catching your breath.

Mostly following the generally dry creekbed, the path occasionally swings up the walls of the gulch, like a bobsled track. The roots and rocks that form the trail surface not only provide a constantly shifting challenge for hikers but also keep the trail visually interesting. On even-numbered days, skilled mountain bikers can be seen descending this section of the trail. The trail is wide and straight enough that the occasional cyclist will not pose a meaningful risk to hikers. In reality, watching the occasional mountain biker navigate the steep, rocky gulch bottom is an impressive sight as well as a good photo opportunity.

At the top of the gulch section of the hike, you'll arrive at a large, flatiron-shaped boulder, next to which is a small wooden sign that indicates the trail options—follow this sign, and the most well-worn path, by making a hard left. After one last minor gain in elevation, you'll intersect the 13-mile Pipeline Trail, one of Salt Lake's most popular trails for hikers, trail runners, and mountain bikers alike.

The historic Pipeline Trail is all that remains of a long-abandoned flume that carried water from Elbow Fork to the erstwhile Mill Creek power station. The wooden pipe that once aided in powering a growing valley may be long gone, but its legacy is a calm trail that now energizes the valley in a whole new way.

The trail quickly bends from north- to southbound as it wraps around Grandeur Peak, another worthwhile hike in the area (see Hikes 17 and 19, pages 91 and 99). The trail, while flat, remains partially shaded for a brief while, until it emerges from the oaks, affording wholly unobstructed views of Mill Creek Canyon. The Pipeline Trail stays on the northern side of the canyon, meaning that you'll be able to see the much more lush and foliated southern side, which is spectacular at any time of year.

Pipeline Overlook (via Rattlesnake Gulch)

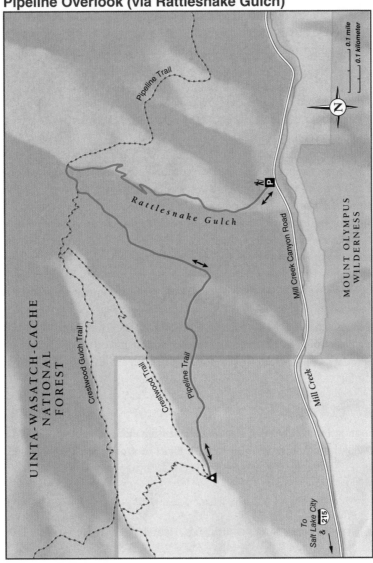

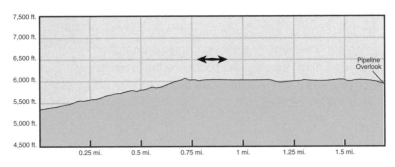

After 0.5 mile on the Pipeline Trail, the path emerges from Rattlesnake Gulch and quickly bends west, paralleling Mill Creek Canyon Road. Soon you'll pass a small wooden sign marking your departure from Uinta-Wasatch-Cache National Forest, just as the canyon opens up towards the valley below.

As you curve along the south face of Grandeur, be sure to look south, just beyond the southern ridgeline of Mill Creek Canyon, and watch as Mount Olympus begins to rise above it. Slowly, as you wander farther and farther west, Mount Olympus takes up a greater portion of your field of view.

After just under a mile on the Pipeline Trail, the pathway emerges from Mill Creek Canyon, terminating on the western slope of the massif that forms Grandeur Peak. The views of the valley below, as well as the Wasatch front writ large, are entirely unobstructed. It is immediately obvious why this trail is so popular with so many outdoor enthusiasts. The calm approach to the overlook allows for a serene entrance into one of the valley's most iconic overlooks. Take some time to sit down, eat a snack, and chat with the other outdoorspeople who are sure to be sharing the space with you.

On the return trip, you have several alternative routes to choose from, but none seem to match the Pipeline Trail for simplicity, vistas, and serenity. This hike, quickly accessed from the downtown area, stands as a fixture in Salt Lake City's outdoor community, not only for its beauty and historical significance but also as a shared locus of outdoor adventure for people from a wide variety of activities and backgrounds.

NEARBY ACTIVITIES

Near the mouth of Mill Creek Canyon, **Momentum Indoor Climbing** (3173 E. 3300 S.; 801-906-2132, momentumclimbing.com) packs in more than 24,000 square feet of climbing terrain, including a 50-foot-tall arch—a fitting feature for a Utah gym.

• •

GPS TRAILHEAD COORDINATES N40° 41.488' W111° 46.148'

DIRECTIONS From the eastern intersection of I-80 and I-215, head south on I-215 and, in 1.2 miles, take Exit 4 for 3900 South. Turn left onto 3900 South and, in 0.1 mile, turn left onto Wasatch Boulevard. In another 0.1 mile, turn right onto Mill Creek Canyon Road and drive 1.4 miles, passing a fee booth at 0.7 mile (you'll pay the canyon use fee here later on your way out). The Rattlesnake Gulch trailhead will be on the left.

19 GRANDEUR PEAK
(via Mill Creek Canyon)

From the summit, peaks to the east can be seen at their best.

GRANDEUR PEAK DELIVERS a lot of bang for the buck. One of the most easily accessible peaks along the Wasatch Front, it offers both great trail conditions and commanding views in all directions.

DESCRIPTION

Imagine a warm Saturday in spring. Snow still flanks most of the high peaks surrounding Salt Lake City. You pull out your hiking boots and decide to bag a mountain summit—something impressive, something grand.

Grandeur Peak is the perfect pursuit. It lies at the forefront of the ridge just north of Mount Olympus and to the south of Parleys Canyon and I-80. It may not be as high as Mount Timpanogos or Pfeifferhorn, or as instantly recognizable to local residents as Mount Olympus, but from nearly anywhere in Salt Lake City, you can be at the trailhead in 20 minutes and on your way to a mountain adventure.

Mill Creek Canyon is Salt Lake City's favorite picnic destination, and Church Fork is the first picnic site you come to when driving up the canyon. If you see cars parked along the canyon road, you can safely assume that the eight parking spaces at the trailhead are already filled. You might as well park on the shoulder of Mill Creek Canyon Road and walk through the Church Fork picnic area to the trailhead, which is marked by a sign pointing to Grandeur Peak.

DISTANCE & CONFIGURATION: 6.8-mile out-and-back

DIFFICULTY: Moderate

SCENERY: Canyon, mountain, and city views. Trail follows creek up a wooded side canyon.

EXPOSURE: Mostly shaded for first mile, mostly exposed for last 1.7 miles to summit

TRAIL TRAFFIC: Heavy

TRAIL SURFACE: Dirt, rock

HIKING TIME: 2.5–4 hours

DRIVING DISTANCE: 11 miles from I-15/I-80 intersection

ELEVATION CHANGE: 5,912'–8,299'

ACCESS: The Church Fork picnic area, from which you access the trailhead, is open daily, 8 a.m.–10 p.m., June–September; at other times, you'll need to park along Mill Creek Canyon Road and walk a short distance to the trailhead. Current use fees for Mill Creek Canyon are $3/car (collected as you leave the canyon) or $40/year. From the trailhead to the switchbacks, you'll be crossing property owned by the Boy Scouts of America.

MAPS: USGS *Mount Aire* and *Sugar House;* Trails Illustrated *Wasatch Front* (709)

FACILITIES: Restrooms and water at trailhead

WHEELCHAIR ACCESS: None

CONTACT: 801-466-6411, fs.usda.gov/uwcnf; 385-468-7275, slco.org/parks/millcreek-canyon

LOCATION: Mill Creek Canyon Road, Salt Lake City, UT 84109

COMMENTS: Dogs must be leashed on even-numbered days; can be unleashed on odd-numbered days

Church Fork is a small side canyon on the north side of Mill Creek. It was originally a placer-mining claim that extended from just above the trailhead to near the ridgeline. This claim was deeded to the Boy Scouts of America in 1918 and remains publicly accessible property owned by the Scouts.

After just 0.1 mile on the trail, you'll cross the Pipeline Trail and take a jog to the left, then continue up the canyon on the Grandeur Peak Trail to the right. The trail leads up a steep canyon shaded by maple conifers and bigtooth maples, with Church Fork Creek descending speedily on your right. Along the creekside, the trail is fragrant with fir, wildflowers, wild mint, and arrowleaf balsamroot.

At 0.8 mile, the path begins a series of switchbacks. As you climb the slope, you emerge from the shaded canopy of maple, oak, and fir. From this point on, the trail is largely unshaded. These switchbacks lead toward a sandstone outcrop on the ridge to the north. Below this outcrop, the trail is dotted and bedded with sandstone—uncharacteristic of most Wasatch trails.

As the switchbacks lead up toward the west, you'll have a beautiful straight-on view of Grandeur Peak in front of you, its slopes ribboned with strands of aspen and white fir. At the top of the switchbacks, you can look to the west and see the entire trail as it leads to the summit. From this point on, the ascent is steady but more gradual as it follows a route just below the ridgeline through a low covering of Gambel oak.

On your route to the top, you'll come to a crest dotted with juniper. After you've passed this false summit, the true summit lies just 0.2 mile straight ahead. You may see a few patches of snow through late May and sometimes into June along the higher trail. Because hikers, dogs, and bikers share busy Mill Creek Canyon, wildlife sightings are less likely, but you may see deer grazing near the summit in spring and fall.

Grandeur Peak (via Mill Creek Canyon)

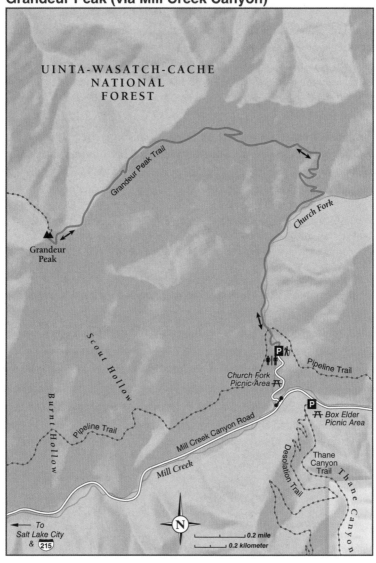

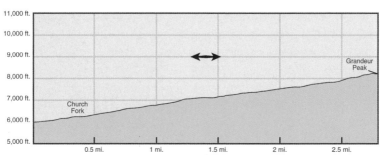

At 8,299 feet in elevation, the Grandeur Peak summit offers great views in all directions. The Salt Lake Valley spreads out below to the west, and Mount Olympus lies at the front of the next ridge to the south. Behind you, to the northeast, are Mountain Dell and Little Dell reservoirs. Soak up the panoramic views; then enjoy a carefree and relaxing descent.

NEARBY ACTIVITIES

Just a few blocks from the mouth of Mill Creek Canyon is **REI** (3285 E. 3300 South; 801-486-2100, rei.com/stores/19). In addition to selling outdoor gear and offering classes, it's home to the Salt Lake City area's Public Lands Information Center, an excellent source of assistance and information about area recreational opportunities.

• •

GPS TRAILHEAD COORDINATES N40° 42.038' W111° 44.552'

DIRECTIONS From the eastern intersection of I-80 and I-215, take I-215 South, drive 1.2 miles, and take Exit 4 for 3900 South. Turn left onto 3900 South and, in 0.1 mile, turn left onto Wasatch Boulevard. In another 0.1 mile, turn right onto Mill Creek Canyon Road, and drive 3.1 miles, passing a fee booth at 0.7 mile (you'll pay the canyon use fee here later on your way out). The Church Fork Picnic area will be on your left. When the gate is open (June–November), turn left and drive 0.3 mile to a small parking area at the end of the road. When the picnic area is closed or the parking area is full, you'll need to park on Mill Creek Canyon Road and walk to the trailhead.

Canyon and valley views abound from the overlook.

HIKING THROUGH A dense forest scented with spruce and fir is just one of the many delights on the Desolation Trail. Climbing over fallen trees and rocky outcrops leads to a direct view of Salt Lake with peaks rising to the north and south.

DESCRIPTION

Don't let the name *Desolation Trail* conjure up images of a harsh, dusty, sun-parched ordeal in the desert. Instead, picture a verdant trail cut along a densely wooded hillside with a bed of needles and cones from the various conifers in the canyon. As one of the most easily accessed trails in Mill Creek Canyon, the Desolation Trail is exceptionally well maintained, especially when you consider the steepness of the slope into which it is carved. For this reason especially, please don't succumb to the urge to cut switchbacks. Combatting man-made erosion is a constant battle on the steep walls of Mill Creek Canyon, and skipping turns on a slope this sheer rapidly damages not only the local flora but also the very trail that passes through it.

You'll find the trailhead at the west end of the small South Box Elder parking area. At 0.1 mile you come to a fork, with the Thayne Canyon Trail leading to the left and the Desolation Trail ascending the hillside to the right—to reach the Salt Lake Overlook, stay to the right, although you also have the extended option of a Thayne

DISTANCE & CONFIGURATION: 4.8-mile out-and-back

DIFFICULTY: Moderate

SCENERY: Wooded canyon, city overview

EXPOSURE: Mostly shaded

TRAIL TRAFFIC: Moderate

TRAIL SURFACE: Dirt, rock

HIKING TIME: 1.5–3 hours

DRIVING DISTANCE: 11 miles from I-15/ I-80 intersection

ELEVATION CHANGE: 5,785'–7,024'

ACCESS: Daily, sunrise–sunset. Current use fees for Mill Creek Canyon are $3/car (collected as you leave the canyon) or $40/year. Bicycles are prohibited on the Desolation Trail.

MAPS: USGS *Mount Aire;* Trails Illustrated *Wasatch Front* (709)

FACILITIES: Restrooms and water at trailhead

WHEELCHAIR ACCESS: None

CONTACT: 801-466-6411, fs.usda.gov/uwcnf; 385-468-7275, slco.org/parks/millcreek-canyon

LOCATION: Mill Creek Canyon Road, Salt Lake City, UT 84109

COMMENTS: This trail traverses a steep hillside that is highly susceptible to erosion—please follow the hike as described, and don't take short-cuts. Dogs must be leashed on even-numbered days; can be unleashed on odd-numbered days.

Canyon–Desolation Trail loop. This option adds several miles to the hike, but along with the extra effort comes with the benefit of a return trip that follows a scenic, tree-lined creek.

The trail navigates a steady series of masterfully crafted and well-groomed switch-backs that reduce the grade on an otherwise precipitous hillside. These northeast slopes provide a cooler, more moist habitat for mosses and a variety of mountain shrubs. In addition to fir and spruce, you'll see maple, Gambel oaks, and wildflowers along the trail at all elevations. Many fallen trees cross the trail, while others lay parallel to the trail, placed there to fortify the slope against erosion.

At 0.6 mile the trail opens up to sunlight with a patch of Gambel oak, although for most of the hike towering conifers shade hikers. At 0.8 mile the path divides at a rock outcrop—take the trail on your right, up through the rocky crag.

If you're hiking with young children, be careful of the steep, unprotected drop-offs in many areas where the trail is only a few feet wide. Also, because you're likely to be paying close attention to your feet and the narrow trail, you might well be surprised by a runner or dog coming in the opposite direction (unleashed dogs are welcome on the trail on odd-numbered days).

You'll often spot deer and squirrels, and the variety of birds makes Mill Creek Canyon a popular birding destination. Early mornings in summer provide good opportunities to spot blue grouse, Steller's jays, scrub jays, and golden eagles.

At 1.3 miles, a clearing in the woods opens to beautiful views up Mill Creek Canyon to the east. But the best view of all comes almost by surprise as the trail circles to the west side of the slope.

For most of the hike, you've been entirely unaware that a million-person city sprawls just beyond the pines, but as the trees clear you'll suddenly have a view into

Desolation Trail to Salt Lake Overlook

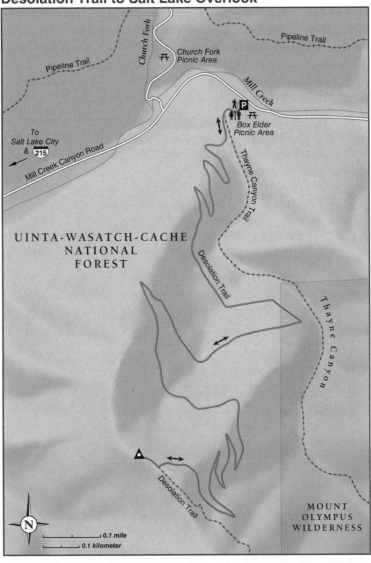

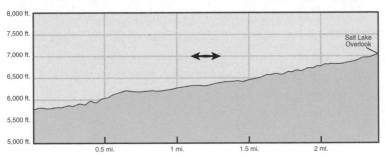

the canyon of Salt Lake City below. To the north is Grandeur Peak, with Mount Olympus and Hobbs Peak to the south. If you're feeling particularly sure-footed on the day of your hike, several large clusters of jagged rocks offer a place to relax, enjoy the view, and have a snack before heading back down the trail.

NEARBY ACTIVITIES

Mill Creek Canyon is Salt Lake City's favorite summer picnic destination. With nine picnic areas within 3–7 miles of the canyon entrance, it's the place to go for a weekend brunch or summer-afternoon lunch. Individual sites abound, and group sites accommodate up to 100 people.

• •

GPS TRAILHEAD COORDINATES N40° 41.850' W111° 44.400'

DIRECTIONS From the eastern intersection of I-80 and I-215, take I-215 South, drive 1.2 miles, and take Exit 4 for 3900 South. Turn left onto 3900 South and, in 0.1 mile, turn left onto Wasatch Boulevard. In another 0.1 mile, turn right onto Mill Creek Canyon Road, and drive 3.3 miles, passing a fee booth at 0.7 mile (you'll pay the canyon use fee here later on your way out). The South Box Elder trailhead parking area will be on the right; a road sign also identifies Desolation Trail 019.

A hiker slowly descends into Mill Creek Canyon.

21 GOBBLERS KNOB
(via Alexander Basin)

The steep climb from the road gives hikers stunning views of Mill Creek Canyon.

THIS POPULAR SUMMIT offers great views in all directions, but the most memorable sight will be of the wildflowers that fill Alexander Basin in spring and summer. Some easy scrambling and route-finding are necessary to navigate a glacial cirque up to the ridge, followed by a short jaunt to the summit.

DESCRIPTION

Although the trail leading to Alexander Basin passes through the Mount Olympus Wilderness, the basin itself is not included in the designated wilderness area. Gobblers Knob is a popular summit climb and Mill Creek is a busy canyon, but Alexander Basin can feel surprisingly remote, even on a summer weekend. Of the four trails most frequently used to reach the Gobblers Knob summit, the Alexander Basin Trail is the shortest and steepest.

As you drive up Mill Creek Canyon, especially past the Elbow Fork area, the road narrows and trees on both sides close in to create a sense of being wrapped up in the woods. From the trailhead parking area, you step onto the trail. Within a few seconds, the road disappears and you're engulfed in woods of Douglas-fir and white fir.

Nobody lost any time cutting switchbacks when making this trail—it shoots directly up the center of the basin and follows a steep track throughout. If you keep a steady pace, you should be at the Bowman Fork junction within 30–40 minutes.

DISTANCE & CONFIGURATION: 4.4-mile out-and-back

DIFFICULTY: Moderate

SCENERY: Wildflowers, alpine basin, summit views

EXPOSURE: Mostly shaded

TRAIL TRAFFIC: Moderate

TRAIL SURFACE: Dirt to the upper bowl, then rocky to the summit

HIKING TIME: 4–5 hours

DRIVING DISTANCE: 15 miles from I-15/I-80 intersection

ELEVATION CHANGE: 7,140'–10,246'

ACCESS: Daily, sunrise–sunset, but the Maple Grove gate across Mill Creek Canyon Road is closed November 1–July 1. During this time, you must park at the Maple Grove picnic area and then hike/ski/snowshoe about 3 miles east to the trailhead. Current use fees for Mill Creek Canyon are $3/car (collected as you leave the canyon) or $40/year.

MAPS: USGS *Mount Aire;* Trails Illustrated *Wasatch Front* (709)

FACILITIES: No drinking water or restrooms at trailhead; creek water can be purified. Restrooms are 1.5 miles west of the trailhead at Elbow Fork and Big Water.

WHEELCHAIR ACCESS: None

CONTACT: 801-466-6411, fs.usda.gov/uwcnf; 385-468-7275, slco.org/parks/millcreek-canyon

LOCATION: Mill Creek Canyon Road, Salt Lake City, UT 84109

COMMENTS: Dogs must be leashed on even-numbered days; can be unleashed on odd-numbered days

At this point you've already covered 0.9 mile and gained more than 1,100 feet in elevation. The Bowman Fork Trail drops down and to your right, but you should continue straight ahead. In another 0.2 mile, the woods thin and the trail opens to views leading up the basin.

In late spring and early summer, wildflowers line the trail every step of the way—even on the rocky upper slopes—but they're most abundant in the woods and in the open areas of the upper basin. Larkspur, cow parsnip, phlox, and bluebells flourish, and you'll spot the elegant and rare white columbine both in the woods and in the open fields.

Alexander Basin is a stairway of tiered basins leading to an upper bowl. Until you reach the middle of the upper bowl, which is covered with patches of snow into mid-summer, the trail proves easy to follow. As you stand in the upper bowl, looking up to the rim, you'll see Gobblers Knob on the right side of the rim. From this point you may have to improvise a bit, but you can usually spot a faint route leading up through the subalpine fir in the bowl's center or, alternatively, another faint cairned route leading up the rocky slope to the right of the trees. If it's at all muddy, choose the rocky slope. Either way, the route will be steep leading to the same destination: the bowl's rim.

Once there, you'll overlook the green expanse of Big Cottonwood Canyon, including many of the prominent peaks along the ridge. From this rim vantage point, look down and make a mental note of your route up the bowl so you'll have a reliable return route.

Now it's just a short climb to the Gobblers Knob summit, on a faint but discernible trail leading up to the west and north along craggy slopes. From the rim it's just

Gobblers Knob (via Alexander Basin)

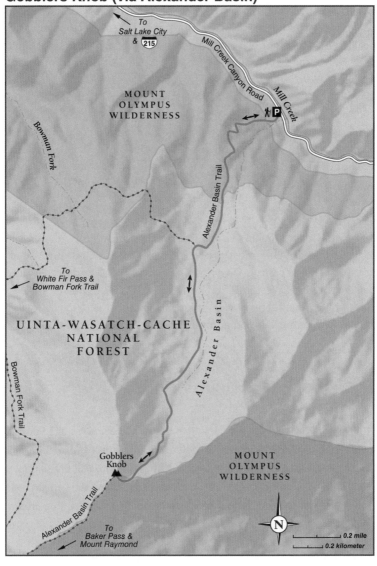

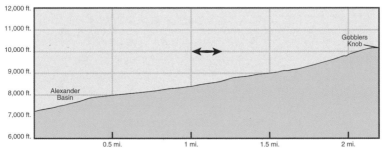

10 minutes of sustained climbing on the dry south-facing slope to the summit. While you can see large slices of the Salt Lake Valley from the top of Gobblers Knob, many of the peaks at the Wasatch's western front block the view. Instead, focus on the most impressive views: the peaks along the southern ridge of Big Cottonwood Canyon and to the east.

Cliff swallows and mountain bluebirds dart in and out of the fir and limber pine at the summit. As you descend to the ridge, look to the west and you'll see a well-worn path leading along the ridge toward Mount Raymond. From the ridge, this trail leads back down to the Terrace Campground and the Bowman Fork trailhead in Mill Creek Canyon. This path is well worth taking if you have a shuttle vehicle waiting or don't mind hiking an additional 3.5 miles up Mill Creek Canyon to your car.

NEARBY ACTIVITIES

Big Water is Mill Creek Canyon's Grand Central Station and provides easy access to many of the upper canyon's most popular hikes. The two large Big Water parking areas, at the top of the canyon where Mill Creek Canyon Road dead-ends, provide easy access to the Great Western Trail, Little Water Trail, and Lower Big Water Trail. These lots, which often fill on weekends, are also popular with cyclists who find Big Water the perfect jumping-off point for the expansive network of trails.

• •

GPS TRAILHEAD COORDINATES N40° 41.493' W111° 40.222'

DIRECTIONS From the eastern intersection of I-80 and I-215, take I-215 South, drive 1.2 miles, and take Exit 4 for 3900 South. Turn left onto 3900 South and, in 0.1 mile, turn left onto Wasatch Boulevard. In another 0.1 mile, turn right onto Mill Creek Canyon Road, and drive 7.7 miles, passing a fee booth at 0.7 mile (you'll pay the canyon use fee here later on your way out). The Alexander Basin trailhead (010) and parking area will be on the right (south) side of the road.

Hikers, dogs, and bikers share the network of trails in the canyon.

A GENTLY ASCENDING TRAIL leads along the upper section of Mill Creek to a ridgeline at the top of the canyon. Enjoy the overview at the saddle or continue up to Murdock Peak for the view from the summit.

DESCRIPTION

Well known and well used by locals, Mill Creek Canyon offers a wealth of year-round recreational opportunities for hikers, dog owners, bikers, cross-country skiers, and snowshoers. Even the farthest reaches of the canyon can get busy on summer weekends. The Upper Big Water trailhead, at the eastern end of Mill Creek Canyon Road, is such a place, with a large parking area that often fills to capacity. But once you get on this trail, the wooded creeksides and rolling hillsides make the upper canyon a place of serenity.

Big Water Gulch offers plenty of trail options and potential destinations. This less-traveled but highly enjoyable trail heads directly east from the upper parking area and follows Mill Creek to its headwaters, connects to the Great Western Trail, and ascends the ridge overlooking Park City. If a summit destination is what you have in mind, you can climb to a higher overlook or even continue to the summit of Murdock Peak.

DISTANCE & CONFIGURATION: 5.2-mile out-and-back to ridgeline saddle, 6.6-mile out-and-back to summit of Murdock Peak

DIFFICULTY: Moderate

SCENERY: Wooded trail with meadows and rounded peaks; ridgeline and summit views to the east

EXPOSURE: Mostly shaded

TRAIL TRAFFIC: Moderate

TRAIL SURFACE: Dirt

HIKING TIME: 2–4 hours

DRIVING DISTANCE: 17 miles from I-15/I-80 intersection

ELEVATION CHANGE: 7,623'–9,602'

ACCESS: Daily, sunrise–sunset, but the Maple Grove gate across Mill Creek Canyon Road is closed November 1–July 1. During this time,

you must park at the Maple Grove picnic area and then hike/ski/snowshoe about 4 miles east to the trailhead. Current use fees for Mill Creek Canyon are $3/car (collected as you leave the canyon) or $40/year.

MAPS: USGS *Mount Aire* and *Park City West;* Trails Illustrated *Wasatch Front* (709)

FACILITIES: Restrooms and drinking water at trailhead

WHEELCHAIR ACCESS: None

CONTACT: 801-466-6411, fs.usda.gov/uwcnf; 385-468-7275, slco.org/parks/millcreek-canyon

LOCATION: Eastern end of Mill Creek Canyon Road, Salt Lake City, UT 84109

COMMENTS: Dogs must be leashed on even-numbered days; can be unleashed on odd-numbered days

Departing on the main trail to the east, known both as Mill Creek Trail and Red Pine Road, follow the route along the creek to a fork—even though the sign points to a trail on the right, take the less-crowded hiking trail, on the left. It will hug the creek bank in a deeply wooded section of the canyon and take you away from the mountain bikers who use the wider trail, on the right. This secluded section of trail is soft dirt carpeted with spruce needles, providing a great walking surface for dogs.

At 0.8 mile, the trail crosses the creek over stepping-stones, then within 0.1 mile crosses again to the south side. At 1.2 miles, the trail crests and drops slightly into a meadow ringed with Douglas-fir and shimmering aspens.

Within a few minutes you'll connect with the Great Western Trail—although the sign at the junction may seem confusing, go left in the direction of Desolation Lake. The path will lead you eastward to the ridge overlooking Park City, at which point the trail eventually turns south toward Desolation Lake.

This section of the Great Western Trail is wide and well traveled, with room for both mountain bikers and hikers. Still, you should be alert, as mountain bikes can often descend the trail at high speeds and can come up on you without warning. Morning hikers may well share the trail with moose and deer, who find a hospitable habitat in these moist meadows.

At 2.2 miles the landscape opens to high meadows, grassy aspen-covered slopes, and rounded hilltops—very different scenery from the Wasatch canyons to the south.

As the trail continues its gentle ascent, you arrive almost without warning at the 8,800-foot ridgeline saddle. The Great Western Trail turns south toward Big Cottonwood Canyon and Desolation Lake. Continuing eastward for just another 100 feet

Mill Creek to Park City Overlook (Including Murdock Peak)

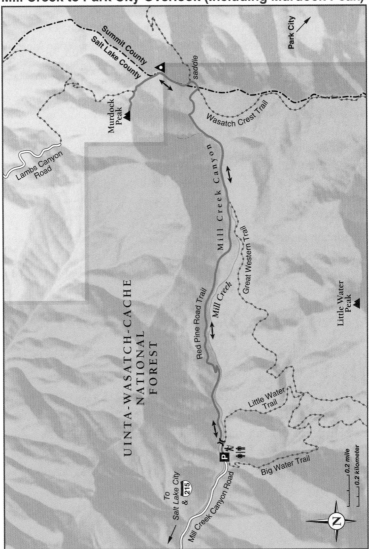

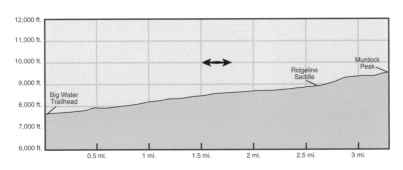

113

gives you a nice view of Park City below, but a quick glance to your left reveals the ridgeline leading up to the higher overlook on the way to Murdock Peak.

No official trail leads to the higher unnamed overlook, or even to Murdock Peak, but the route is clear and the bushwhacking along game trails through low-lying sage and juniper is easy. At a steady pace, you'll arrive at the first overlook about 10 minutes after leaving the saddle. From the 9,300-foot overlook, you're above the Park City ski lifts and have a sweeping view of the valley below.

Another 10–15 minutes and 300 feet of elevation gain will put you on the summit of Murdock Peak, along the ridge to the west. While the overlook and the summit are both rewarding destinations, the most beautiful parts of the hike can be found in the meadows, gentle slopes, and wooded creeksides of the upper canyon.

NEARBY ACTIVITIES

Park City Mountain Resort is a premier summer and winter recreational destination just 30 minutes east of Salt Lake City. Summer attractions include an alpine slide, an elevated alpine coaster, an exhilarating zip line, and lift-assisted hiking and mountain biking. For information call 435-649-8111 or visit parkcitymountain.com.

· ·

GPS TRAILHEAD COORDINATES N40° 41.083' W111° 38.815'

DIRECTIONS From the eastern intersection of I-80 and I-215, take I-215 South, drive 1.2 miles, and take Exit 4 for 3900 South. Turn left onto 3900 South and, in 0.1 mile, turn left onto Wasatch Boulevard. In another 0.1 mile, turn right onto Mill Creek Canyon Road, and drive 9.2 miles, passing a fee booth at 0.7 mile (you'll pay the canyon use fee here later on your way out). Just past the Lower Big Water parking area on your right, park in the Upper Big Water lot, straight ahead at the end of the road.

Neffs Canyon is hikable even in the early spring.

THIS SPUR CANYON just south of Mill Creek Canyon has led its life in the shadows of Mount Olympus, so its beauty and history are often overlooked. The steep trail ascends along one of the many canyon streams to a high aspen-ringed meadow surrounded by towering peaks.

DESCRIPTION

The canyons that slice through the Wasatch Mountains not only provide water to the Salt Lake Valley but also powered many of its early industries. One 1847 Mormon pioneer, John Neff, brought his milling machinery with him to the Salt Lake Valley. He built the first mill in the valley at the mouth of Mill Creek, and by 1848 he was producing flour. In his lifetime he built 30 mills, including one near the canyon that bears his name.

Today the Olympus Cove neighborhood has grown up around the access point to Neffs Canyon, and only locals regularly use the trailhead. In all likelihood, fewer people know about Neffs Canyon today than 150 years ago, when it was a hotbed of mining, timber, and grazing activity. The mills, mining, and timber operations have been gone for nearly 100 years, but you can still see one of the old millstones at the Utah State Capitol, along with other pioneer relics.

DISTANCE & CONFIGURATION: 5.5-mile out-and-back

DIFFICULTY: Strenuous

SCENERY: Wooded canyon, meadow with surrounding peaks

EXPOSURE: Mostly shaded

TRAIL TRAFFIC: Light

TRAIL SURFACE: Dirt, rock

HIKING TIME: 4-5 hours

DRIVING DISTANCE: 9 miles from I-15/I-80 intersection

ELEVATION CHANGE: 5,624'–8,069'

ACCESS: Daily, 6 a.m.–10 p.m.; no fees or permits. Much of the hike lies within Mount Olympus Wilderness Area.

MAPS: USGS *Sugar House* and *Mount Aire;* Trails Illustrated *Wasatch Front* (709)

FACILITIES: None

WHEELCHAIR ACCESS: None

CONTACT: 801-733-2660, fs.usda.gov/uwcnf

LOCATION: End of White Way, Salt Lake City, UT 84124

COMMENTS: Neffs Canyon is a great snowshoe destination, but stay in the lower canyon where the routes aren't so steep and rocky. Motorized vehicles and bicycles are prohibited within the wilderness area; dogs allowed off-leash.

Standing at the trailhead looking up the canyon, you can tell that it's going to be a beautiful setting. What you can't discern is the number of natural springs that dot the canyon, the various routes taken by the streams, and the water flow's steep gradient.

From the large parking area, take the well-marked trail to the east, which rises quickly to a graded service road in just 100 feet. This road continues a gentle incline along the north side of the canyon, passing a water tank on the left at 0.3 mile. At 0.5 mile, the graded road ends as it comes to a wide stream crossing, where you can easily step across on rocks without ever getting wet. After the crossing, the trail continues up the canyon on an old roadbed used by wagons more than 100 years ago. At 1.1 miles, the old roadbed ends and the trail continues as a steep singletrack among Gambel oaks and bigtooth maples.

Because of the canyon's long history, dozens of trails follow its springs and streams. Worth exploring, these trails lead through some beautiful conifer wooded areas. If you find yourself on the south side of the canyon, on a faint trail, and up against a rock slab, you're on your own. You'll enjoy nice overlooks and some great rock climbing, but it's not the main trail to the meadow. Although the road may not be the most romantic route, it is reliable and easy to follow. The Neff Canyon Trail doesn't believe in switchbacks, and even if it did, there's not much room for them in this narrow canyon.

At 1.5 miles the trail enters the Mount Olympus Wilderness Area. The trail, by now a well-worn dirt track, steepens considerably. After climbing steadily through spruce and fir, the trail crosses the stream over a log bridge at 1.8 miles. As the trail gains elevation, you enter large stands of quaking aspens blended with conifers and maples.

Eventually the steep ascent lets up just a bit as the trail reaches the crest and enters the meadow at 2.5 miles. Another 0.2 mile and you're at the upper, eastern end of the meadow. Bounded by a dense aspen forest on the south, you have perfect views of Mount Raymond and Hobbs Peak above the aspens.

Neffs Canyon

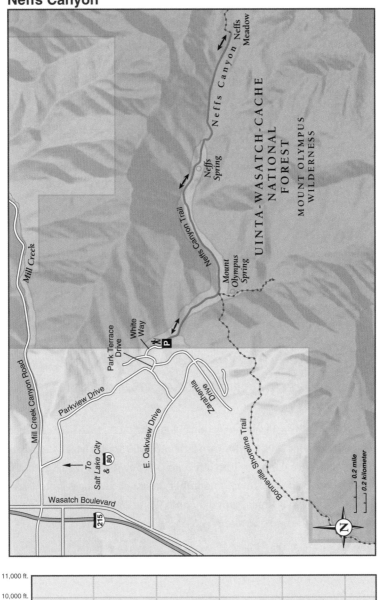

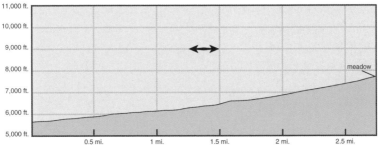

Another little-known feature on one of the slabs to the south of the meadow is Neffs Canyon Cave, a designated National Natural Landmark. At 1,165 feet, it's one of the deepest caves in the United States. Because it's also extremely risky to explore—with most passages dipping steeply at a 45- to 60-degree slope—the U.S. Forest Service grants admission only to experienced cavers (the entrance is gated to prevent unauthorized access).

The meadow is a great place to enjoy a snack or to sit quietly and watch for wildlife—especially deer, moose, and elk—as it comes to the stream at the south side of the meadow. The return to the trailhead takes about 1.5 hours. From the meadow you can also follow the trail as it curves to the north. Within a mile it intersects the Thayne Canyon Trail, which descends into Mill Creek.

NEARBY ACTIVITIES

On the northeast side of the trailhead parking area are a well and pumping station for **Mount Olympus Spring Water.** The water, which was originally bottled in 1899, is low in dissolved solids and high in oxygen, with a slightly sweet taste. Stainless steel tankers transport the water from Neffs Canyon to a bottling plant in Salt Lake City; from there, it's distributed to offices, homes, and retail outlets throughout the Mountain West.

• •

GPS TRAILHEAD COORDINATES N40° 40.620' W111° 46.578'

DIRECTIONS From the eastern intersection of I-80 and I-215, take I-215 South, drive 1.2 miles, and take Exit 4 for 3900 South. Turn left onto 3900 South, which quickly becomes Jupiter Drive, and drive 0.9 mile. Turn left onto Oakview Drive/4280 South and, in 0.4 mile, turn left onto Parkview Drive. In another 0.2 mile, turn right onto Park Terrace Drive/4260 East; then, in 0.1 mile, turn right onto White Way. The trailhead parking area is 0.3 mile ahead, at the end of White Way.

With the valley as a backdrop, Mount Olympus offers plentiful photo ops.

MOUNT OLYMPUS IS the best-known and most recognizable peak on Salt Lake City's eastern skyline. Geologically, it's a mammoth anticline of purple quartzite slabs jutting out nearly a mile above the valley floor. Physically, it's a steep, demanding trail capped by a Class 3 scramble to the rocky summit, where exceptional views await.

DESCRIPTION

True to its name, Mount Olympus inspires many locals to describe climbing it in mythic terms. Its foreboding, craggy summit appears to be unclimbable from the valley floor. Typically, however, it's not the final rock scramble but the steep trail to the saddle that brings unconditioned and unprepared hikers down for the count.

How you handle the trail's first 100 yards best predicts whether you'll make it to the summit. This initial stretch accurately represents the entire trail in terms of steepness—if you need to stop and rest after 100 yards, multiply those stops by 60 and you'll have some sense of what the hike entails. As the trail ascends the canyon and leads toward the summit, it becomes more wild and beautiful, but its steep angle doesn't ease up one bit. The trail's lower portions consist of Bonneville Shoreline alluvium studded with quartzite talus and boulders from above.

DISTANCE & CONFIGURATION: 7-mile out-and-back

DIFFICULTY: Strenuous

SCENERY: Exceptional views of the valley, with Big Cottonwood Canyon peaks to the south and east

EXPOSURE: Largely exposed to sun for first mile; mostly shaded in canyon for next 2 miles, then mostly exposed on the scramble to the summit

TRAIL TRAFFIC: Heavy

TRAIL SURFACE: Dirt, rock

HIKING TIME: 5–7 hours

DRIVING DISTANCE: 10 miles from I-15/I-80 intersection

ELEVATION CHANGE: 4,966'–9,030'

ACCESS: Daily, 6 a.m.–10 p.m.; no fees or permits. Hike lies within the Mount Olympus Wilderness Area.

MAPS: USGS *Sugar House;* Trails Illustrated *Wasatch Front* (709)

FACILITIES: None; creek water can be purified

WHEELCHAIR ACCESS: None

CONTACT: 801-733-2660, fs.usda.gov/uwcnf

LOCATION: Wasatch Boulevard just east of I-215, Holliday, UT 84121

COMMENTS: Because the summit scramble is mostly exposed, *do not attempt this hike if there is even a chance of lightning or rain.* Motorized vehicles and bicycles prohibited within the wilderness area; dogs allowed off-leash.

Because the Mount Olympus Trail begins just a stone's throw from I-215, you may find it disturbing to hear the roar of freeway traffic in a federally protected wilderness area. But that disturbance lasts for just the first mile or so.

At 0.5 mile the trail curves to the left around a quartzite outcrop, then proceeds up Tolcats Canyon to the east. At 0.7 mile the path enters the Mount Olympus Wilderness Area, marked by a sign. Eventually, at a point fairly deep in the canyon and 1.7 miles from the trailhead, you'll cross a small creek. The crossing's elevation is 6,256 feet, a 1,290-foot gain from the trailhead. The shade and boulders surrounding the creek make this a popular rest stop.

Beyond the creek crossing, the trail continues its steep ascent to the head of the canyon, aided by several series of switchbacks. Deep in the canyon, at 2.4 miles from the trailhead, conifers begin to appear, and at higher elevations stands of aspen line the trail. This section of trail is particularly beautiful, rocky, and steep.

Soon you approach the saddle, at an elevation of 8,400 feet. The trail levels and turns north through a peaceful grove of Douglas-fir. Take a minute and walk 20 feet or so over to the eastern side of the saddle. The view to the east, a maze of rocky crags, looks absolutely inaccessible and deserving of the wilderness designation.

Because of the trail's popularity and its proximity to the city, wildlife sightings are rare—but rattlesnakes appear fairly often, both on the trail and on the lower sections of the summit scramble. As you're climbing through this area, use extra caution when placing your hands on rocky ledges so as not to surprise a rattler.

From the saddle, follow the trail north toward the summit. Within 100 yards of traversing the saddle, the grove of Douglas-fir gives way to rocky slopes, and soon you'll be climbing hand over hand. The trail becomes faint, but it's generally discernible with some careful scouting. No exceptionally difficult or technical movements

Mount Olympus

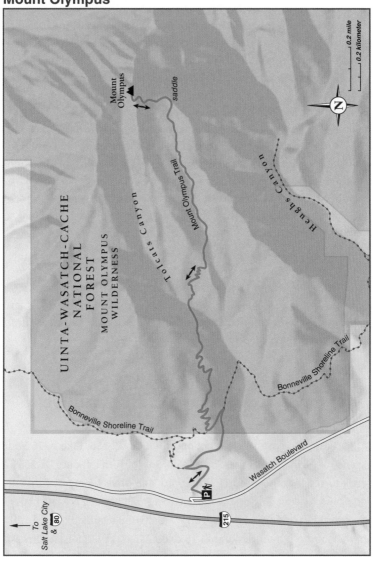

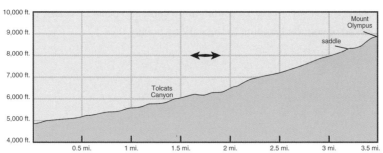

are required, so if you come to an insurmountable point, just retrace your steps and relocate the trail.

The route from the saddle to the summit entails 15–20 minutes of sustained scrambling. This section is prone to rockfall, so be careful not to dislodge rocks onto climbers below.

The summit of Mount Olympus consists of an enormous rockpile of angular quartzite boulders. As you'd expect, spectacular views of the Salt Lake Valley await. On a clear day, they extend far up the Great Salt Lake to the northwest and to Deseret Peak (see Hike 56, page 256) in the distant west. The views of the Twin Peaks Wilderness to the south are equally striking.

Remember that descending from the rocky summit is generally more dangerous and more time-consuming than the climb up, so take your time and save your strength for the jarring downhill return.

NEARBY ACTIVITIES

Just 5 miles from the Mount Olympus trailhead, **Wheeler Historic Farm** in Salt Lake City (6351 S. 900 E.; 385-468-1755, wheelerfarm.com) offers tours, tractor rides, wagon rides, and demonstrations of agriculture and Salt Lake County's rural lifestyle from 1890 to 1920. Open year-round.

• •

GPS TRAILHEAD COORDINATES N40° 39.115' W111° 48.373'

DIRECTIONS From the eastern intersection of I-80 and I-215, take I-215 South, drive 2.1 miles, and take Exit 5 for UT 266 South/4500 South. Turn left onto UT 266 East; then immediately turn right onto Wasatch Boulevard, and drive 1.5 miles. Turn left onto an unmarked paved road leading up the hillside to a small parking area. On busy summer weekends, overflow parking is available on Wasatch Boulevard.

From the southern intersection of I-15 and I-215, take I-215 East, drive 4.6 miles, and take Exit 6 for UT 190 East. Turn right onto UT 190 East/Big Cottonwood Road, and drive 0.7 mile; then turn left onto Wasatch Boulevard, and drive 1.7 miles. Turn left onto the unmarked paved road leading to the parking area.

Aspens line the shore of Dog Lake, which is far prettier than its name suggests.

A SMALL, PEACEFUL LAKE ringed by quaking aspens lies at the junction of several trails leading to other peaks and canyons. A well-used mountain biking trail, the Dog Lake Trail is wide and easy to follow.

DESCRIPTION

Dog Lake, which lies within Big Cottonwood Canyon, is both remote and accessible, out of the way yet simple to find. It can easily be accessed from Mill D North Fork, as described here, or Butler Fork in the Mount Olympus Wilderness Area; it's also frequently accessed from Mill Creek Canyon. If you're armed with a good trail map of the area, it's easy to plan a canyon-to-canyon hike with Dog Lake as the centerpiece.

The trip to Dog Lake from Big Cottonwood's Mill D North Fork is one of the few hikes in the Wasatch without a single switchback. In a little more than 2 miles, the trail ascends steadily but never too steeply. Because of its gradual incline, the trail is popular with mountain bikers. Hikers also love the wide, easily followed trail, which readily accommodates those who want to chat and walk side by side. Because the route cuts through aspen and meadows, visibility is good, allowing hikers and bikers to see one another on its long, straight stretches. Even so, be sure to keep your gaze up, as a silently approaching mountain bike could easily spell a quick and painful end to an otherwise beautiful hike.

DISTANCE & CONFIGURATION: 4.6-mile out-and-back

DIFFICULTY: Easy

SCENERY: Wooded canyon and lake

EXPOSURE: Mostly shaded

TRAIL TRAFFIC: Moderate

TRAIL SURFACE: Dirt

HIKING TIME: 2–3 hours

DRIVING DISTANCE: 22 miles from I-15/I-80 intersection

ELEVATION CHANGE: 7,295'–8,747'

ACCESS: Daily, sunrise–sunset; no fees or permits

MAPS: USGS *Mount Aire;* Trails Illustrated *Wasatch Front* (709)

FACILITIES: Restrooms across the street from trailhead

WHEELCHAIR ACCESS: None

CONTACT: 801-733-2660, fs.usda.gov/uwcnf

LOCATION: UT 190/Big Cottonwood Canyon Road, Salt Lake City, UT 84121

COMMENTS: You'll be sharing the trail with cyclists, as this is a popular mountain-biking trail. Dogs prohibited in Big Cottonwood Canyon, a protected watershed.

From the Mill D North Fork trailhead, the trail quickly ascends to the north, then immediately turns right to rise parallel to the canyon road on your right. The trail parallels the road for 0.4 mile before curving to the left and entering Mill D North Fork. At this point the trail is already far above the canyon floor, and it maintains a gentle ascent for another 0.8 mile until it joins Mill D Creek.

Mill D has more-moderate and less-rugged slopes than other Big Cottonwood side canyons. While it's not as dramatic or rocky as Big Cottonwood, it is beautiful, especially in fall as the aspens turn bright yellow. In the summer, daisies and alpine asters line the path.

At 1.7 miles from the trailhead, you arrive at a signed junction and the Desolation Trail. The path to the right leads to Desolation Lake (see next hike)—take the route to the left, which takes you directly to Dog Lake, just 0.6 mile farther. This trail leads through more aspens sprinkled with Douglas-fir. As you near the lake, the gradient increases a bit, but never long enough to become tiring. With a steady pace, you should arrive at Dog Lake, which lies at an elevation of 8,544 feet, about an hour after you leave the trailhead.

A still, shallow, circular basin ringed by aspens and conifers, Dog Lake may be too small to be called a lake and too large to be called a pond. Because it's shielded from wind, the lake typically has a glassy surface that reflects the surrounding trees like a flawless mirror. Bring your camera, walk around the lake, and enjoy the peaceful setting.

At the north end of the lake is a marked junction on the Desolation Trail. Continuing to the west for 2.8 miles will lead down Butler Fork and back to Big Cottonwood Canyon; from the Butler Fork trailhead, it's just 0.8 mile up the canyon road back to the Mill D North Fork trailhead.

Dog Lake

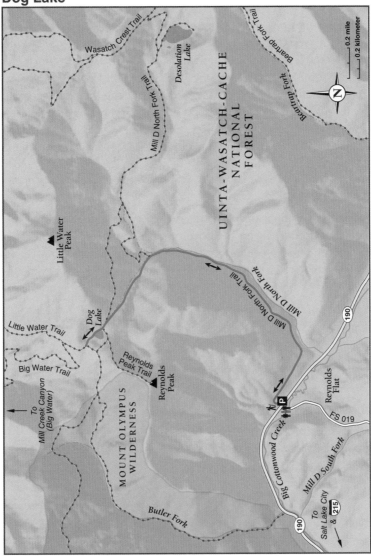

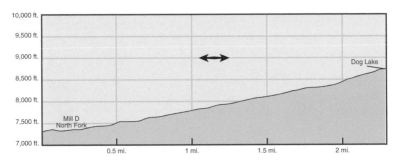

If you're adventurous and energetic, you can take the Big Water Trail over the ridge into Mill Creek Canyon. This is a beautiful alternative route, but unless you have a shuttle vehicle awaiting you, it will be a long walk back to your car.

Note that some hikers trek to Dog Lake from Mill Creek Canyon on the Big Water Trail, thinking that it allows them to bring along their canine companions, which are forbidden in Big Cottonwood Canyon—a protected area that serves as a water source for Salt Lake City—but welcome in Mill Creek Canyon. Unfortunately, the lake lies within the watershed's boundaries, and accessing it from a nonprotected area is not an exception to this rule.

NEARBY ACTIVITIES

Storm Mountain is the imposing barrier that sits 2.5 miles up Big Cottonwood Canyon and made access to the canyon so difficult for early pioneers. The **Stairs Gulch Trail** leads 0.5 mile up a rocky couloir at the base of the mountain. To access the trail, park near the geology sign on the right side of the road 100 yards beyond the Storm Mountain Picnic Area. Follow the trail up and to the west before turning south into Stairs Gulch.

· ·

GPS TRAILHEAD COORDINATES N40° 38.978' W111° 38.893'

DIRECTIONS From I-215 on Salt Lake City's east side, take Exit 6 and turn right onto UT 190 East/Big Cottonwood Canyon Road. Drive 1.7 miles; then turn left onto UT 190 East/Big Cottonwood Canyon Road, and drive 9 miles. The Mill D North Fork trailhead and parking area will be on the left side of the road.

The creek next to the trail supports a rich variety of plant and wildlife.

A GENTLE CANYON TRAIL ascends to a high-alpine lake, then leads to a ridge overlooking Park City and Big Cottonwood Canyon. A steep descent of a little-known canyon returns you to the Big Cottonwood Canyon floor.

DESCRIPTION

The 17-mile Desolation Trail stretches from the mouth of Mill Creek Canyon to the top of Big Cottonwood Canyon—from canyon floor to ridgeline. While few hikers ever follow the complete trail from end to end, sections of this scenic trail are popular as a means of connecting various canyons, lakes, and trailheads.

A hike to Desolation Lake—labeled as Lake Desolation on USGS maps—is an excellent orientation hike to Big Cottonwood Canyon because it leads hikers through two side canyons (Mill D North Fork and Beartrap Fork), ascends a panoramic ridgeline, and affords a stop at Desolation Lake. Dog Lake (see previous hike) can also be included in this hike by means of a short side trip.

From the Mill D North Fork trailhead, you'll ascend quickly to the north and then immediately turn right to rise parallel to the canyon road on your right. The trail parallels the road for 0.4 mile before curving left and entering Mill D North Fork. At this point the trail is already far above the canyon floor, and it maintains a gentle ascent for another 0.8 mile until it joins Mill D Creek.

DISTANCE & CONFIGURATION: 6.6-mile point-to-point or 8.2-mile loop, plus optional 1.2-mile out-and-back spur to Dog Lake

DIFFICULTY: Moderate

SCENERY: Canyons, alpine lake, ridgeline views

EXPOSURE: Mostly shaded

TRAIL TRAFFIC: Moderate

TRAIL SURFACE: Dirt, rock

HIKING TIME: 3–4 hours

DRIVING DISTANCE: 22 miles from I-15/I-80 intersection

ELEVATION CHANGE: 7,295'–9,760'

ACCESS: Daily, sunrise–sunset; no fees or permits

MAPS: USGS *Mount Aire* and *Park City West;* Trails Illustrated *Wasatch Front* (709)

FACILITIES: Restrooms across the street from trailhead

WHEELCHAIR ACCESS: None

CONTACT: 801-733-2660; fs.usda.gov/uwcnf

LOCATION: UT 190/Big Cottonwood Canyon Road, Salt Lake City, UT 84121

COMMENTS: You'll be sharing the trail with cyclists, as Mill D North Fork and the Desolation Trail are popular mountain biking trails. The descent down Beartrap Fork is more secluded than the previous section. Dogs prohibited in Big Cottonwood Canyon, a protected watershed.

As you ascend Mill D, you'll notice that the slopes on both sides of the canyon are more moderate and less rugged than slopes in other Big Cottonwood side canyons. While Mill D is not particularly dramatic or rocky, it is beautiful, especially in fall as the aspens turn bright yellow. In the summer, daisies and alpine asters line the path.

At 1.7 miles from the trailhead, you arrive at a signed junction and the Desolation Trail. Before continuing on the path to the right, which leads to Desolation Lake, consider a side trip to Dog Lake, just 0.6 mile farther along the path to your left. The Dog Lake option adds another 30 minutes and 1.2 miles to your trip.

From the junction, continue another 1.9 miles along the north slope of a small canyon as it leads through aspens in its ascent to Desolation Lake. The lake lies at an elevation of 9,232 feet in a broad, shallow bowl ringed by a treeless shoreline—hence *desolation.* In actuality, the meadow to the north and the trees on the upper slopes create a peaceful openness that is anything but desolate. It's not uncommon to see deer and elk feeding near Desolation Lake.

A trail ringing the lake makes a pleasant extension if you want to visit the woods on the lake's south side. From the north side, you can turn around and retrace your ascent route to return to the Mill D North Fork trailhead, or you can continue up to the ridge on the east for an interesting variation leading back to Big Cottonwood Canyon.

From Desolation Lake, take the trail from the northeast shore of the lake as it leads up to the ridgeline along an extended switchback. Within a few minutes, you'll be at the top of the ridge on the Great Western Trail leading toward Guardsman Pass and approaching a jagged section popularly known among mountain bikers simply as "the spine." Along this ridge you'll have fine views down into Park City to the east. Passing the spine, the trail leads south to the right of a knoll and continues along a level contour. As the Great Western Trail begins to curve to the left, you'll notice a

Desolation Lake

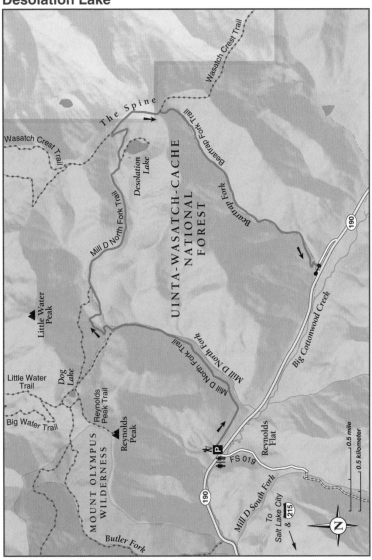

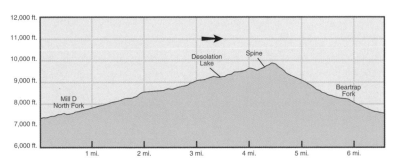

faint, unmarked trail that leads to the southwest, down a grassy slope into a canyon. This is Beartrap Fork, a quiet side canyon on the north side of Big Cottonwood.

Continuing down the trail, you'll soon connect with a seasonal creekbed at the bottom of Beartrap Canyon. Follow this creek as it leads toward the floor of Big Cottonwood Canyon. The total distance from the Great Western Trail junction through Beartrap Fork down to Big Cottonwood Canyon is 2.2 miles.

Once you arrive at the canyon floor and near the road, you'll pass around a metal gate, but no signs indicate that you've just descended Beartrap Fork. Unless you've left a shuttle vehicle outside the Beartrap Fork gate, you'll need to walk 1.6 miles west down the canyon road back to the Mill D North Fork trailhead.

NEARBY ACTIVITIES

A few miles east on Big Cottonwood Canyon Road, **Solitude Mountain Resort** is well known for its winter skiing but also offers a varied summer program. Featured activities include lift-served hiking, mountain biking, mountain scooters, disc golf, and casual dining. For information, call 801-534-1400 or visit skisolitude.com.

* *

GPS TRAILHEAD COORDINATES
Mill D North Fork: N40° 38.978' W111° 38.893'
Beartrap Fork: N40° 38.289' W111° 37.283'

DIRECTIONS From I-215 on Salt Lake City's east side, take Exit 6 and turn right onto UT 190 East/Big Cottonwood Canyon Road. Drive 1.7 miles; then turn left onto UT 190 East/Big Cottonwood Canyon Road, and drive 9 miles. The Mill D North Fork trailhead and parking area will be on the left side of the road. The Beartrap Fork gate is 1.6 miles farther, also on the left; the gate stays locked, however, so if you want to leave a shuttle vehicle here, you'll have to park wherever space is available nearby on either side of the road.

Aspens mix with conifers to provide a shady approach to Mount Raymond.

ADMITTEDLY, NEIGHBORING GOBBLERS KNOB (see Hike 21, page 107) is 5 feet higher in elevation and has a more interesting name, but Mount Raymond is the more interesting hike. Groves of aspen blanket the lower trail, and a variety of conifers clings to a rocky knife ridge leading to the summit. You'll have great views in all directions.

DESCRIPTION

A hike to the summit of Mount Raymond exemplifies the interconnectedness of many Wasatch trails. As you browse the summit log, you may find that most of the other hikers arrived by some other route. The path described here departs from the Butler Fork trailhead in Big Cottonwood Canyon, but you could just as easily use the Mill B North Fork trailhead or one of several Mill Creek Canyon trailheads. The Butler Fork route attains the summit with the least vertical ascent, though, and still offers an appealing approach. Along the route to the summit, you'll come to five trail junctions, and while you'll want to explore them all, you may have to save some for another day.

From the small roadside parking area, follow the trail leading north along the west side of a small stream. The trail immediately crosses to the east side of the stream and enters the Mount Olympus Wilderness Area, marked by a large U.S. Forest Service sign. At 0.5 mile from the trailhead, you'll come to a junction marked by

DISTANCE & CONFIGURATION: 8-mile out-and-back

DIFFICULTY: Strenuous

SCENERY: Wooded drainage, aspen slopes, high ridgeline ascent to a 10,241' peak with great views

EXPOSURE: Mostly shaded for first 2 miles, partially shaded to summit

TRAIL TRAFFIC: Moderate

TRAIL SURFACE: Dirt, rock

HIKING TIME: 4.5–5.5 hours

DRIVING DISTANCE: 21 miles from I-15/I-80 intersection

ELEVATION CHANGE: 7,170'–10,241'

ACCESS: Daily, sunrise–sunset; no fees or permits

MAPS: USGS *Mount Aire;* Trails Illustrated *Wasatch Front* (709)

FACILITIES: None

WHEELCHAIR ACCESS: None

CONTACT: 801-733-2660, fs.usda.gov/uwcnf

LOCATION: UT 190/Big Cottonwood Canyon Road, Salt Lake City, UT 84121

COMMENTS: This hike lies within both the federally designated Mount Olympus Wilderness Area and Big Cottonwood Canyon, a protected watershed. Pets, horses, bicycles, motorized vehicles, and open campfires are prohibited.

a small USFS sign indicating a trail to Dog Lake on the right and Mill A Basin on the left. Go to the left, up into the aspen-lined drainage.

Within 100 yards the aspens give way to a clearing about the size of a football field. This area will be your best chance to see moose, especially in the early morning. Never approach a moose—instead, try to work your way around it or wait for it to move. Never come between a moose cow and her calf or between a moose and the water.

From the clearing, the trail continues up the slope through a series of switchbacks. At 1.6 miles from the trailhead, you arrive at a saddle. A faint trail, normally blocked by fallen limbs to steer hikers along the main trail, takes off to the left. It leads to Circle All Peak, an 8,707-foot outcrop overlooking Big Cottonwood Canyon and also Mount Raymond. It's just 0.2 mile to the viewpoint and an elevation gain of 150 feet from the junction. It's certainly worth 10 minutes of your time, and if you're rushed for time it could be a suitable alternate destination for a hike of less than 2 hours.

Back on the main trail, continue along a gently ascending slope to another sign pointing to Dog Lake on the right and Mill A on the left. Follow the trail left as it sweeps along the upper slope of the Mill A Basin. This is a particularly enjoyable section of the hike, with excellent views of Mount Raymond directly to the west. These slopes also provide abundant habitat for many birds, including American redstarts and yellow warblers, which you should be able to hear even if you can't see them.

As you near the top of the Mill A Basin, a faint trail, normally unmarked, takes off along a level contour to the west and leads down to the Mill B North Fork Trailhead. Stay to the right as the trail continues another 0.2 mile up to the saddle of Baker Pass.

From Baker Pass (9,340') you have your first views into Mill Creek Canyon and west to the Great Salt Lake. Four separate trails meet at this pass. If you turn to the right, a fairly straightforward walk ascends 900 feet in 0.8 mile to the summit of Gobblers Knob. To the left a more rigorous climb ascends 900 feet in 0.6 mile to the

Mount Raymond (via Butler Fork)

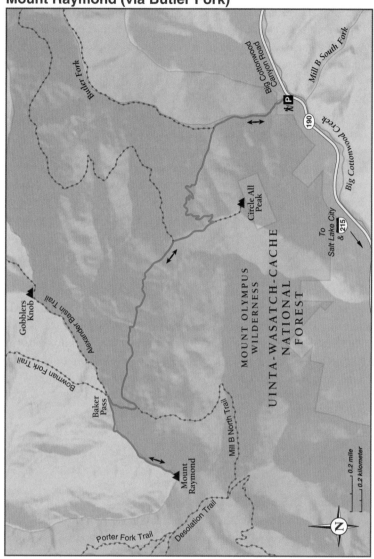

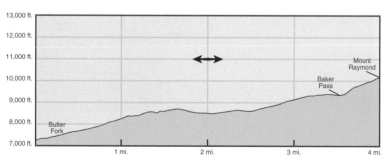

summit of Mount Raymond. Many hikers do both on the same hike, and that's certainly an option you can consider—you can bag two summits in one afternoon.

Departing Baker Pass and walking toward Mount Raymond to the west, you'll see an amazing variety of conifers, including Douglas-fir, limber pine, bristlecone pine, and subalpine fir. Some are firmly planted in soil, and others cling tenaciously with exposed roots hugging the rocks. The first 0.3 mile from the pass offers some beautiful steep ascents along a grassy alpine ridge trail. Then the trail ends and you're face to face with a fractured ridge of angular limestone and quartzite. It's a good scramble with some exposure, but nothing that would demand protective equipment or technical-climbing experience. There's just enough maneuvering to make it fun.

As you might expect, the summit offers excellent views in all directions. You'll enjoy seeing Mount Olympus from the less familiar back side, and Twin Peaks and Dromedary Peak to the south. At the summit you'll find a USGS marker and a summit log. You'll probably share the views with a handful of other hikers and a few interested chipmunks.

NEARBY ACTIVITIES

Big Cottonwood Canyon trails are known for their steep ascents to towering peaks and shimmering lakes. An enjoyable introduction to the canyon is the **Mill B South Interpretive Trail,** which follows rushing Big Cottonwood Creek for a 0.7-mile out-and-back. The trail is paved and wheelchair accessible, and there are restrooms at the trailhead. Start at the Mill B South Fork Trailhead parking lot, just 4.3 miles up the canyon as you enter the S-curves.

• •

GPS TRAILHEAD COORDINATES N40° 38.967' W111° 39.717'

DIRECTIONS From I-215 on Salt Lake City's east side, take Exit 6 and turn right onto UT 190 East/6200 South/Wasatch Boulevard; then, in 1.7 miles, turn left to continue on UT 190 East/Big Cottonwood Canyon Road, and drive 8.2 miles. Look for a small parking area on the left side of the road.

The footbridge across Broads Fork

BROADS FORK OFFERS HIKERS the chance to quickly ascend from the busy Mill B trailhead into a quiet corner of the canyon. Hikers are rewarded not only with a quiet walk but also with stunning views of the canyon, as well as a beautiful glacial cirque.

DESCRIPTION

On a sunny day, Big Cottonwood Canyon is filled with thousands of adventurers, each trying to find a quiet slice of serenity in the wilderness around Salt Lake Valley. Starting from a trailhead as popular as Mill B might seem like a counterintuitive way to achieve this end, but the lesser known Broads Fork Trail quickly gets away from the madness of the canyon bottom and ascends into quiet fir and aspen forests, far from the madding crowds.

From the Mill B South parking area, walk to the west end of the lot, where a small sign marks the beginning of the trail. The initially westbound trail ascends rapidly from the parking lot—a telling glimpse into many of the physical challenges that are soon to come on this hike.

As you proceed down the trail, the hike may sometimes feel like a high-intensity interval exercise: 5- to 10-minute bursts of arduous, steep trail interspersed with similarly timed periods of calm, relaxing flatness. As you ascend this gigantic staircase,

DISTANCE & CONFIGURATION: 4.5-mile out-and-back

DIFFICULTY: Moderate

SCENERY: Wooded canyon, glacial valley

EXPOSURE: Mostly shaded

TRAIL TRAFFIC: Medium

TRAIL SURFACE: Dirt, rock

HIKING TIME: 2–3 hours

DRIVING DISTANCE: 17 miles from I-15/ I-80 intersection

ELEVATION CHANGE: 6,205'–8,435'

ACCESS: Daily, sunrise–sunset; no fees or permits

MAPS: USGS *Mount Aire* and *Dromedary Peak;* Trails Illustrated *Wasatch Front* (709)

FACILITIES: Vault toilet at trailhead; no drinking water, but creek water can be purified

WHEELCHAIR ACCESS: None

CONTACT: 801-733-2660, fs.usda.gov/uwcnf

LOCATION: UT 190/Big Cottonwood Canyon Road, Salt Lake City, UT 84121

COMMENTS: Dogs prohibited in Big Cottonwood Canyon, a protected watershed

use the easier stretches with minimal elevation change as a chance to rest, take pictures, and look around at the rapidly changing scenery.

The trail initially heads west, but after 0.1 mile the trail bends around the ridge and quickly curves back to the east, seemingly taking you back up the canyon, toward the ski resorts. After less than 0.25 mile, however, the trail finally curves southward and enters the Twin Peaks Wilderness area, which lies within the Uinta-Wasatch-Cache National Forest. Most of the remainder of the hike is largely southward, vaguely following eponymous Broads Fork, a stream that has carved a deep gulch for itself. The gulch, combined with the thick tree cover, results in few actual views of the river; hikers are mainly alerted of its proximity by the occasional sound of the rushing waters cascading toward Big Cottonwood Creek, the defining natural feature of the area.

Broads Fork Trail benefits from plenty of shade, making for not only happy hikers but also a rich and rewarding microclimate. The trapped moisture gives rise to flora that are unusual for Utah. Mossy rocks and thick undergrowth give the area a rich color, texture, and smell that further add to the beauty of the surrounding peaks.

The silence created by the thick tree cover is occasionally broken by the sound of Broads Fork. While not large, the river is very steep and thus quite loud at times. The sound of the rushing water slowly grows from a whisper to a roar as you approach the only stream crossing of the hike, which you accomplish on a sturdy and elegant footbridge. Take some time here to enjoy the soundscape that this river creates in chorus with the local bird populations. This crossing occurs just before the halfway point of this ascent, both in terms of distance and elevation gain.

As you continue along the staircase-like trail, the undergrowth slowly becomes thicker and more encroaching. For this reason, many hikers will be glad that they wore pants instead of shorts, regardless of the weather.

Over the next 0.7 mile, more and more deciduous trees appear between the thinning firs. Suddenly—almost as if the trail were landscaped—the conifers that

Broads Fork

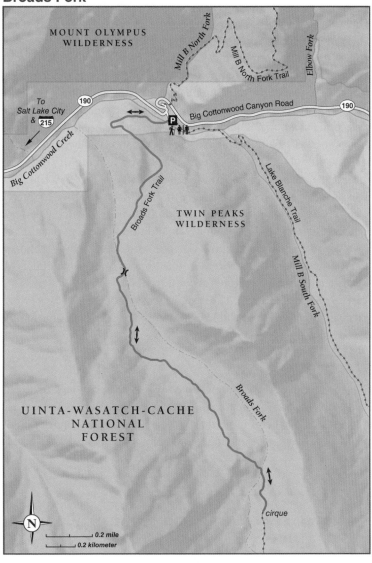

MOUNT OLYMPUS
WILDERNESS

Mill B North Fork

Mill B North Fork Trail

Elbow Fork

To
Salt Lake City
& 215

190

Big Cottonwood Canyon Road

190

Big Cottonwood Creek

Broads Fork Trail

TWIN PEAKS
WILDERNESS

Lake Blanche Trail

Mill B South Fork

Broads Fork

UINTA-WASATCH-CACHE
NATIONAL
FOREST

cirque

N

0.2 mile
0.2 kilometer

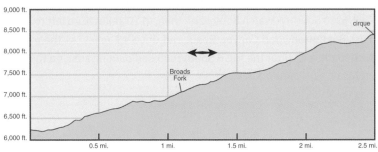

defined the trail give way to shimmering aspens. In the fall, these upper reaches of the trail become brightly colored with a bed of fallen aspen leaves.

Less than 0.25 mile from the first large aspen grove, the trail clearly forks. Each branch of the trail will take you to one side or the other of a grassy, tree-capped hill. This hill marks the end of the trail and offers the best views of the hike. Look down the hill to see sweeping views of the verdant, bustling canyon, or look upwards toward the lofty peaks for a view that is quintessentially Wasatch. The cirque is surrounded by large summits such as Twin Peaks, Dromedary Peak, and O'Sullivan Peak.

More-adventurous hikers may be drawn in by the maze of trails that winds around the cirque, many choosing to use the Broads Fork Trail as a launching point for some of the previously mentioned summits. But hikers tempted to travel onward should carefully assess their level of preparation, as the trail quickly deteriorates in terms of surface, safety, and navigability. In addition, a large population of rattlesnakes calls the rocky talus field home. Anyone who inadvertently wanders off the faint trail will quickly find themselves in thistles and scree, surrounded by rattlesnakes who are unlikely to be thrilled about intruders.

Be careful on the hike down. The steepest sections of the trail can spring up suddenly, leaving inattentive hikers sliding and stumbling. Take your time in the steeper sections, and enjoy the views northward.

NEARBY ACTIVITIES

A fixture at the mouth of Big Cottonwood Canyon, **Porcupine Pub & Grille** (3698 Fort Union Blvd.; 801-942-5555, porcupinepub.com) has been serving food and libations to weary skiers and hikers for more than 20 years. Stop in for a quick pint of one of Utah's many local beers, or stay longer and enjoy one of Salt Lake's most famous après-ski meals.

• •

GPS TRAILHEAD COORDINATES N40° 37.998' W111° 43.417'

DIRECTIONS From I-215 on Salt Lake City's east side, take Exit 6 and turn right onto UT 190 East/6200 South/Wasatch Boulevard; then, in 1.7 miles, turn left to continue on UT 190 East/Big Cottonwood Canyon Road, and drive 4.3 miles. As the road makes a hairpin turn to the left, enter the Mill B South trailhead parking area, on the right.

Doughnut Falls is one of the most popular destinations in Big Cottonwod Canyon.

DOUGHNUT FALLS IS UNIQUE: a waterfall that plunges through a hole in the rock and into a grotto before cascading down the rocky drainage below. The hike to the falls is short and popular with families and youth groups. If you want to climb to the top of the falls, you'll face a challenging but rewarding scramble.

DESCRIPTION

Doughnut Falls is irresistible. In less than a mile of easy walking, you come to a rocky chasm with a waterfall that drops through a hole in the rock. The sight is so intriguing that you are compelled to climb as close as possible to see where all that water goes.

As you drive up Big Cottonwood Canyon, you'll notice signs referring to Mill B, Mill C, and so on. This naming system dates back to the 1850s, when the side canyons in Big Cottonwood Canyon were named alphabetically, A–F, with a lumber mill placed at the mouth of each canyon. Doughnut Falls is on the Mill D South Fork. As you get closer to the trailhead, the canyon widens into a large, open meadow called Reynolds Flat, site of the Jordan Pines picnic area.

After a visitor fell through Doughnut Falls to his death in 1990, signs directing people there were removed, giving some visitors the impression that the falls were off-limits. Likewise, some disputes with private-land holders in the area have resulted in a number of PRIVATE PROPERTY and NO TRESPASSING signs being put up,

DISTANCE & CONFIGURATION: 1.4-mile out-and-back

DIFFICULTY: Easy

SCENERY: Spruce forest, stream, and waterfall

EXPOSURE: Mostly shaded

TRAIL TRAFFIC: Heavy

TRAIL SURFACE: Dirt, rock

HIKING TIME: 1–2 hours

DRIVING DISTANCE: 22 miles from I-15/I-80 intersection

ELEVATION CHANGE: 7,493'–7,830'

ACCESS: Daily, no fees or permits; gate to Jordan Pines picnic area is closed winter–early spring, necessitating an 0.8-mile walk to the trailhead

WHEELCHAIR ACCESS: None

MAPS: USGS *Mount Aire*

FACILITIES: Vault toilet at trailhead; no drinking water, but creek water can be purified

CONTACT: 801-733-2660, fs.usda.gov/uwcnf

LOCATION: UT 190/Big Cottonwood Canyon Road, Salt Lake City, UT 84121

COMMENTS: The road to the trailhead passes through private property with NO TRESPASSING signs posted, but access to the falls is open to the public. Dogs prohibited in Big Cottonwood Canyon, a protected watershed.

leading some to believe that the falls are closed to the public. In 2007, Salt Lake City purchased Doughnut Falls and about 144 surrounding acres as a watershed. The U.S. Forest Service's management of the area preserves public access to the falls.

From the trailhead parking area, the wide trail leads up the canyon through a forest of white, blue, and yellow spruce, dotted with limber pine and the occasional Douglas-fir. Stands of quaking aspen brighten the trail, especially in the fall as they turn lemon yellow. At 0.2 mile the wide trail constricts and veers off to the right. At 0.4 mile the trail enters an open area shaded by large conifers. From here, cross the bridge over Mill D South Fork to your right, then immediately turn left onto the old mining road and continue up the canyon with the stream at your left. At 0.1 mile past the bridge, you'll arrive at a fork in the mining road, where you'll stay to the left, following the stream up the canyon.

Almost instantly, the canyon becomes a rocky chasm. By staying close to the stream, you'll be drawn into the boulder-filled drainage below the falls. In the spring, the snow-fed stream spans the chasm, and continuing up toward the falls will require some boulder-hopping and scrambling up steep rock ledges. Getting wet is almost inevitable. In the summer, as the stream flow is reduced, some scrambling will be required, but it's easier to avoid getting wet. Even though Doughnut Falls is a popular family hike, the climb to the falls may be too risky to attempt with children younger than age 6.

As you weave through the large boulders below the falls and scale the rocky ledges leading up to them, be sure to stay on the west side of the stream, to the right of the falls. This will give you the safest access and put you face to face with the falls' intriguing layout.

Doughnut Falls plunges through a hole about 6 feet in diameter and drops into a grotto about 20 feet long and 10 feet wide. You'll want to get close—and most

Doughnut Falls

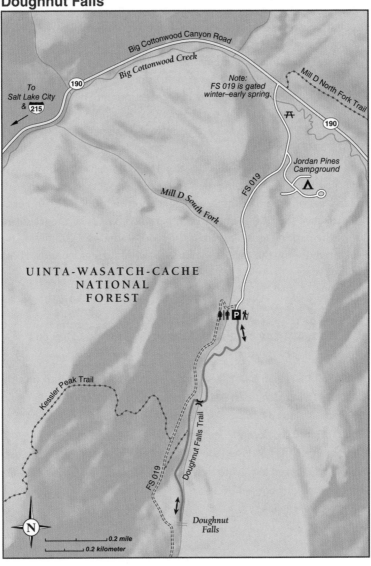

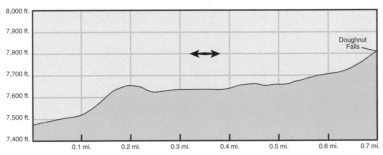

visitors get within a few feet of the grotto—but be careful. It's easy to spend an hour or more playing around here.

On your way to the falls and back, be on the lookout for moose, who find a luxurious habitat in this drainage. Beavers still appear in the stream, and foxes occasionally dart behind trees. But the most likely sightings will be ground squirrels and chipmunks in a lush home of spruce and aspen.

NEARBY ACTIVITIES

As long as you're visiting Doughnut Falls, don't miss **Hidden Falls** on your way up the canyon—it's just 100 yards from the road and takes just a few minutes to visit. As you come to the S-curve, 4.3 miles up the canyon, enter the Mill B North Fork parking area, 100 yards past the Mill B South Fork parking area. Take the trailhead on the north side of the parking area, and cross the road. Rather than following the Mill B North Fork Trail, follow the creek to your left—within a few seconds, Hidden Falls appears as if by magic.

• •

GPS TRAILHEAD COORDINATES N40° 38.375' W111° 39.087'

DIRECTIONS From I-215 on Salt Lake City's east side, take Exit 6 and turn right onto UT 190 East/6200 South/Wasatch Boulevard; then, in 1.7 miles, turn left to continue on UT 190 East/Big Cottonwood Canyon Road, and drive 9 miles. Turn right on Forest Service Road 019 into the Jordan Pines picnic area, and continue 0.8 mile to the trailhead parking area, on the left. When the FS 019 gate is closed for the season or the parking area is full, you'll need to walk to the trailhead—additional parking is available just outside the gate on both sides of UT 190.

Lake Blanche nestles at the base of Sundial Peak.

LAKE BLANCHE IS A classic glacial tarn at the base of a cirque. The hike to the lake begins at the Big Cottonwood Canyon floor and follows the dramatically glaciated side canyon to an exceptionally scenic and remote alpine setting. It's one of the most popular hikes in the Salt Lake area—and justifiably so.

DESCRIPTION

It's entirely possible to walk out of a meeting in the Fort Union business and financial district and, within 15 minutes, be following a roaring stream up a glacial canyon in a federally designated wilderness area. And that's only the beginning. The highlight, Lake Blanche, awaits under a glacial cirque at the top of the canyon. No wonder this is such a popular hike.

The parking area at the Mill B South Fork trailhead holds 24 cars, but you can also park along the road. The parking lot serves both the Broads Fork trailhead at the west end of the lot (see Hike 28, page 135) and the Mill B South Fork (Lake Blanche) trailhead at the east side of the lot, to the left of the vault toilet. Take this paved trail as it parallels Big Cottonwood Creek to your left. Within about 0.2 mile and just before the paved trail crosses a bridge, the Lake Blanche Trail departs the paved trail, bearing to the right and becoming a rocky path.

DISTANCE & CONFIGURATION: 5.8-mile out-and-back

DIFFICULTY: Moderate

SCENERY: Canyon with glacial geology, stream, glacial lakes, surrounding peaks

EXPOSURE: Mostly shaded up to lake, then partially shaded

TRAIL TRAFFIC: Heavy

TRAIL SURFACE: Dirt, rock

HIKING TIME: 3.5–5 hours

DRIVING DISTANCE: 17 miles from I-15/I-80 intersection

ELEVATION CHANGE: 6,240'–8,910'

ACCESS: Daily, sunrise–sunset; no fees or permits

MAPS: USGS *Mount Aire, Dromedary Peak;* Trails Illustrated *Wasatch Front* (709)

FACILITIES: Vault toilet at trailhead; no drinking water, but water from stream and lake can be purified

WHEELCHAIR ACCESS: None

CONTACT: 801-733-2660, fs.usda.gov/uwcnf

LOCATION: UT 190/Big Cottonwood Canyon Road, Salt Lake City, UT 84121

COMMENTS: This hike lies within both the federally designated Twin Peaks Wilderness Area and Big Cottonwood Canyon, a protected watershed. Pets, horses, bicycles, motorized vehicles, and open campfires are prohibited.

After 0.1 mile on the Lake Blanche dirt trail, you'll cross a bridge to the east side of the Mill B South Fork and continue up a switchback to the north. Within another 0.2 mile, you'll enter the Twin Peaks Wilderness Area with the stream at your right as you head up the canyon.

The trail steadily ascends the canyon in a shaded forest. Soon, within the upper area of the canyon, you'll pass through several acres of avalanche damage, where hundreds of trees have been toppled like so many toothpicks. Follow the course of destruction by looking at the release area on the denuded, avalanche-prone slope to the west. Observe how the avalanche crossed the stream and took out trees on the opposite slope from where you stand. Above and below the avalanche zone, the trail is largely shaded by a blanket of aspen and dotted with Douglas-fir.

Near the top of Mill B South Fork, you ascend the slope above the aspen to the eastern side of the canyon. Along the high switchbacks, you can catch a narrow glimpse of the Salt Lake Valley through the canyon's mouth. At 2.4 miles from the trailhead, you come to a talus slope composed of quartzite boulders. The trail skirts the large rock pile and continues up to the south. Within 100 yards of the first talus field, the trail crosses another quartzite field.

As you approach the large quartzite formation at the top of the canyon, you'll begin to notice evidence of glacial activity. As glaciers transported rocks and debris over the surface of the formation, they left striations on the quartzite's surface that are still clearly visible.

As you crest the formation, Lake Blanche comes into full view. As you look across the lake, Sundial Peak stands at the center of the cirque. While the quartzite formation forms the northern shore of the lake, the remains of a concrete reinforced rock dam are visible on both sides of the quartzite dome. This dam was built in the 1930s to contain a much larger reservoir. Many of the upper Wasatch lakes were

Lake Blanche

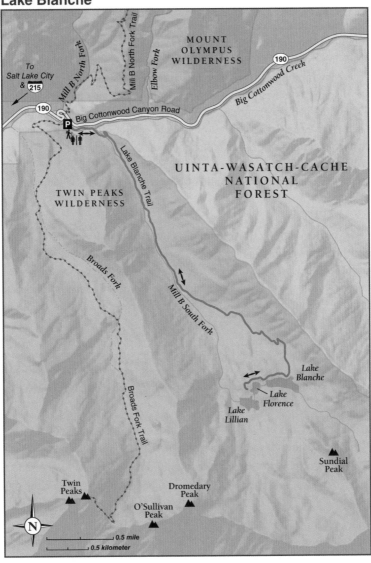

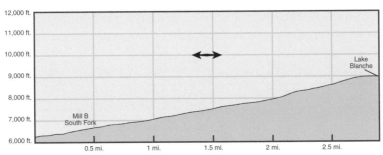

controlled and maintained as reservoirs to ensure a consistent supply of water to the city throughout the summer. The Lake Blanche dam broke along the western rim in 1983, leaving the lake at its present size. If you're tempted to take a dip in the icy waters, *don't:* swimming is prohibited in watershed lakes.

Lake Blanche is a destination resort in the wilderness. Take your time, walk around, study the geology, count the wildflowers, look for waterfalls, and explore the woods at the far end of the lake. Allow at least an hour at and around the lake. As you walk to the western side of Lake Blanche, you'll discover two smaller tarns—Lake Florence and Lake Lillian—in a lower glacial bowl. These more-remote lakes get less traffic, provide a quiet place to rest, and offer better chances for viewing wildlife.

NEARBY ACTIVITIES

As you drive back down Big Cottonwood Canyon following your hike, you may want to stop at the **Storm Mountain Picnic Area.** Near the picnic sites is the Storm Mountain Amphitheater, which can be reserved for private programs and concerts. The amphitheater holds up to 200 people and offers a dramatic setting for a business or organizational event. Open mid–May–August; for reservations (available in 4-hour blocks), call 877-444-6777 or go to recreation.gov.

• •

GPS TRAILHEAD COORDINATES N40° 37.968' W111° 43.415'

DIRECTIONS From I-215 on Salt Lake City's east side, take Exit 6 and turn right onto UT 190 East/6200 South/Wasatch Boulevard; then, in 1.7 miles, turn left to continue on UT 190 East/Big Cottonwood Canyon Road, and drive 4.3 miles. As the road makes a hairpin turn to the left, enter the Mill B South trailhead parking area, on the right.

During the winter the aspens shed their leaves, opening up spectacular ridgeline views.

THIS SHORT, LITTLE-KNOWN HIKE leads to a high meadow and lake. Situated at the top of Big Cottonwood Canyon, Willow Heights is filled with wildflowers and wildlife, but despite its lush flora and astonishing views of the southern ridge and canyon below, this quick hike attracts few people.

DESCRIPTION

You'll find that most hikes leading to lakes in Big Cottonwood Canyon are well marked, have ample trailhead parking, and are often crowded. Willow Lake has none of these attributes. Because there's no marked trailhead, you'll need to park on the south side of the road (UT 190), cross to a residential drive leading 0.1 mile to the west, and then switchback another 0.1 mile to the east. As the pavement ends, the trail begins.

The wide path leads through a hillside of aspens, sprinkled with just a few young firs. Occasionally the trail steepens, but it's never too strenuous. At 0.8 mile you come to Willow Creek, which can be crossed on a crude bridge of fallen branches or on stepping-stones several feet upstream. The creek is small and swells only slightly in the springtime, so regardless of how you cross the creek, you need not worry about your feet getting wet.

DISTANCE & CONFIGURATION: 1.5-mile out-and-back

DIFFICULTY: Easy

SCENERY: Aspen forest, meadows, a quiet lake

EXPOSURE: Mostly shaded

TRAIL TRAFFIC: Moderate

TRAIL SURFACE: Paved for first 0.2 mile, then dirt to meadow and lake

HIKING TIME: 1–1.5 hours

DRIVING DISTANCE: 24 miles from I-15/I-80 intersection

ELEVATION CHANGE: 7,815'–8,490'

ACCESS: Daily, sunrise–sunset; no fees or permits

MAPS: USGS *Park City West*

FACILITIES: None

WHEELCHAIR ACCESS: None

CONTACT: 801-733-2660, fs.usda.gov/uwcnf

LOCATION: UT 190/Big Cottonwood Canyon Road, Salt Lake City, UT 84121

COMMENTS: This is a great snowshoe hike or backcountry ski tour in winter. Dogs prohibited in Big Cottonwood Canyon, a protected watershed.

Within 0.1 mile the aspen grove opens to a large meadow and views of the upper canyon and ridgeline to the east. As you follow the trail to the upper end of the meadow, you come to a fork. Turning left will lead you to Willow Lake in less than 100 yards. Continuing straight will lead to aptly named Dry Lake, about 0.5 mile to the northeast.

While Willow Lake may be a short hike, don't make it a fast one. Take your time as you approach the lake: explore, walk around the shore, and watch for wildlife. It's the perfect place to spot moose and deer, especially in the early morning and at dusk. A large beaver lodge rises from the middle of the shallow lake, and ducks nest and live near the water in spring and summer. Cliff swallows skim the surface of the lake, and raptors circle high overhead.

Regardless of which season you hike during—and this truly is as wonderful and quick a snowshoe adventure as it is a hike—Willow Heights offers an astonishing density of photography opportunities. In the summer, the lake and meadow are lush and alive. Teeming with wildlife eager to pose for their close-up. The deciduous-heavy tree cover makes the area burst with color as soon as fall descends on the canyon. And in the wintertime, the aspens shed their foliage and the white branches that remain tangle together to create a stained glass view of the south ridge of Big Cottonwood Canyon.

Several primitive campsites await on the north side of the lake for those wanting a short hike to a setting of solitude and natural beauty. If you choose to make this an overnight destination, the well-hidden trailhead ensures that, even on busy weekends in the canyon, you will be treated to a quiet night, blissfully unaware that you are just minutes from a million-person city. Note, however, that Willow Lake and the meadow can be buggy in summer, so come prepared with insect repellent.

The meadow and the flatlands around the lake are alive with wildflowers in spring and summer. Phlox is the most abundant, while larkspur and penstemon are also common.

Willow Heights, the open area encompassing both the meadow and the lake, makes a wonderful short morning hike. You can be up to the lake before the sun rises

Willow Heights

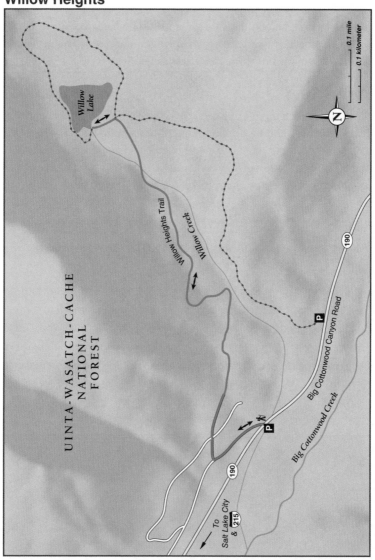

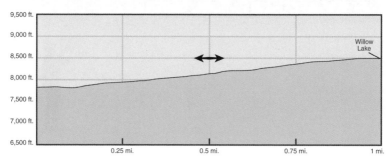

over the ridge, watch the wildlife awaken, and still be back to your nearby lodge or cabin before breakfast. In winter or early spring, a midday snowshoe hike exposes the wildlife as the sun beams through leafless aspen.

NEARBY ACTIVITIES

A great choice for lunch or an extended stay, **Silver Fork Lodge** offers nearby access to skiing, hiking, fishing, and mountain biking. It has a patio and indoor casual dining that you can enjoy without having to get dressed up—even if you've just come off the trail or the ski slopes. The lodge has seven rustic rooms without phones or TVs, plus an outdoor hot tub. For reservations, call 888-649-9551 or go to silverforklodge.com.

• •

GPS TRAILHEAD COORDINATES N40° 37.928' W111° 36.518'

DIRECTIONS From I-215 on Salt Lake City's east side, take Exit 6 and turn right onto UT 190 East/6200 South/Wasatch Boulevard; then, in 1.7 miles, turn left to continue on UT 190 East/Big Cottonwood Canyon Road, and drive 11.1 miles to Silver Fork Lodge, on the right. Continue another 0.2 mile up the canyon, and park on the right side of the road. The trail begins across the street on a narrow, paved road leading to a residential area.

The lake at the top of the hike allows for unobstructed views and stunning photos.

In addition to waterfowl, chukars can be seen along the parkway.

Photo: BirdPhotos/iStockPhoto.com

THE JORDAN RIVER PARKWAY stays close to the river, passing along and through a riparian habitat and floodplain. You can easily reach the trail at dozens of points: parks, street crossings, and residential neighborhoods. The parkway in its entirety extends almost 50 miles from the Utah County line to the south to the Davis County line to the north. The section featured here is particularly beautiful, exhibiting some of the path's most accessible and enjoyable scenery.

DESCRIPTION

The Jordan River, Utah Lake's outlet, is one of the three major rivers that empty into the Great Salt Lake. Originally named the Utah River, it was renamed by Mormon pioneer Heber C. Kimball, who likened the river to its Holy Land namesake, which also flows from a freshwater lake into an inland salt sea.

The Jordan River Parkway was an ambitious urban trail project to undertake. The section described here can easily be accessed at Gardner Village to the south, at Redwood Trailhead Park to the north, and at dozens of points in between.

The trail snakes its way around the various inlets and marshes that dress the banks of the river, making the trail even more circuitous than the river itself. As the crow flies, this section measures only 7.7 miles in length, but as the trail follows the meandering

DISTANCE & CONFIGURATION: 11-mile point-to-point (full trail is almost 50 miles)

DIFFICULTY: Easy

SCENERY: The Jordan River and its surrounding wetlands

EXPOSURE: Partial shade

TRAIL TRAFFIC: Heavy

TRAIL SURFACE: Completely paved and striped

HIKING TIME: Varies greatly based on the distance selected

DRIVING DISTANCE: 5 miles from I-15/I-80 intersection

ELEVATION CHANGE: 4,290' at trailhead, with no significant rise

ACCESS: Daily, sunrise–sunset; no fees or permits

MAPS: Available at slco.org/parks/trails

FACILITIES: Restrooms, water, food, and other services at the trailhead and throughout the hike

WHEELCHAIR ACCESS: Yes

CONTACT: 801-535-7800, slc.gov/parks

LOCATION: 1100 W. 7800 S., West Jordan, UT 84088 (Gardner Village); eastern end of Cesar Chavez Drive/2320 South, 1 mile east of UT 68/Redwood Road, West Valley City, UT 84119 (Redwood Trailhead Park)

COMMENTS: Dogs allowed on leash

river, it covers a distance of more than 11 miles. While the Jordan does wind and meander, dropping only about 5 feet per mile, it still flows at a surprisingly fast clip.

Leaving Gardner Village just north of 7800 South, the trail heads north along the west bank of the Jordan until 6300 South. As the river flows north, the trail makes several river crossings and also manages to adeptly avoid most major thoroughfares and two freeways with some well-placed underpasses. For the most part, road noise is easy to escape along the trail.

When early pioneers arrived in the Salt Lake Valley, they noted that the cottonwood- and willow-lined river corridor stood in sharp contrast to the treeless, sage-covered plains on either side. They soon built settlements along the river and shared the land with wolves and coyotes, while beavers built dams along the river. All are gone today, but foxes, skunks, raccoons, and muskrats still live in the wooded areas near the river.

More than any other species, you'll see waterfowl. Mallards, grebes, coots, Canada geese, and great blue herons make the parkway marshlands their permanent home. Ring-necked pheasants, chukars, and quail can also be spotted year-round.

As late as 1910, the riverbanks provided seasonal camping for Ute, Paiute, and Shoshone tribes. American Indians traded tanned skins and dried meat for supplies. Trailhead markers provide interpretive background on the natural history of the area, as well as insights into pioneer homesteads and early settlements along the river.

The growth of the Salt Lake Valley, industrialization, dredging, and channeling have not always been kind to the Jordan River—many of its rich riparian and wetland areas have been lost over the last 100 years. Today, natural-resource damage-settlement funds from the Sharon Steel Superfund Site are being used to restore more than 270 acres of river corridor and floodplain by removing invasive plants, putting in native plants, and contouring some sections of the riverbank.

Jordan River Parkway

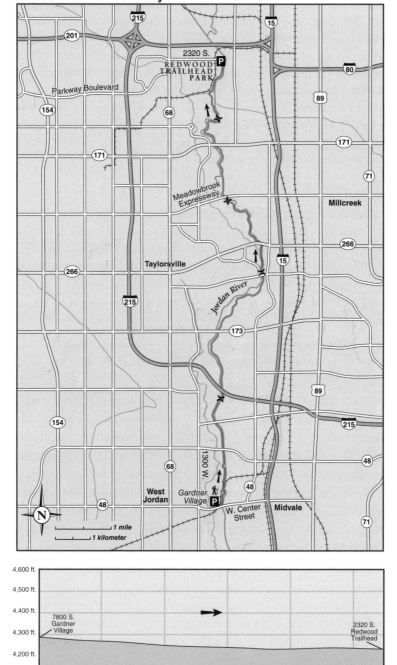

A number of spur trails and oxbow divisions mark the trail. At some points, the trail divides into a pedestrian portion, while bicycles stay on the paved route. The West Valley City Cross Towne Trail and other spurs connect the main trail to nearby neighborhoods. These poorly marked spurs typically follow a diversion canal or side channel. When in doubt, stay on the trail nearest the river.

North of Redwood Trailhead Park, the parkway continues unobstructed for another 2 miles, but the surrounding area loses much of its natural beauty and scenic appeal. The setting becomes more industrial with less shade—and, of concern to cyclists, more thorns to flatten your tires.

NEARBY ACTIVITIES

Gardner Village, an early-Utah-themed shopping village (1100 W. 7800 S.; 801-566-8903, gardnervillage.com), got its start in 1853, when the first flour mill in the South Salt Lake Valley was built on the site. Today, specialty shops, a restaurant, bakery, and day spa cluster in a historical setting linked by brick paths, gardens, and a covered bridge.

· ·

GPS TRAILHEAD COORDINATES
Redwood Trailhead Park: N40° 43.212' W111° 55.290'
Gardner Village: N40° 36.576' W111° 55.341'

DIRECTIONS *Redwood Trailhead Park (ending trailhead):* From I-15 South near the southern intersection of I-15 and I-80, take Exit 305A and merge onto UT 201 West. (From I-80 West, take Exit 123A for UT 201 West.) Drive 0.8 mile; then take Exit 15B/15C, turn left onto UT 68 South/Redwood Road, and drive 0.2 mile. Turn left onto Cesar Chavez Drive/2320 South, and drive 1 mile. Trailhead parking is at the end of the road on the right.

Gardner Village (starting trailhead): After leaving a shuttle at the trailhead parking lot, backtrack to Cesar Chavez Drive/2320 South, turn left, and drive 0.1 mile. Turn right onto 1070 West, which becomes 2240 South and then 2200 South, and drive 0.9 mile. Make a quick right onto Redwood Road, and immediately bear right onto the entrance ramp for UT 201 East. In 1.1 miles, shortly after crossing the Jordan River, use the left two lanes to merge onto I-15 South. In 7.4 miles, take Exit 297; then, in another 0.4 mile, bear right at the fork onto UT 48/7200 South. Drive 0.5 mile, and turn left onto Bingham Junction Boulevard; then, in 0.8 mile, turn right onto West Center Street/7800 South. Drive 0.4 mile, and turn right into the parking lot for Gardner Village. Access the trail from the parking lot's southeast corner.

In addition to these starting and ending trailheads, more than a dozen official trailheads supply public parking and easy trail access along the way.

Tiny wildflowers speckle the trail all the way to the summit.

THE GREAT WESTERN TRAIL is a corridor of trails traversing 4,455 miles through Arizona, Utah, Idaho, Wyoming, and Montana. Within Utah, the Great Western Trail roughly follows the Wasatch ridge running north and south. A short hike from Guardsman Pass to Clayton Peak follows a section of the trail along a scenic ridgeline.

DESCRIPTION

Ridgeline hikes have the benefit of delivering panoramic views and enabling you to put the surrounding peaks and canyons in perspective. This small section of the Great Western Trail demonstrates how interconnected Wasatch canyons are and how easy it is to connect to trails in Park City and Heber Valley to the east. With most of the hike being above 10,000 feet in elevation, there's not much to block the view.

Guardsman Pass offers a high-elevation start for the hike. The area is popular with mountain bikers—once parking is gone, very few alternatives are available nearby, so consider doing this hike early in the day or on a weekday if possible.

From the trailhead parking area, take a look around in all directions. Summit County and Park City lie to the north and east, Wasatch County and Heber Valley lie to the south and east, and Big Cottonwood Canyon lies directly below to the west. The trail leading to Clayton Peak stretches in front of you to the south. A wider and

DISTANCE & CONFIGURATION: 2.2-mile out-and-back

DIFFICULTY: Moderate

SCENERY: Mountain scenery, panoramic views

EXPOSURE: Partially shaded

TRAIL TRAFFIC: Light

TRAIL SURFACE: Dirt, rock

HIKING TIME: 2–2.5 hours

DRIVING DISTANCE: 29 miles from I-15/I-80 intersection

ELEVATION CHANGE: 9,706'–10,721'

ACCESS: Daily, sunrise–sunset, but Guardsman

Pass Road is closed to cars late fall–early spring; no fees or permits

MAPS: USGS *Brighton*

FACILITIES: Restrooms at Guardsman Pass Road winter gate, about 2.3 miles west of trailhead

WHEELCHAIR ACCESS: None

CONTACT: 801-733-2660, fs.usda.gov/uwcnf

LOCATION: Guardsman Pass Road, Salt Lake City, UT 84121

COMMENTS: Dogs permitted on trail from Guardsman Pass eastward but prohibited in Big Cottonwood Canyon, a protected watershed, to the west

better-groomed quickly descends toward the lakes just east of the ridgeline. Don't let this trail confuse you—the trail to Clayton Peak stays cleanly along the ridge, seldom deviating by more than a dozen yards.

Like most Wasatch trails, this one rises quickly from the trailhead. After less than 30 minutes of hiking at a steady pace, you've already covered 0.6 mile and gained more than 700 feet of elevation. You'll find yourself on top of an unnamed knoll along the ridgeline at an elevation of 10,420 feet. The views are great, but Clayton Peak still looms in the distance to the south. Descend the slope on a faint trail and continue along the ridge, dropping more than 300 feet of hard-earned elevation gain.

Along the way, you can't help but notice the many lakes in the basin to the east. Little-known to most Wasatch hikers, they include Bloods Lake, Lake Brimhall, Silver Lake, Silver Lake Islet, and Lackawaxen Lake. You can reach them on trails leading down from the ridgeline, in particular as part of a loop hike returning to Guardsman Pass.

As you work your way up the ridge, a quick glance to the right will surprise you with a view of the Brighton ski lift just 50 feet below, but this is only a brief distraction and doesn't significantly alter the feeling of remoteness. About halfway up the northern slope of Clayton Peak, the trail turns from a rocky path to a ridge made entirely of rock. For the final stretch leading to the summit, you'll be navigating boulders at a slow pace.

Most Wasatch hikes focus on westward views to the Salt Lake Valley. Clayton Peak offers panoramic views, but the most interesting vistas here are those to the east, with Heber Valley in the forefront and the Uintas Mountains off in the distance.

Even near the summit, aspens and firs rise near the trail. At this elevation, snow can cover the ridge into mid-June, and the aspens often change colors in the first

Great Western Trail (Guardsman Pass to Clayton Peak)

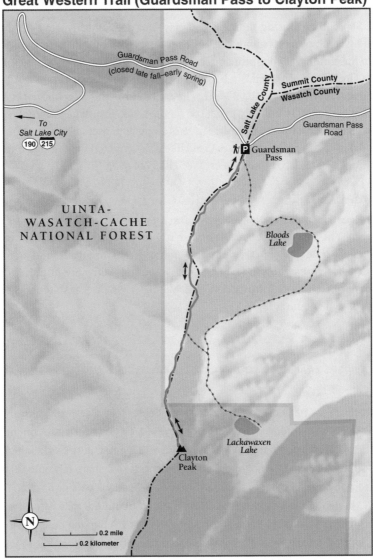

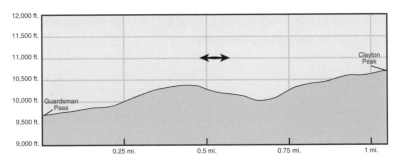

week of September. During summer, you may spot deer and coyotes near the ridge, and you'll see chipmunks along the entire trail. Clark's nutcrackers favor the high slopes in the summer, and raptors often circle nearby.

The Great Western Trail is a hike for aspiring peak baggers and a good way to train and acclimatize above 10,000 feet. The trail follows the ridgeline, so even when it becomes faint, you're unlikely to get too far off-track. From the Clayton Peak summit, you can either return to Guardsman Pass along your ascent route or extend your hike by dropping to Brighton Lakes (see Hike 35, page 163) or forging on to Sunset Peak, along the ridge to the southwest (see Hike 36, page 167).

NEARBY ACTIVITIES

Wasatch Mountain State Park in Midway is just 10 miles down Guardsman Pass Road to the east. The 22,000-acre park is a year-round mountain retreat with a USGA-sanctioned 27-hole golf course, camping, hiking and nature trails, and an interpretive center. In winter, snowshoeing and cross-country skiing are popular activities. For reservations or more information, call 435-654-1791 or visit stateparks.utah.gov /parks/wasatch-mountain.

• •

GPS TRAILHEAD COORDINATES N40° 36.402' W111° 33.297'

DIRECTIONS From I-215 on Salt Lake City's east side, take Exit 6 and turn right onto UT 190 East/6200 South/Wasatch Boulevard; then, in 1.7 miles, turn left to continue on UT 190 East/Big Cottonwood Canyon Road, and drive 13.8 miles. Just past Solitude Mountain Resort and Redman Campground on your right, take a sharp left onto Guardsman Pass Road, and drive 3.1 miles to the Guardsman Pass Overlook parking area, on the right.

Note: In winter Guardsman Pass Road is gated about 0.8 mile after the turnoff, about 0.3 mile past a hairpin turn south along the road. A parking pullout with a restroom is located on the right side of the road adjacent to the gate, but in winter it's reserved for snowmobile trailers, so if you're not snowmobiling you'll need to find parking where you can nearby—making sure to heed the NO PARKING signs where posted—and then hike, ski, or snowshoe to the trailhead.

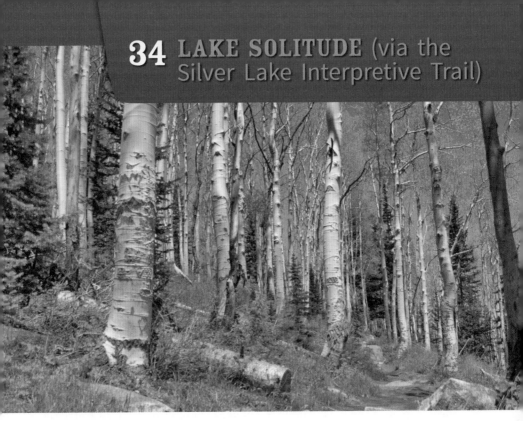

Thick, towering aspens surround the trail.

TWO HIKES FOR THE PRICE OF ONE: the Silver Lake Interpretive Trail circles the alpine marsh around Silver Lake, and the connected Lake Solitude Trail leads through a forest of fir and aspen to a small glacial tarn. You'll get a hands-on education in alpine ecosystems in a scenic mountain setting.

DESCRIPTION

Silver Lake has been one of Salt Lake City's most popular summer recreation areas since July 23, 1849, when more than 2,000 residents escaped the valley's summer heat to hold their first Pioneer Day celebration here. The Brighton ski area remains a great summer getaway, and Silver Lake is the ideal short family hike.

Silver Lake, a shallow alpine lake surrounded by wetlands, teems with life during its short season. A brilliantly conceived trail, the Silver Lake Interpretive Trail allows visitors to explore the fragile wetlands ecosystem without ever getting wet or damaging the marshy areas. In the wooded areas along the lake's southern shore, the trail leaves the boardwalk and enters moist woods of fir and aspen along a dirt path.

Start your adventure at the Silver Lake Visitor Center, staffed in summer by the U.S. Forest Service. (In winter, the visitor center becomes the Solitude Nordic Center, where cross-country skiers can access 12 miles of trails.) From here you can follow the circular path in either direction, although most traffic seems to flow

DISTANCE & CONFIGURATION: 3.5-mile loop with out-and-back

DIFFICULTY: Easy

SCENERY: Alpine lake with surrounding mountains

EXPOSURE: Partially shaded on Silver Lake Interpretive Trail, mostly shaded on Lake Solitude Trail

TRAIL TRAFFIC: Heavy

TRAIL SURFACE: Boardwalk and dirt

HIKING TIME: 1.5–2 hours

DRIVING DISTANCE: 27 miles from I-15/I-80 intersection

ELEVATION CHANGE: 8,720'–9,220'

ACCESS: Daily, sunrise–sunset; no fees or permits

MAPS: USGS *Brighton*

FACILITIES: Restrooms and water at trailhead; store and restaurant across the street; visitor center open daily, June–September, 10 a.m.–5 p.m.

WHEELCHAIR ACCESS: The Silver Lake Interpretive Trail is wheelchair accessible

CONTACT: 801-733-2660, fs.usda.gov/uwcnf

LOCATION: Brighton Resort, South Brighton Loop Road, Brighton, UT 84121

COMMENTS: Bicycles prohibited on Silver Lake boardwalk; dogs prohibited in Big Cottonwood Canyon, a protected watershed

counterclockwise. Along the way, signs and displays describe the area's flora, fauna, and ecosystems, as well as watershed and drinking-water concerns. Rainbow trout and small brook trout stock the lake, making it an ideal destination for young anglers going after their first catch.

Winters are long and life is hard in this alpine environment. With an average of 33 feet of snow each winter, plants and animals have adapted to survive. The quaking aspen photosynthesizes through its bark and doesn't leaf out until mid-June in order to conserve energy. Snowshoe hares turn snow white in winter and float over the snow with their giant feet. The Uinta ground squirrel, whose burrows line the path, hibernates for eight months of the year.

Wildlife flourishes around the lake and in the wetlands during the summer. Ducks find welcome habitat in the willows, sparrows nest in the nearby trees, and raptors soar overhead. Early-morning visitors may find moose munching on wetland vegetation, while those who arrive later in the day will certainly see their tracks in the boggy marsh. Squirrels start bulking up with seeds and vegetation early in the spring before returning to their sleep cycle in mid-July.

On the west side of Silver Lake, a wide, well-marked trail leads into woods toward Twin Lakes Reservoir and Lake Solitude. Soon, after crossing a Forest Service road, the trail forks, with the Lake Solitude Trail taking off to the right.

Mature spruce, subalpine fir, and aspen shade the fragrant trail, which is lined with fir needles. Columbine, mountain bluebell, shooting star, monkshood, and other flowers dot the slopes. Patches of snow often cover the trail into late June.

While bikes aren't allowed on the boardwalk, you can expect to see mountain bikers on the Lake Solitude Trail and connecting roads and trails. You'll also pass signs for ski trails, cross ski-resort service roads, and even pass directly under a Solitude ski-resort lift.

Lake Solitude (via the Silver Lake Interpretive Trail)

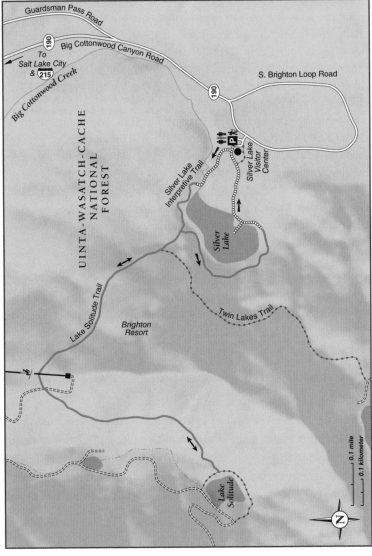

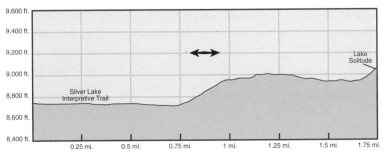

Nearing the lake, the trail steepens somewhat but never becomes punishing. Occasionally you'll have to surmount fallen trees, but this only makes the trail more appealing to youngsters. Arriving at the lake, you'll want to explore at least some of the shoreline to the west. Lake Solitude lies at the head of the Mill F South Fork, and you'll cross the stream outlet on the tarn's northwest rim. Mount Evergreen rises above to the south.

As you return to the Silver Lake Interpretive Trail, you'll want to complete the loop and continue your education in alpine ecology. The south shore is more wooded and has several landings that extend into the lake. They are ideal for fishing, but remember that this is a protected watershed, and swimming—or even dangling your feet in the water—is prohibited. From Silver Lake's south side, you can literally watch snowmelt flow into trickles, then into small streams that enter the lake. Within days, you'll be drinking this water at home or in restaurants throughout the valley.

NEARBY ACTIVITIES

Brighton Store and Cafe, across the street from the Silver Lake Visitor Center, provides a convenient stop for a drink, snack, or lunch after your hike (8019 S. Brighton Loop Road; 435-649-9156). You can relax at the outdoor eating area and take in the views.

* *

GPS TRAILHEAD COORDINATES N40° 36.213' W111° 35.083'

DIRECTIONS From I-215 on Salt Lake City's east side, take Exit 6 and turn right onto UT 190 East/6200 South/Wasatch Boulevard; then, in 1.7 miles, turn left to continue on UT 190 East/Big Cottonwood Canyon Road, and drive 14 miles. About 0.3 mile south of the turnoff to Guardsman Pass (see previous hike), the road forks—bear right onto South Brighton Loop Road. The Silver Lake Recreation Area and parking are 0.2 mile ahead on your right.

During the winter, visitors at Brighton Resort can ski past the lakes.

EXPLORE A CHAIN of pristine alpine lakes at the top of Big Cottonwood Canyon. It's a favorite hike for families and couples in search of remote mountain scenery, fir-scented woods, and photogenic lakes—all within 30 minutes of your car. Lake Mary may be the most popular alpine hike in the Salt Lake area, with hundreds of hikers enjoying its beauty on any given summer Saturday, but only a small percentage of those hikers go on to Lake Martha or Lake Catherine, where you can often find yourself completely alone. The section from just below Lake Mary to Lake Catherine is part of the Great Western Trail.

DESCRIPTION

Silver mining brought William Stuart Brighton to the upper bowl of Big Cottonwood Canyon in the 1870s. But he soon realized that a better living could be made feeding and housing miners than in actually mining silver.

After spending three summers in a tent, he built a hotel in 1874 near the shores of Silver Lake and soon developed the area into a popular mountain resort. His wife, Catherine, would serve the trout she had caught in Silver Lake with hot buttermilk biscuits.

In winter, Brighton's sons, Will and Dan, made crude skis out of wood just to get around in the deep snow. But skiers would have to wait until 1936 before a towrope was installed to create Brighton, Utah's first ski resort.

DISTANCE & CONFIGURATION: 2.2-mile out-and-back to Lake Mary + 0.6-mile out-and-back to Lake Martha + 1.4-mile out-and-back to Lake Catherine + 0.3-mile out-and-back to Dog Lake

DIFFICULTY: Moderate

SCENERY: Conifer woods, alpine lakes, glacial cirque

EXPOSURE: Partially shaded

TRAIL TRAFFIC: Heavy

TRAIL SURFACE: Dirt, rock

HIKING TIME: 2.5–3.5 hours

DRIVING DISTANCE: 27 miles from I-15/I-80 intersection

ELEVATION CHANGE: 8,762'–9,962'

ACCESS: Daily, sunrise–sunset; no fees or permits

MAPS: USGS *Brighton*

FACILITIES: Restrooms and water at Silver Lake Visitor Center

WHEELCHAIR ACCESS: None

CONTACT: 801-733-2660, fs.usda.gov/uwcnf; 801-532-4731, brightonresort.com

LOCATION: Brighton Resort, South Brighton Loop Road, Brighton, UT 84121

COMMENTS: Dogs prohibited in Big Cottonwood Canyon, a protected watershed

Your hike to the beautiful chain of glacial lakes that dot the southern side of Big Cottonwood's upper bowl departs from the base of Brighton Resort's Majestic chairlift. A large sign in front of the lift (at the parking lot's southeast edge) displays the route, marked as the Lake Mary–Catherine Pass Trail.

The trail is steep as it passes beneath two chairlifts and ascends some of Brighton's ski slopes. At 0.6 mile, the trail leaves the slopes and enters a wooded area, offering more of a wilderness feel. At 0.9 mile you come to a gateway of gray granite that forms the bowl of Lake Mary. A large sign at a trail junction marks the spur that leads to Dog Lake. Within moments, a concrete dam—which enlarges and regulates Lake Mary—appears in front of you on the trail. At this point, note an unmarked trail leading off to the right about 30 feet before the dam. It accesses Lake Mary's western side and also leads to Twin Lakes.

The trail ascends to the left of the dam, and within minutes you'll find yourself in the exquisite granite basin that contains Lake Mary. The one-way distance from the trailhead to the Lake Mary shore is 1.1 miles. Even if your ultimate destination is Lake Catherine, you'll want to stop to enjoy the beauty of Lake Mary's granite shoreline. It offers lots of coves, nooks, and smooth granite outcrops where you can pause for a snack and enjoy the view.

The trail continues along Lake Mary's eastern shore for 0.3 mile before arriving at Lake Martha, at an elevation just 38 feet higher than Lake Mary. Lake Martha lacks Lake Mary's granite lining but is perfectly charming and provides more solitude.

At this point, Lake Catherine is just 0.7 mile up the trail, so it would be a shame to miss it. Departing Lake Martha, the crowds thin considerably and the trail, now part of the Great Western Trail, becomes more moist and wooded. Your chances of seeing wildlife—especially moose, deer, and porcupine—increase.

Continuing upward, the trail ascends to the east of Lake Martha, then switches back to the north and comes to a ridgeline promontory overlooking the upper bowl

Brighton Lakes

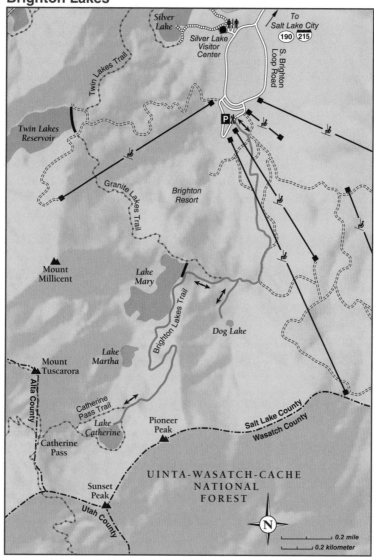

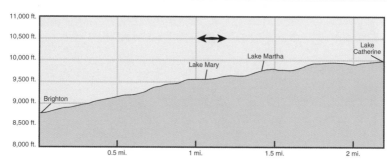

of Big Cottonwood Canyon. The trail continues 0.6 mile past Lake Martha, through alpine forests of spruce and fir, before coming to a crest and a fork in the trail. To the right is the Catherine Pass Trail, which leads over the rim of the cirque into Little Cottonwood Canyon. To the left, the trail arrives at the shore of Lake Catherine in less than 0.1 mile.

In a fitting tribute, William Brighton named the jewel of upper Big Cottonwood Canyon after his wife. Lake Catherine is a perfectly inviting place for a picnic, a rest, or a relaxing afternoon of fishing. Be sure to walk to the top of the granite formation at the north end of the lake, where you'll find the ideal overview of Lake Martha and Lake Mary. On your return trip, Dog Lake is just 700 feet off the main trail below Lake Mary. Although less scenic than the other lakes, it's a great place to watch for moose, particularly in the early morning.

NEARBY ACTIVITIES

Big Cottonwood Canyon provides a field course in Wasatch geology. As you drive up the canyon, a series of large blue-and-brown signs at roadside turnouts provides interpretive information about the canyon. Explaining specific features like folding, faulting, and glaciation, these signs will enrich your hiking experience and give you a better appreciation for the canyon.

· ·

GPS TRAILHEAD COORDINATES N40° 35.893' W111° 35.068'

DIRECTIONS From I-215 on Salt Lake City's east side, take Exit 6 and turn right onto UT 190 East/6200 South/Wasatch Boulevard; then, in 1.7 miles, turn left to continue on UT 190 East/Big Cottonwood Canyon Road, and drive 14 miles. About 0.3 mile south of the turnoff to Guardsman Pass (see Hike 33, page 155), the road forks—bear right onto South Brighton Loop Road. The trailhead and parking are about 0.4 mile ahead on the south side of Brighton Loop Road, at the base of Brighton ski resort's Majestic chairlift.

The thick deciduous cover makes for great autumn hiking.

THE HIKE TO SUNSET PEAK is one of the most popular summit trails in the Wasatch. It's a great jaunt, suitable for hikers of all skill levels. Wildlife, wildflowers, and rewarding views along the trail and at the summit justify its popularity.

DESCRIPTION

With a high-elevation trailhead at the top of Little Cottonwood Canyon, a hike from Albion Basin to Catherine Pass offers a chance for nearly any hiker, regardless of skill level or conditioning, to ascend to a high-mountain ridge near the tree line and gaze down at alpine lakes and off to distant ranges. From the Catherine Pass ridgeline, a short climb on to 10,648-foot Sunset Peak delivers even more expansive views stretching east to the Uintas.

The large trailhead parking area fills quickly on weekends, so be sure to arrive early. An early arrival will also give you the best chance to spot the moose that browse the verdant meadows.

From the trailhead parking area, just south of an Alta chairlift, cross the U.S. Forest Service road and follow the marked trail leading to Catherine Pass. At 0.2 mile the trail comes to a ski-resort utility road. Turn left onto the road and follow it

DISTANCE & CONFIGURATION: 4.2-mile out-and-back

DIFFICULTY: Easy

SCENERY: Wildflowers, alpine scenery, panoramic views from summit

EXPOSURE: Partially shaded

TRAIL TRAFFIC: Heavy

TRAIL SURFACE: Dirt, rock

HIKING TIME: 2–3 hours

DRIVING DISTANCE: 27 miles from I-15/ I-80 intersection

ELEVATION CHANGE: 9,379'–10,648'

ACCESS: Daily, sunrise–sunset; the Albion Basin gate above Alta Ski Area is generally open July 1– November 1. The resort charges a $6 road-access fee in season.

MAPS: USGS *Brighton;* Trails Illustrated *Wasatch Front* (709)

FACILITIES: Restrooms in trailhead parking lot

WHEELCHAIR ACCESS: None

CONTACT: 801-733-2660, fs.usda.gov/uwcnf; 801-359-1078, alta.com

LOCATION: Alta Ski Area, Albion Basin Road, Alta, UT 84092

COMMENTS: Dogs prohibited in Little Cottonwood Canyon, a protected watershed

up and to the left. Leaving the road, the trail soon crosses a granite outcrop and then ascends to the right.

At 0.5 mile the trail traverses a small wooden bridge and then narrows. It quickly crests at an outcrop, then dips a bit before continuing its ascent. At 0.7 mile a spur trail leads off to the right to give hikers a nice overview of the Albion Basin, with views of Baldy, Sugarloaf, and Devil's Castle to the left.

Albion Basin is famous for the variety and density of its wildflowers. With more than 50 feet of snow per year and a short growing season, the basin is home to dwarf species that have adapted to the harsh environment. An example is alpine asters, with blooms about half the size of the normal species. Both golden and bald eagles can be seen riding the updrafts that rise from the basin to the ridgeline.

At 0.9 mile the trail ascends into a draw with gentle slopes on both sides before entering a small basin meadow. At the upper (east) end of the meadow, the trail climbs a few switchbacks dotted with granite boulders as it makes its way up to Catherine Pass.

At the pass the trail merges with the Great Western Trail (see Hike 33, page 155) and ascends to the right along a fine, sandy surface leading to Sunset Pass to the south. Here the Great Western Trail continues along the ridge to the south, while the trail to Sunset Peak turns left and to the east. This ridge forms the boundary of Salt Lake and Utah Counties.

The trail ascends steadily along a timberline route dotted with subalpine fir; soon it curves to the left and arrives at the summit. Sunset Peak is the only point in the area to form the boundary of three counties: Salt Lake County to the north and west, Utah County to the south, and Wasatch County to the east. On a clear day you can enjoy excellent views of Mount Timpanogos to the south and Heber Valley to the east. In the distant east, the flat-topped Uintas appear on the horizon. To the north,

Sunset Peak

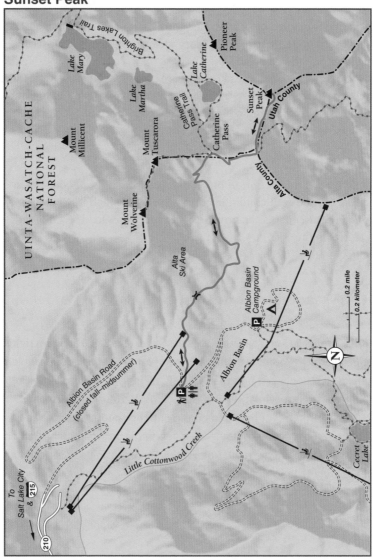

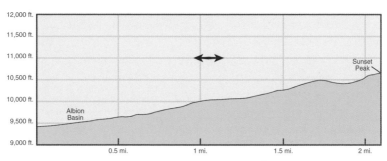

Lake Catherine is cradled by Mount Tuscarora on the left and Pioneer Peak on the right. Lakes Catherine, Martha, and Mary glisten below and almost appear to be adjoining lakes on the same plane.

You can return to the trailhead parking area the way you came, or at Sunset Pass take a trail that descends to the west, leading into Albion Basin Campground. From here it's an easy 0.5-mile stroll along the Forest Service road back to the Catherine Pass parking area.

NEARBY ACTIVITIES

The **Alta Ski Area** entrance station on Albion Basin Road is a good source of information on hikes and trail conditions in the area. Although it's staffed only during the summer, the attendants can provide maps, brochures, and recommendations for other activities in the area.

• •

GPS TRAILHEAD COORDINATES N40° 34.967' W111° 37.107'

DIRECTIONS From I-215 on Salt Lake City's east side, take Exit 6 and turn right onto UT 190 East/6200 South. Continue south and then east 14.1 miles, during which UT 190 becomes Wasatch Boulevard and then UT 210, taking you up into Little Cottonwood Canyon. (Alternatively, begin at the intersection of UT 209 and UT 210, and drive east on UT 210 for 10.1 miles.) At the Albion Basin entrance booth and gate above Alta Ski Area, stay left at the fork and continue 1.9 miles on the dirt road to the Catherine Pass trailhead parking area, on the right. *Note:* When Albion Basin Road is closed and gated (November 1–July 1), look for a parking spot along Little Cottonwood Canyon Road just outside the gate, and hike, ski, or snowshoe to the trailhead.

In the midsummer, Cecret Lake offers a relaxing destination and stunning wildflowers.   *Photo: Greg Witt*

ALBION BASIN IS ABLAZE with wildflowers and wildlife in summer. This popular and easy hike travels along a well-marked interpretive trail through flowered meadows to a rock-rimmed alpine lake at the head of Little Cottonwood Canyon.

DESCRIPTION

In its heyday, Alta was a hotbed of silver mining activity. In the 1870s, thirsty miners had 26 saloons to choose from. Many of those miners came from Great Britain and named the area at the head of Little Cottonwood Canyon Albion Basin, evoking an ancient poetic name for their native England.

Today the most valued natural resource in the area is water. Albion Basin receives more than 50 feet of snow per year and provides almost 15 percent of Salt Lake City's drinking water. Cecret Lake, the small glacial tarn above Albion Basin to the south, serves as the headwaters of Little Cottonwood Creek.

The other treasured natural resource in the Albion Basin is wildflowers. More than 120 different species bloom in the basin during the short summer season. They start to appear as soon as the snow begins to melt and reach their climax in August. More than 20,000 people come to Albion Basin every summer, so it becomes each

DISTANCE & CONFIGURATION: 1.6-mile out-and-back

DIFFICULTY: Easy

SCENERY: Wildflowers, alpine lake, mountain scenery

EXPOSURE: Partially shaded

TRAIL TRAFFIC: Heavy

TRAIL SURFACE: Dirt, rock

HIKING TIME: 1–2 hours

DRIVING DISTANCE: 27 miles from I-15/I-80 intersection

ELEVATION CHANGE: 9,410'–9,875'

ACCESS: Daily, sunrise–sunset; the Albion Basin gate above Alta Ski Area is generally open July 1– November 1. The resort charges a $6 road-access fee in season.

MAPS: USGS *Brighton;* Trails Illustrated *Wasatch Front* (709)

FACILITIES: Water and restrooms at campground near trailhead

WHEELCHAIR ACCESS: None

CONTACT: 801-733-2660, fs.usda.gov/uwcnf; 801-359-1078, alta.com

LOCATION: Alta Ski Area, Albion Basin Road, Alta, UT 84092

COMMENTS: Dogs prohibited in Little Cotton-wood Canyon, a protected watershed

visitor's responsibility to tread lightly, stay on the trail, and protect this fragile natural environment.

From the large Cecret Lake parking area, just north of Albion Basin Campground, take the trail that leads south. It quickly crosses a small brook fed by seasonal runoff from the snow patches that remain well into summer. At 0.1 mile you'll cross under an Alta ski-resort chairlift before the trail turns onto a dirt road. At 0.2 mile you'll pass beneath a second Alta chairlift.

At 0.4 mile the trail leaves the service road and veers left. Along the way you'll see several interpretive signs describing the alpine environment and the delicate balance of life that exists in the area. As you pass through this meadow you'll likely see moose grazing on the plant life, especially in the early morning.

At an elevation of around 9,500 feet, winters are long and the growing season is short. Wildflowers bloom in a rapid and predictable sequence with sprays of yellow, red, blue, purple, and white. Each color of flower attracts different birds and insects, which then pollinate the flower, enabling it to seed and return the following year. Flies and beetles are drawn to green and brown foliage and flowers, hummingbirds prefer red, and bees will go to any color.

As you walk along the main trail, you'll see many side trails leading into the meadow. Most of these work their way back to the campground or the main trail and are always worth exploring.

At 0.6 mile the trail leaves the flowered basin and crosses a rocky field before ascending a steep slope along a switchback into the upper basin, home to Cecret Lake. Near the northeast side of the lake is a small outlet that allows the water to cascade down the slope and through the meadow below. The headwaters of Little Cottonwood Creek, this outlet continues to be fed by many forks and creeks along the way as it swells to a raging torrent just 10 miles downstream.

Cecret Lake

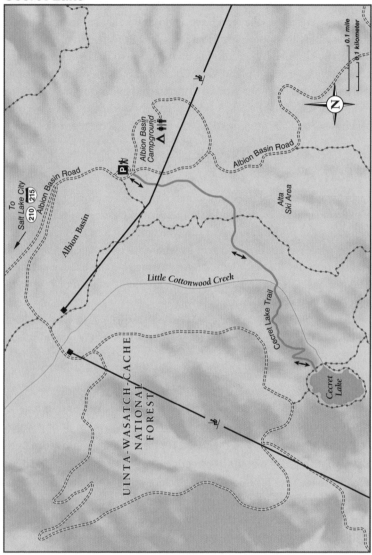

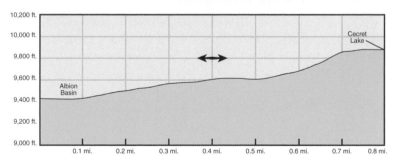

Once you arrive at the lake, you'll see a faint track that circles the shore, crossing boulder fields and talus slopes. Sugarloaf Peak, at 11,051 feet in elevation, lies to the south and can be climbed by scrambling up the slope to the left of the summit.

Moose rarely approach the shores of Cecret Lake, as they find most of their food in the lush lower meadows, but ground squirrels and marmots love the rocky regions near the lake. Because of the lake's popularity, these rodents have become accustomed to humans and are quite bold. If you leave a pack on the rocks near the lake, expect a squirrel to come nosing around looking for some trail mix or crackers.

NEARBY ACTIVITIES

Albion Basin Campground is a perfectly situated base for exploring the upper reaches of Little Cottonwood Canyon. In addition to providing overnight camping, it's also available for day use mid-July–August (daily, 6 a.m.–10 p.m.; no fees), making it an ideal meeting place for families and groups who want to escape the heat in the valley below and spend a day hiking, picnicking, and enjoying the beauty of Albion Basin. Each campsite has a fire grill, parking spur, and picnic table. For reservations, call 877-444-6777 or visit recreation.gov.

• •

GPS TRAILHEAD COORDINATES N40° 34.673' W111° 36.782'

DIRECTIONS From I-215 on Salt Lake City's east side, take Exit 6 and turn right onto UT 190 East/6200 South. Continue south and then east 14.1 miles, during which UT 190 becomes Wasatch Boulevard and then UT 210, taking you up into Little Cottonwood Canyon. (Alternatively, begin at the intersection of UT 209 and UT 210, and drive east on UT 210 for 10.1 miles.) At the Albion Basin entrance booth and gate above Alta Ski Area, stay left at the fork and continue 2.5 miles on the dirt road to the Cecret Lake trailhead parking area, on the left. *Note:* When Albion Basin Road is closed and gated (November 1–July 1), look for a parking spot along Little Cottonwood Canyon Road just outside the gate, and hike, ski, or snowshoe to the trailhead.

Valley and canyon views materialize quickly as you ascend toward the lake.

SURPRISE—HERE'S A GLACIAL LAKE in Little Cottonwood Canyon that can be reached along a gently ascending trail. The open trail leads to wonderful canyon views, a glacial cirque dotted with alpine vegetation, and one of the prettiest lakes in Utah.

DESCRIPTION

The loggers and miners who worked Big Cottonwood and Little Cottonwood Canyons in the late 1800s and early 1900s were an ambitious lot. They built the first two timber slides in White Pine Canyon and adjoining Red Pine Canyon. Loggers cut Engelmann spruce, which they called white pine, and Douglas-fir, which they called red pine.

After the loggers came miners in search of silver, lead, and zinc. They never made much money, but the miners left their mark in the canyons by building many of the roads to access the mines. The White Pine Trail follows the route of a mining road built in the early 1900s. Don't worry about hiking on jeep trails, though: the U.S. Forest Service closed the road more than 50 years ago, and now it's almost completely reclaimed. It looks and feels like a wide trail, not a rutted jeep trail, allowing you to walk side by side with your hiking companion. Its openness reduces the chances of getting lost, so the hike is well suited and safe for inexperienced hikers

DISTANCE & CONFIGURATION: 9.8-mile out-and-back

DIFFICULTY: Moderate

SCENERY: Deep glacial valley rising to high glacial lake

EXPOSURE: Mostly shaded to 9,700', partially shaded above 9,700' and at lake

TRAIL TRAFFIC: Moderate

TRAIL SURFACE: Dirt, rock (mostly rock above 9,800')

HIKING TIME: 5–7 hours

DRIVING DISTANCE: 22 miles from I-15/I-80 intersection

ELEVATION CHANGE: 7,698'–10,150'

ACCESS: Daily, sunrise–sunset; no fees or permits

MAPS: USGS *Dromedary Peak;* Trails Illustrated *Uinta National Forest* (701) and *Wasatch Front* (709)

FACILITIES: Restrooms at trailhead

WHEELCHAIR ACCESS: None

CONTACT: 801-733-2660, fs.usda.gov/uwcnf

LOCATION: UT 210/Little Cottonwood Canyon Road, Alta, UT 84902

COMMENTS: Bicycles are permitted on the trail all the way to the lake, although you can expect some rocky terrain. Dogs prohibited in Little Cottonwood Canyon, a protected watershed.

and children who are capable of the distance. Because the trail began as a road, the gradient is not as steep as most trails', but the route is longer and more circuitous.

The trail departs from the south side of the large White Pine trailhead parking lot. Even though the parking lot accommodates 35 cars, it often fills on summer weekends, and latecomers may find themselves having to park along Little Cottonwood Canyon Road. From the parking area the trail dips, and within 100 yards you cross Little Cottonwood Creek and begin your ascent.

Immediately after crossing the bridge, the trail passes through an area damaged by avalanches. Looking at some of the leveled aspens with trunk diameters in excess of a foot, you get a sense of the power and force of snow thundering down the mountain. The White Pine Trail is a popular snowshoeing and cross-country-skiing area, but only after the avalanche danger has passed.

At 0.9 mile you arrive at a junction with the Red Pine Trail. With the White Pine Fork at your right, continue along the wide trail as it makes a sharp turn to the left and ascends along a straight course. At the top of this stretch you arrive at a canyon overlook at 8,200 feet in elevation before making a hairpin turn and continuing through forests of conifer and aspen.

By now the trail is high above the canyon floor, following a well-crafted path along the eastern side of White Pine Fork. Along the way, numerous springs and creeks cross the trail. Wildflowers, including white columbine and buttercups, dot the side of the trail.

At 3.4 miles the trail enters a large, open meadow, and the upper reaches of the glacial bowl become more apparent. Soon the terrain changes from dense spruce and fir forests to a rocky glacial terrain. Near the top of the canyon, the trail crosses a wide talus slope, often covered by a snowfield into early summer. Once you cross the slope, the trail remains on glacial moraine to the rim above the lake. As the trail nears the lake, at an elevation just under 10,000 feet, the trail sweeps widely to the east, then

White Pine Lake

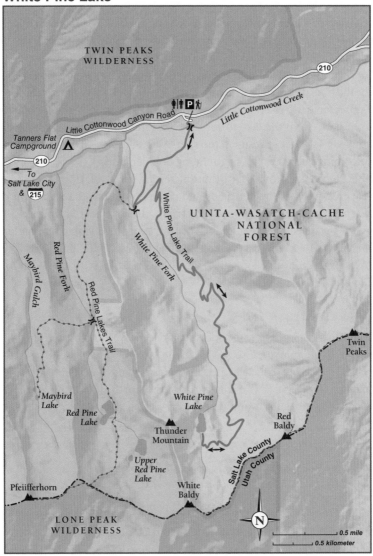

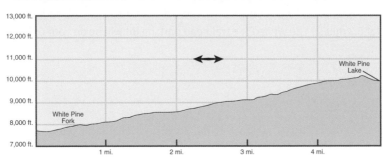

turns west as it rounds the bowl and heads toward the lake. You might think it faster to scramble the slope to the west and drop down directly into White Pine Lake, but even though the trail looks long, you can move quickly along its gradual ascent.

Within minutes you'll be at the rim overlooking White Pine Lake, the high elevation for the hike. From here a downhill stroll of 0.2 mile will put you at the water's edge. If you're an early riser, you can sit on one of the smooth granite boulders and watch trout jump from the lake to snag live flies. If you look up the drainage to the south, you may see deer grazing on the sparse high grasses. Marmots and pikas also find a welcoming habitat in the surrounding boulder fields.

White Pine Lake provides a beautiful setting for a relaxing lunch before you return. By crossing the boulder fields and ridge directly to the west, you can also drop into the Red Pine Lake basin and return to the trailhead from there. The traverse involves some scrambling and navigating your way along an unmarked route before arriving at Red Pine Lake, about 360 feet below White Pine Lake's elevation. This makes for an enjoyable loop hike, but come prepared with a detailed topo map and solid route-finding skills.

NEARBY ACTIVITIES

The White Pine Trail offers some spectacular scenery and a beautiful lake, but no major waterfalls. If you yearn to see a canyon stream spraying and cascading over granite cliffs, check out **Lisa Falls,** just 2.5 miles down the canyon from the White Pine trailhead. The Lisa Falls trailhead is on the north side of the road. The path climbs along the stream for 0.1 mile before arriving at the falls.

• •

GPS TRAILHEAD COORDINATES N40° 34.537' W111° 40.868'

DIRECTIONS From I-215 on Salt Lake City's east side, take Exit 6 and turn right onto UT 190 East/6200 South. Continue south and then east 10.9 miles, during which UT 190 becomes Wasatch Boulevard and then UT 210, taking you up into Little Cottonwood Canyon. (Alternatively, begin at the intersection of UT 209 and UT 210, and drive east on UT 210 for 5.3 miles.) The White Pine trailhead parking lot will be on your right.

39 PFEIFFERHORN
(via Red Pine Lake)

The sun rises over the northern ridge of Little Cottonwood Canyon.

THE TREK TO THE PFEIFFERHORN is one of the best summit hikes in the Wasatch. A scenic canyon trail leads to a glistening alpine lake. A challenging traverse over a saddle of large boulders, along with a steep scramble to the 11,326-foot summit, offers wonderful views.

DESCRIPTION

The Pfeifferhorn (identified as Little Matterhorn Peak on USGS maps) is recognizable from the floor of both Salt Lake Valley and Utah Valley by its distinctive pyramidal shape and its location behind Lone Peak, on Little Cottonwood Canyon's southern ridge. Lying within the rugged Lone Peak Wilderness Area, the mountain was named in honor of Chuck Pfeiffer, an early leader of the Wasatch Mountain Club.

A climb of the Pfeifferhorn offers hikers an excellent variety of trail scenery, alpine lakes, boulder hopping, and a challenging scramble to the top. In spite of the challenges, the Pfeifferhorn remains one of the most popular summit climbs in the Wasatch.

From the White Pine trailhead parking lot, the trail descends to the south to cross Little Cottonwood Creek over a wooden bridge, then begins a steady ascent along an old mining road into the mouth of White Pine Canyon. An early start will

DISTANCE & CONFIGURATION: 7-mile out-and-back to Red Pine Lake, 10-mile out-and-back to Pfeifferhorn summit

DIFFICULTY: Strenuous

SCENERY: Wooded canyon, alpine lakes, summit views

EXPOSURE: Mostly shaded to Red Pine Lake; partially shaded to saddle; no shade from saddle to summit

TRAIL TRAFFIC: Moderate

TRAIL SURFACE: Dirt and rock to lake, mostly rock from lake to summit

HIKING TIME: 7–9 hours

DRIVING DISTANCE: 22 miles from I-15/I-80 intersection

ELEVATION CHANGE: 7,698'–11,326'

ACCESS: Daily, sunrise–sunset; no fees or permits

MAPS: USGS *Dromedary Peak*

FACILITIES: Restrooms and water at trailhead

WHEELCHAIR ACCESS: None

CONTACT: 801-733-2660, fs.usda.gov/uwcnf

LOCATION: UT 210/Little Cottonwood Canyon Road, Alta, UT 84902

COMMENTS: Dogs prohibited in Little Cottonwood Canyon, a protected watershed. The canyon is subject to occasional avalanche closures November–May.

give you the best opportunity to spot deer and moose on the trail below Red Pine Lake; it will also give you plenty of time to reach the summit.

At 0.8 mile you arrive at a junction where the mining road ascends to the left on its way to White Pine Lake—avoid this route by continuing straight ahead for another 20 feet. Here the trail climbs to the left before immediately turning right and crossing a bridge over White Pine Fork. After the bridge crossing, the trail ascends to the northwest as it makes its way around the canyon wall to enter Red Pine Canyon. As the trail moves up into the canyon, you'll have a fleeting glimpse of the Pfeifferhorn to the south.

At 2.1 miles from the trailhead, you'll arrive at a steep stretch littered with boulders and marked by avalanche scarring. Soon the trail unites with Red Pine Creek and levels out a bit. At 2.5 miles you'll pass the cutoff and bridge to Maybird Gulch, on your right.

Immediately after the cutoff, the trail passes through a boggy meadow where the stream spills onto the trail and passes mine tailings on the left. A steep, rocky section of trail brings you to the shores of Red Pine Lake. With a steady pace, you can hike from the trailhead to the lake in just under 2 hours.

Once on the north shore of Red Pine Lake, take a moment to enjoy the view and plan your route to the summit. The Pfeifferhorn is not visible from Red Pine Lake, but it lies to the southwest, obscured by the rocky slopes to the west of the lake. The easiest, most reliable route to the summit starts by following the trail along the east side of the lake—although it may look more direct and very appealing, you want to avoid the talus field to the west of the lake.

Arriving at the south end of the lake, you pass a large rock slab the size of a school bus on your right. Cross the creek that descends from Upper Red Pine Lake and climb a beautiful section of steep trail leading through fragrant stands of spruce.

Pfeifferhorn (via Red Pine Lake)

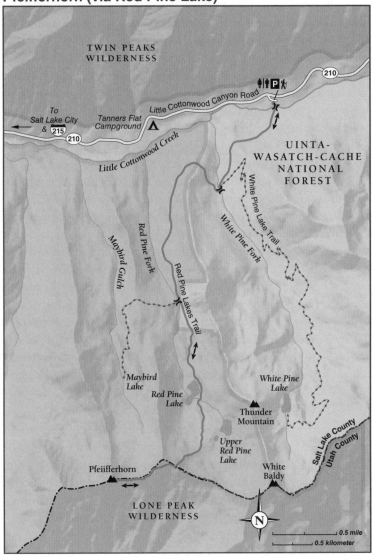

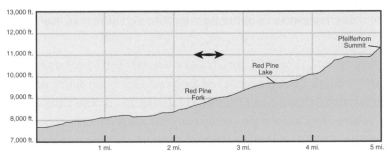

This trail winds its way up and to the southwest, eventually rising above the wooded area onto a steep, rocky slope leading toward the saddle.

The most impressive feature of the climb from Red Pine Lake to the Pfeifferhorn summit is the quality of the rock. Often mistaken for granite, the talus slopes, saddle, and summit of the Pfeifferhorn are composed almost entirely of quartz monzonite, an intrusive igneous rock. Quartz monzonite provides an excellent climbing and nonskid hiking surface, making boulder-hopping on the route a true delight.

Once at the saddle, you'll have a clear view of the Pfeifferhorn down the ridgeline to the west. But before ascending the final 500 feet to the summit, you need to traverse a 100-yard-long, knife-edged, boulder-capped saddle. Although technical-climbing equipment is unnecessary, navigation does require moving carefully over and around large boulders with some exposure. You'll want to stow your trekking poles in your pack and consider bringing along a pair of gloves to protect your hands. Most hikers pick a route that stays primarily to the right or north side of the ridge.

Once off the boulders, the trail resumes its steep climb up a chute to the left of the peak's southeast ridge. From the massive slabs that form the small summit platform, you'll have great views into the populated valleys. The most intriguing views, though, are those directly below as you survey the wild, rocky, and rugged terrain of the Lone Peak Wilderness. From the Pfeifferhorn summit, you'll find some challenging descent routes into Maybird Gulch and Bells Canyon to the north and west, but most day hikers are content with a return to Red Pine Lake and back to Little Cottonwood Canyon.

NEARBY ACTIVITIES

The brilliant quartz monzonite that graces the summits of both Pfeifferhorn and Lone Peak was also prized by early Mormon pioneers, who quarried the stone used to build the Salt Lake Temple. The **Temple Quarry Trail,** a 0.3-mile, wheelchair-accessible interpretive loop, will give you a greater appreciation for the monumental effort involved in quarrying stone. The trailhead is at the mouth of Little Cottonwood Canyon on UT 209 just south of its intersection with UT 210, the main canyon road.

• •

GPS TRAILHEAD COORDINATES N40° 34.537' W111° 40.868'

DIRECTIONS From I-215 on Salt Lake City's east side, take Exit 6 and turn right onto UT 190 East/6200 South. Continue south and then east 10.9 miles, during which UT 190 becomes Wasatch Boulevard and then UT 210, taking you up into Little Cottonwood Canyon. (Alternatively, begin at the intersection of UT 209 and UT 210, and drive east on UT 210 for 5.3 miles.) The White Pine trailhead parking lot will be on your right.

American Fork Twin Peaks tower over Snowbird ski resort.

Photo: Mitch Johanson/Shutterstock

THIS CHALLENGING ROUTE ALONG a knife ridge and up a steep, rocky slope leads to the dual summit that forms the highest peak in Salt Lake County. In just over a mile one-way, you'll achieve a first-class mountaineering scramble capped by commanding views in all directions.

DESCRIPTION

Let's begin with a pop quiz: What is the most frequently summited 11,000-plus-foot peak in Utah?

If you guessed Mount Timpanogos or even Kings Peak, you're thinking clearly, but neither of those peaks comes close to the hundreds of skiers and summer visitors who reach the summit of 11,000-foot Hidden Peak, at the top of Snowbird ski resort's Aerial Tram. The highest lift-accessed peak in the Wasatch, Hidden Peak is also a convenient trailhead for climbing American Fork Twin Peaks along the ridge to the southwest. In spite of the crowds that ride the tram to the top of Hidden Peak, very few ever make the traverse to the summit of Twin Peaks. You might have the entire route to yourself—even on a summer weekend.

American Fork Twin Peaks lies across the canyon and to the east of Broads Fork (or Salt Lake) Twin Peaks. The East Twin is 11,433 feet and the West Twin is 11,489 feet, making the West Twin the highest peak in Salt Lake County. The ridgeline

DISTANCE & CONFIGURATION: 2.2-mile out-and-back

DIFFICULTY: Moderate

SCENERY: High-alpine rock slopes and spectacular views

EXPOSURE: No shade on trail

TRAIL TRAFFIC: Light

TRAIL SURFACE: Dirt, rock

HIKING TIME: 2.5–3 hours

DRIVING DISTANCE: 28 miles from I-15/I-80 intersection

ELEVATION CHANGE: 11,000'–11,660'

ACCESS: The hike lies on U.S. Forest Service land accessed through Snowbird ski resort. You must buy a ticket to ride the Snowbird Aerial Tram to the Hidden Peak summit (see page 186 for additional information).

MAPS: USGS *Dromedary Peak;* Trails Illustrated *Wasatch Front* (709)

FACILITIES: Restrooms and water at Hidden Peak trailhead and Snowbird Center (tram base)

WHEELCHAIR ACCESS: None

CONTACT: 801-933-2222, snowbird.com

LOCATION: 9385 S. Snowbird Center Dr., Snowbird, UT 84092

COMMENTS: You can also climb Twin Peaks unassisted from Snowbird's Gad Valley. Dogs prohibited in Little Cottonwood Canyon, a protected watershed.

constitutes the county line, with Utah County lying to the south. The scramble from Hidden Peak to Twin Peaks is one of the more challenging sections of a longer hike from Albion Basin to Red Pine Lake known as the Bullion Divide.

The Snowbird Aerial Tram achieves 2,900 feet of vertical lift in about 1.6 miles. From the top of the tram, walk down the road to the southwest that leads into Mineral Basin. About 0.1 mile down the road, the rocky thumb of a ridge forms to the west. Ascend the ridge along a faint trail as it becomes rockier and more jagged. An occasional subalpine fir or limber pine will dot the ridgeline's rocks, but for the most part the route is treeless, even as it dips below the 11,000-foot tree line.

As the knife ridge dips down to an elevation of about 10,800 feet, you'll encounter the most challenging sections of the trail, with some exposure and long sections that require the use of both hands and some basic climbing moves. Along the way you may be tempted to take a lower route, but you'll find that the ridgeline rocks are large and stable, while the rocks just 8–10 feet below the ridge are small and loose.

As you near the end of the ridgeline scramble, a formation of black rock leads up toward the eastern slope of East Twin. Follow this dike while still staying close to the top of the ridge. Use extreme caution: the black rock has particularly sharp edges. Even the slightest fall could result in severe injury.

The 100-yard ascent from the knife ridge to the summit of East Twin follows a faint but discernible trail that zigzags up the steep, rocky slope. You'll often spot mountain goats grazing on these slopes. From the bald, rounded summit of East Twin, it's a leisurely 10-minute stroll along rocky tundra to the West Twin summit.

Another route from East Twin leads to a little-known and rarely visited South Twin, at the end of a gentle tundra ridge 0.3 mile to the south. Most summer days will be clear and refreshing at the summit, but don't come if storm clouds form: with

American Fork Twin Peaks

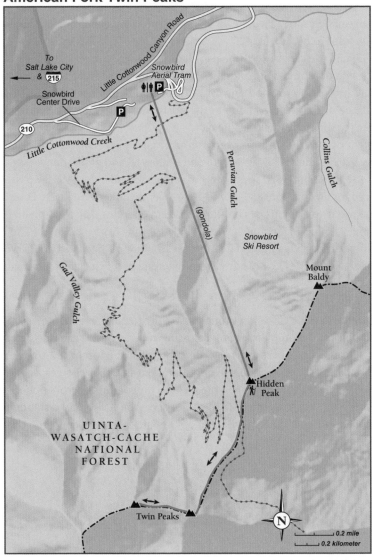

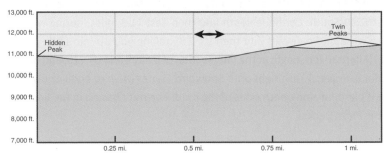

any chance of lightning, Twin Peaks' exposed ridge and expansive summit is the last place you want to be.

You'll find the views exceptional in all directions. Some of the highlights include the back side of Mount Timpanogos, Heber Valley to the east, and the many peaks along the Little Cottonwood and Big Cottonwood ridgelines. From the summit, descend one of the steep couloirs to the north into Gad Valley or return along the ridge back to the tram at Hidden Peak.

Note: Prices to ride the Snowbird Aerial Tram are as follows: on weekdays single rides are $20 for adults, $17 ages 7–16 and seniors 65 and older; on weekends single rides are $24 for adults, $20 ages 7–16 and seniors 65 and older. All-day passes can be purchased for an additional $1–$6. Kids age 6 and younger ride free. Discounts are available when you buy passes online. The tram operates daily, 9 a.m.–3:30 p.m. in winter and 11 a.m.–5 p.m. on weekends in late spring/early summer. (The resort is generally open late November–late May or early June.) Prices and hours are subject to change, so call 801-933-2222 or visit snowbird.com for the latest information.

NEARBY ACTIVITIES

Snowbird offers a wide variety of summer activities for all ages and interests. Whether you rent bikes and mountain scooters or bring your own, you can ride on easy trails near the base or on expert trails that descend from the top of the tram. ATV and horseback riding tours are available in Mineral Basin. Other choices: spend the day riding the alpine slide, zip line, and mechanical bull or doing acrobatics on the bungee trampoline; then visit the Cliff Spa to recover. You'll also find restaurants, shopping, and accommodations on-site. For a schedule of events, concerts, classes, and activities, visit snowbird.com.

· ·

GPS TRAILHEAD COORDINATES
Hidden Peak summit: N40° 33.640' W111° 38.727'

DIRECTIONS From I-215 on Salt Lake City's east side, take Exit 6 and turn right onto UT 190 East/6200 South. Continue south and then east 11.9 miles, during which UT 190 becomes Wasatch Boulevard and then UT 210, taking you up into Little Cottonwood Canyon. (Alternatively, begin at the intersection of UT 209 and UT 210, and drive east on UT 210 for 6.3 miles.) Turn right onto Snowbird Center Drive to enter Snowbird resort; parking is plentiful along both sides of the road. The tram base is in the Snowbird Center, on the Plaza Deck.

Visiting the waterfall is a fun option for this hike.

BELLS CANYON IS LONG, deep, and beautiful, with cascading falls, lush vegetation, and a rocky cirque. The trail is steep and challenging, but the varied views and granite setting are spectacular.

DESCRIPTION

Rising from the valley floor to a high glacial bowl below the summit of Lone Peak, Bells Canyon is as appealing to geologists as it is to hikers. Because the glacier that formed this canyon reached the foot of the mountains and the elevation of Lake Bonneville, Bells Canyon is geologically unique. This allows geologists to study glacial advance and the lake's rising elevation. Equally fascinating are the exposed Precambrian rocks at the mouth of Bells Canyon, some of the oldest rocks on Earth.

Immediately south of Little Cottonwood Canyon, within the federally protected Lone Peak Wilderness Area, Bells Canyon is easily accessible from a low-elevation suburban trailhead. From the parking area, the trail makes a steep switchback ascent onto the moraine of the glacier that once filled the canyon.

After 0.7 mile of sage-and-oak-covered foothills, you'll come to a dirt utility road leading up toward the mouth of the canyon. The shallow waters of the drained Lower Bells Canyon Reservoir are on the right. You can easily descend to the edge of the reservoir. While the water feature itself is overshadowed—literally and figuratively—by

DISTANCE & CONFIGURATION: 5.6-mile out-and-back to upper waterfall, 8.4-mile out-and-back to Upper Bells Canyon Reservoir

DIFFICULTY: Strenuous

SCENERY: Deep wooded canyon, waterfalls, towering canyon walls, some valley views

EXPOSURE: Mostly shaded

TRAIL TRAFFIC: Light

TRAIL SURFACE: Dirt, rock

HIKING TIME: 2.5–3 hours to upper falls, 6–8 hours to Upper Bells Canyon Reservoir

DRIVING DISTANCE: 16 miles from I-15/I-80 intersection

ELEVATION CHANGE: 5,239'–9,388'

ACCESS: Daily, sunrise–sunset; no fees or permits

MAPS: USGS *Draper;* Trails Illustrated *Wasatch Front* (709), *Uinta National Forest* (701)

FACILITIES: Restrooms and water at trailhead

WHEELCHAIR ACCESS: None

CONTACT: 801-733-2660, fs.usda.gov/uwcnf

LOCATION: 3470 E. Little Cottonwood Rd., Sandy, UT 84092

COMMENTS: Dogs prohibited in Bells Canyon, a protected watershed

the scenery that surrounds it, you can frequently see migrating waterfowl such as ducks and Canada geese around the pondlike remains, as well as grazing deer on the slopes above it.

After 100 yards on the utility road, take the trail that leads off to the left. This trail ascends gently at first through bigtooth maple and curly-leaf mountain mahogany. At 1.3 miles from the trailhead, the path crosses a sturdy wooden footbridge to the south side of a stream.

The trail enters the mouth of Bells Canyon along a granite-strewn pathway that is sometimes overgrown but easy to follow. As you ascend the canyon, conifers become more predominant and aspens begin to appear. Along the way, several spur trails depart from the main trail, but stay on the main trail, defined by the granite boulders.

At about 1.7 miles from the trailhead, you'll come to a junction with a spur trail leading off to the left. A steep descent on this spur takes you to the base of the lower falls; you may want to make this your destination for a short day hike.

From the lower falls, the main trail continues its vertical ascent along a staircase of granite boulders. After 2.2 miles from the trailhead, the steps ease up a bit, but the dirt trail is still punctuated with plenty of granite.

At 2.6 miles the trail meets the stream on the left and a large granite slab on the right—follow the trail across the slab, and within a few minutes you'll arrive at the smaller upper falls. This is a great destination in its own right and certainly worth a rest stop and trail snack. At this elevation the forest is dense and moist; ferns and moss line the trail, and spruce and aspen provide the canopy.

To continue upward, look for a crude log bridge 100 feet below the waterfall. The bridge crosses the stream to the north side of the creek. This trail leads initially through a dense passage of fern before it ascends a granite slope. The trail passes through a meadow and then crosses the creek over another log bridge on its way to the Upper Bells Canyon Reservoir.

Bells Canyon

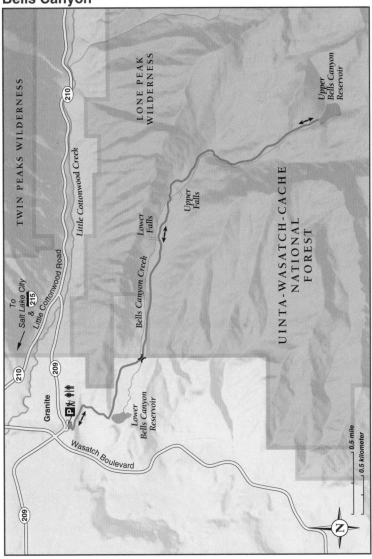

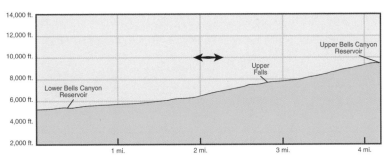

Within a rocky cirque, the upper reservoir is a remote, pristine glacial lake at an elevation of 9,388 feet. The reservoir is surrounded by Lone Peak, Bearstooth, and Thunder Mountain. Any routes leading beyond the reservoir in the direction of those peaks require difficult scrambling and technical-climbing expertise. The most reliable way out of the canyon is to retrace your route and descend the steep granite stairs back to the trailhead.

NEARBY ACTIVITIES

The **Rocky Mouth Canyon Trail** is a short, scenic hike through a slot canyon to a beautiful waterfall. The trailhead address is 11300 S. Wasatch Blvd. in Sandy. (Be sure to park at the trailhead and not in the neighborhood.) The first 0.25 mile follows a sidewalk to a dirt trail, which continues another 0.25 mile to the waterfall.

• •

GPS TRAILHEAD COORDINATES N40° 34.305' W111° 47.813'

DIRECTIONS From I-215 on Salt Lake City's east side, take Exit 6 and turn right onto UT 190 East/6200 South. Continue south 4 miles, during which UT 190 becomes Wasatch Boulevard; then turn right to stay on Wasatch Boulevard, and drive 1.1 miles. Turn left onto Little Cottonwood Road and, in 0.1 mile, turn right into the parking area.

Hikers weave around the boulders that dot the upper reaches of Lone Peak.

Photo: Greg Witt

THIS IS THE TOUGHEST and perhaps the most rewarding of these 60 hikes. A Lone Peak ascent demands a long, dry, steep approach into a beautiful rock bowl surrounded by towering cliffs. The final climb to the summit over massive rock slabs offers spectacular views.

DESCRIPTION

Lone Peak is the prominent summit that dominates both the south end of the Salt Lake Valley and the north end of Utah Valley. Its west-lying ridge trails off into the valley at Point of the Mountain. The jagged spires and sheer rock face of the 11,253-foot summit are identifiable from miles around. But only those who hike into the Lone Peak Wilderness Area and approach the mountain's higher reaches can appreciate the impressive and inspiring qualities of Lone Peak.

While many routes lead to the summit of Lone Peak, all are difficult and require 5,000–6,000 feet of vertical elevation gain. Population growth in Draper, where residential subdivisions abut national forest, has diminished access to some trails. The Jacobs Ladder Trail, starting at the Ghost Falls trailhead, has emerged in recent years as one of the more popular and accessible summit routes. Like other Lone Peak trails, Jacobs Ladder, leading to the Draper Ridge, is long, dry, and steep.

DISTANCE & CONFIGURATION: 12-mile out-and-back

DIFFICULTY: Strenuous

SCENERY: Rocky high-alpine basins, rock cliffs, exceptional summit views

EXPOSURE: Partial shade in lower bowl between 9,200' and 10,000'. Remainder of trail is fully exposed. Dry, exposed south-facing slopes can be particularly hot in summer.

TRAIL TRAFFIC: Moderate

TRAIL SURFACE: Dirt, rock

HIKING TIME: 8–11 hours

DRIVING DISTANCE: 20 miles from I-15/I-80 intersection

ELEVATION CHANGE: 5,793'–11,253'

ACCESS: Corner Canyon Road is open daily, 6 a.m.–10 p.m., up to the Ghost Falls trailhead; no fees or permits

MAPS: USGS *Draper;* Trails Illustrated *Uinta National Forest* (701)

FACILITIES: Vault toilet at trailhead

WHEELCHAIR ACCESS: None

CONTACT: 801-733-2660, fs.usda.gov/uwcnf

LOCATION: Upper Corner Canyon Road 2.6 miles south of Orson Smith Park, Draper, UT 84020

COMMENTS: The long distance, lack of water, and exposed rock-scrambling to the summit make this hike unsuitable for dogs.

From the trailhead parking area, continue up the road another 50 yards to an opening in the fence on your left. Take this singletrack mountain bike trail as it winds through scrubby woods to a low-lying ridgeline. The unmarked trail follows this ridge in an easterly direction as it parallels, merges, and diverges from various bike tracks.

In less than 1 mile, the trail approaches a chalky white outcrop and curves north along a much narrower trail to begin the Jacobs Ladder climb. It's a steep ascent through Gambel oak, sage, and curly-leaf mountain mahogany.

At 3.3 miles, the Jacobs Ladder Trail meets the Draper Ridge Trail on a dry slope at an elevation of 9,120 feet. At this point you've been climbing for about 2 hours, and you've gained more than 3,300 feet, or about two-thirds of your overall vertical ascent for the hike. Take a short rest on the nearby log and know that the toughest part of the trail is behind you—and that the most beautiful section is right in front of you.

From the Draper Ridge junction, the trail descends slightly into a meadow dotted with quartz monzonite and lined with conifers. As it rises above the meadow, the trail crosses giant slabs of rock, appropriately marked by cairns. From the meadow to the summit, the trail surface is predominately rock, dotted with spruce and fir, then alpine tundra nearing the tree line. Crossing exposed slabs before entering a narrow, boulder-strewn draw, the trail leads to the upper cirque. Along this rock route, it's easy to lose the trail, but as long as you keep ascending in a northeasterly direction toward the upper cirque, you're on track.

Arriving at the cirque, you'll be awestruck by the full view of Lone Peak's summit cliffs on the right. As you stand in the cirque facing due north, the cliffs will be at 3 o'clock. Either follow the cairns or walk up toward the boxy chute at 1 o'clock. Some easy Class 3 scrambling will lead you up the chute, known as The Chimney.

As you emerge from The Chimney on the west side of the ridge, the trail crosses over the ridge and follows a faint route up a rocky slope to the large boulders that

Lone Peak (via Jacobs Ladder)

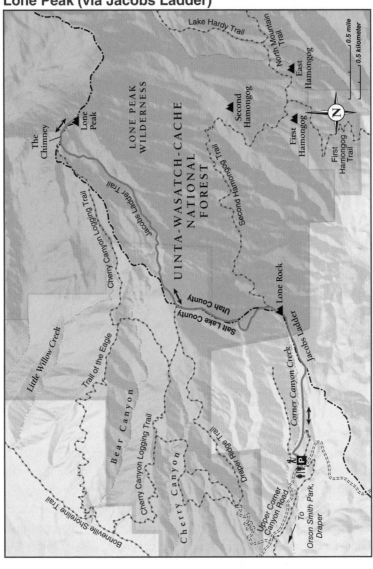

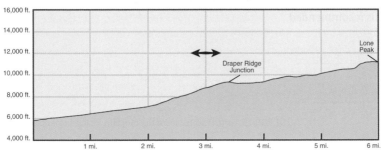

compose the summit formation. As you make your final approach to the summit, cautiously weaving your way through the massive angular slabs, it's hard to ignore the stunning majesty of the peak and cliffs in front of you. Lone Peak is one of the most breathtakingly beautiful summits in the United States.

The summit block of Lone Peak has enough space for just a few climbers to sit and enjoy the views. Lone Peak is not the highest peak in the Wasatch—it's not even the highest peak in the Lone Peak Wilderness Area—but it does have the most commanding views. Because of its forefront position, Lone Peak is one summit from which you have unobstructed views of every other major peak in the Wasatch, as well as extended views to the north and south. Take time to enjoy these views before beginning your long, dry descent back to the trailhead.

NEARBY ACTIVITIES

The trailhead in Draper's **Orson Smith Park** (12625 Highland Drive) provides a convenient and well-maintained starting point for many area hikes. The park has restrooms, water, picnic tables, and signs showing the area's trail system. From the trailhead you can access the Bonneville Shoreline Trail, the Aqueduct Trail, the Orson Smith Trail, and other connector trails. You can also reach two Lone Peak trails—Little Willow and Cherry Canyon—from here.

• •

GPS TRAILHEAD COORDINATES N40° 29.655' W111° 49.002'

DIRECTIONS From the southern intersection of I-215 and I-15, take I-15 South and, in about 7 miles, take Exit 291. Keep left at the fork, and turn left onto UT 71 North/East 12300 South. In 1.4 miles, turn left onto 900 East, go 0.1 mile, and turn right onto Pioneer Road. In 0.7 mile, take the second exit off the traffic circle to stay on Pioneer Road. In 1 mile, turn right onto Highland Drive/2000 East; then, in another 0.2 mile, turn left into the parking area for Orson Smith Park. From here, turn right on Upper Corner Canyon Road, a dirt road that leads south, and continue 2.6 miles to the Ghost Falls trailhead parking area. Note that this road is very rough and bumpy—a high-clearance vehicle is recommended.

OPPOSITE: Lone Peak is one of the most imposing summits in the Wasatch.
Photo: Greg Witt

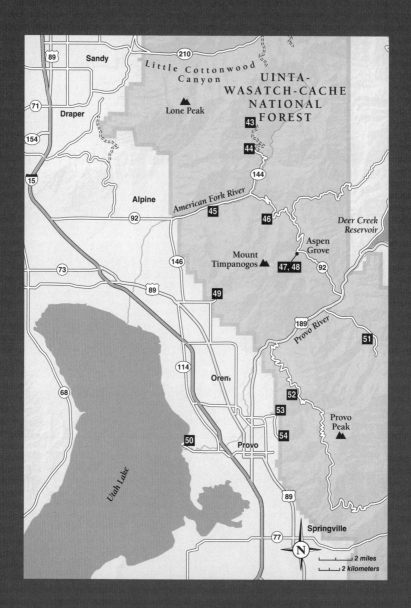

SOUTH
(Utah County)

Silver Lake comprises a wide variety of colors and textures.

BREATHTAKING ALPINE SCENERY, abundant wildlife, and a well-designed new trail to a blue lake nestled in a glacial bowl make Silver Lake one of the most perfect hikes in Utah County. It's a great day hike, but you'll want to stay longer.

DESCRIPTION

What begins as a pleasant and shaded uphill stroll concludes with one of the most dramatic wilderness settings in Utah. You'll think you've been transported to Yosemite in the Sierra Nevada. It has all the iconic elements of that far-more-famous national park: towering gray-granite walls, blue glacial lakes, spruce and fir trees, cascading waterfalls, glistening streams, and moose—lots of moose.

The 3 miles of dirt road leading to the trailhead and its location within the Lone Peak Wilderness Area discourage many less-serious hikers from visiting Silver Lake. As a result, the hike is not as crowded as one might expect for a jewel of this magnitude. The dirt road from Granite Flat to the trailhead at Silver Lake Flat is rugged but passable for most passenger vehicles—just watch out for large, protruding rocks.

From the trailhead parking area on the north side of Silver Lake Flat Reservoir, take the well-marked trail to the right of the restrooms. The trail ascends through

DISTANCE & CONFIGURATION: 4.4-mile out-and-back

DIFFICULTY: Moderate

SCENERY: Alpine lake, granite ridgeline, canyon views, woodlands

EXPOSURE: Mostly shaded for first mile, partially shaded for second

TRAIL TRAFFIC: Moderate

TRAIL SURFACE: Dirt

HIKING TIME: 2.5–3.5 hours

DRIVING DISTANCE: 39 miles from I-15/I-80 intersection

ELEVATION CHANGE: 7,536'–8.985'

ACCESS: Daily, sunrise–sunset, but road access is limited early fall–late spring, when UT 92 is

closed. This hike lies within both Lone Peak Wilderness Area (see Comments) and American Fork Canyon, a fee-charging area. Current access fees are $6/1–3 days, $12/week, and $45/year; America the Beautiful passes honored (see page 15).

MAPS: USGS *Dromedary Peak;* Trails Illustrated *Uinta National Forest* (701)

FACILITIES: Restrooms at trailhead

WHEELCHAIR ACCESS: None

CONTACT: 801-785-3563, fs.usda.gov/uwcnf

LOCATION: Trailhead is just north of Silver Lake Flat Reservoir on FS 008/Silver Lake Rd., 17 miles northwest of American Fork, UT

COMMENTS: Motorized vehicles and bikes prohibited in Lone Peak Wilderness Area; dogs allowed on leash

a beautiful, shaded grove of aspen dotted with Douglas-fir. Large granite boulders, many the size of cars, also appear throughout the Silver Creek drainage.

Birds fill the woodland in the spring and summer. Red-tailed hawks and golden eagles nest in the conifers; American robins and black-headed grosbeaks share the deciduous groves.

At 0.4 mile from the trailhead, you'll pass a clearing on the right where beavers have leveled an acre or so of aspen for their dams. At 0.5 mile you enter the Lone Peak Wilderness Area, marked by a sign. Throughout this lower drainage, you can often see deer feeding on the lush undergrowth.

At 1.1 miles the trail rises above the creek and moves up the dry slope to the east. As you emerge from the shade of the aspens, you'll find striking views of the canyons and ridgeline to the south. Along this section of the trail, watch for chokecherry bushes with their white flowers in spring and reddish-purple berries in summer.

When you reach the upper drainage, below the granite bowl that cradles Silver Lake, you may well spot mountain goats and moose. Both can be temperamental and aggressive if approached or provoked, so keep a safe distance and make sure that dogs are leashed and under control at all times.

Just below Silver Lake, you'll pass a cascading waterfall along Silver Creek to the left as it drains from the lake. Subalpine fir makes its appearance at this higher elevation. Within 5 minutes you crest the large granite boulders that form the rim of the lake, and you've instantly arrived at the shore. Depending on the amount of snowfall and the spring temperatures, Silver Lake may well be frozen into May, and occasionally into June.

By quickly scanning the shore, you'll often spot moose grazing on the aquatic plant life in the lake. Also, keep your eyes peeled for mountain goats on the rocky

Silver Lake

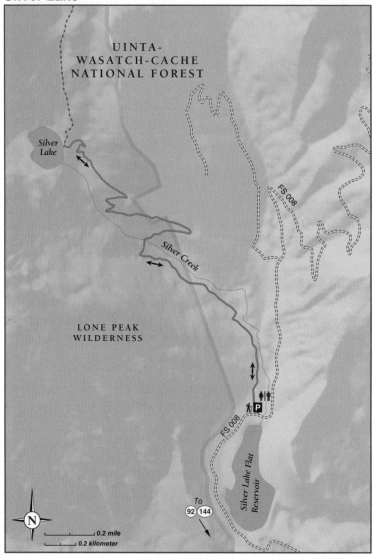

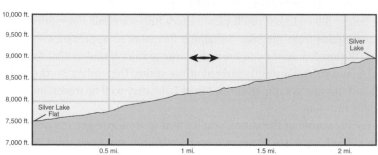

slopes above the lake. The Yosemite-quality granite cathedral towering over the northeast side of the lake is White Baldy. At 11,321 feet, it is one of the highest but least visited peaks on the ridge. A good scramble that is typically approached from Red Pine Lake in Little Cottonwood Canyon, the White Baldy hike can also be approached from Silver Lake.

Once you've hiked the 2.2 miles from the trailhead to the shores of Silver Lake, circle the lake through the maze of granite boulders at its rim. You can also ascend another 0.7 mile and 900 vertical feet to the northeast and discover the smaller Silver Glance Lake with an even rockier, more rugged setting. But most visitors are content to find a natural granite countertop on which to enjoy a snack and take in the mesmerizing beauty of this alpine treasure.

NEARBY ACTIVITIES

American Fork Canyon is a year-round scenic wonder and recreational playground that's popular with outdoors enthusiasts of all types and all ages. You'll find a wide range of camping options, with both wilderness and improved campgrounds as well as many picnic and day-use facilities. Hiking, rock climbing, fishing, ATV riding, snowmobiling, cross-country skiing, horseback riding, and mountain biking are all popular pursuits here.

• •

GPS TRAILHEAD COORDINATES N40° 30.420' W111° 39.380'

DIRECTIONS From the southern intersection of I-215 and I-15 in Salt Lake City, take I-15 South about 14.4 miles to Exit 284 for Highland/Alpine. Keep left at the fork; then turn left onto UT 92 East, and drive 12.6 miles. Turn left onto UT 144/Forest Service Road 085 toward Tibble Fork. Drive 2.5 miles to the east end of Tibble Fork Reservoir; then turn left onto paved FS 010. In 0.7 mile, just before you enter Granite Flat Campground, turn right onto FS 008 toward Silver Lake Flat Reservoir. Continue 3.2 miles on this dirt road to Silver Lake Flat Reservoir, where you'll find trailhead parking on your left, at the north end of the lake.

Note: From early fall to late spring, UT 92, aka the Alpine Loop Scenic Backway, is closed to cars in the area covered by this hike, but in winter the highway is groomed periodically by **The Utah Nordic Alliance** for hikers, runners, cyclists, snowshoers, cross-country skiers, and snowmobilers. Be aware, however, that snowmobiles and other motorized vehicles are prohibited in Lone Peak Wilderness Area, which you enter just beyond the trailhead. Visit utahnordic.com/skiing/locations/sr92 for the latest information.

Deciduous cover gives way to conifers on the upper reaches of Box Elder Peak.

ONE OF THE lesser-known big peaks of the Wasatch, Box Elder Peak offers exceptional mountain-wilderness scenery and wildlife-viewing. Most fit hikers can achieve the adventurous off-trail scramble to the summit.

DESCRIPTION

Tucked amid slightly larger and more frequently climbed peaks, including Lone Peak, Pfeifferhorn, and Mount Timpanogos, Box Elder Peak is easily overlooked—even with its 11,101-foot triangular summit. Although marked trails ring the peak, no official trail leads to the summit. As a result, Box Elder gives hikers the opportunity to enjoy a stunning alpine wilderness setting at the lower elevations and then experience the challenge of a summit quest involving some scrambling and route-finding on rarely used routes.

A popular route to Box Elder Peak from the north is the Deer Creek–Dry Creek Trail (045), which can be accessed from the town of Alpine to the west or from Granite Flat Campground to the east. The route described, however, accesses the peak from the south using the Box Elder Trail (044), which also starts at the campground. The main advantage of the Box Elder Trail is that it offers a more favorable ridge route to the summit and makes getting lost or dropping into the wrong drainage

DISTANCE & CONFIGURATION: 9.8-mile out-and-back

DIFFICULTY: Strenuous

SCENERY: Mountain wilderness, glacial terrain, excellent views from summit

EXPOSURE: Mostly shaded below 8,700', partially shaded to ridgeline, fully exposed above 9,700'

TRAIL TRAFFIC: Light

TRAIL SURFACE: Dirt, becoming rockier toward summit

HIKING TIME: 6.5–8 hours

DRIVING DISTANCE: 37 miles from I-15/I-80 intersection

ELEVATION CHANGE: 6,778'–11,101'

ACCESS: Daily, sunrise–sunset, but road access is limited early fall–late spring, when UT 92 is closed; Granite Flat Campground gate is open 8 a.m.–10 p.m. in season. The trail, which lies within the Lone Peak Wilderness Area (see Comments), can be reached from American Fork Canyon, a fee-charging area, or from the city of Alpine on the Dry Creek and Phelps Canyon Trails (no fees or permits). American Fork Canyon fees: $6/1–3 days, $12/week, and $45/year; America the Beautiful passes honored (see page 15).

MAPS: USGS *Timpanogos Cave;* Trails Illustrated *Uinta National Forest* (701)

FACILITIES: Restrooms at trailhead; water at nearby campsites

WHEELCHAIR ACCESS: None

CONTACT: 801-785-3563, fs.usda.gov/uwcnf

LOCATION: Granite Flat Campground, FS 010 about 13 miles east of Alpine, UT

COMMENTS: Motorized vehicles and bikes prohibited in Lone Peak Wilderness Area. Dogs allowed on leash but should be used to strenuous hiking. Doing this hike in winter requires mountaineering experience.

less likely on the descent. It also offers greater solitude, better wildlife-viewing, and some less frequently visited mountain scenery along the way.

A sign for the Box Elder Trail lies at the north end of the Sandwagon parking lot in Granite Flat. Within 100 yards of the trailhead, you'll pass a sign marking your entrance into the Lone Peak Wilderness Area.

The path rises steeply through successively higher meadows linked by stands of aspen and conifer, but no box elder trees. By entering these meadows slowly and quietly, visually scanning the rim, you'll have a good chance of spotting deer and occasionally moose. At 1.8 miles you'll come to a natural spring trickling down the side of a rock to the right of the trail. At 2.3 miles you'll see the remains of an old cabin on the left side of the trail. This cabin must have been "property with a view," as it's perched near a ledge overlooking Wide Hollow, a deep, glacial side canyon.

Shortly after passing the cabin, you'll come to a sign marking the White Canyon Trail (188), which heads north and connects with the Deer Creek–Dry Creek Trail—stay on the Box Elder Peak Trail to the left as it dips into Wide Hollow and crosses the seasonal runoff. As the trail crosses Wide Hollow and rises above the 8,700-foot level, you leave the mostly shaded woodland for partially shaded alpine meadows and ridges. Snowpack often remains into midsummer in the bowls and on the north-facing slopes at these higher elevations. You're in the wilderness, and along the trail you're just as likely to see bear tracks as boot tracks. It's important to trust the trail, because the route is unintuitive and the summit doesn't come into sight until you cross the upper ridge.

Box Elder Peak

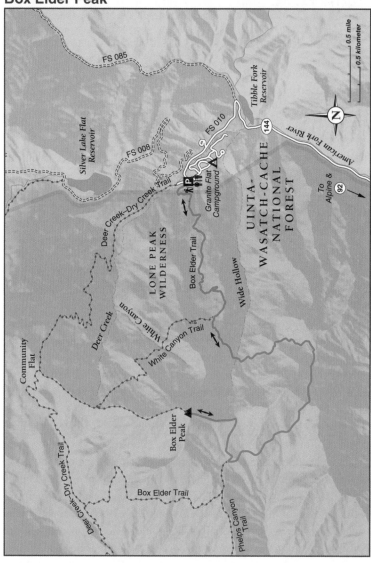

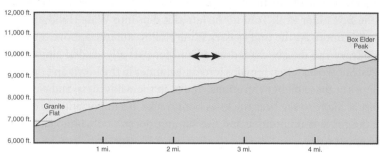

When you arrive at the saddle, views of the Utah Valley open to the west. The trail continues to the northwest along a level contour near 9,700 feet. Here you'll see the summit, and you must determine the best place to depart the trail and head for it. One good choice appears after crossing a steep shale slope. A faint ridgeline leads up to the northwest, and while the ascent is steep, it provides better footing than some of the scree slopes.

On the way to the summit, and often once you're there, you can see a herd of mountain goats that find safety from predators in this high, rocky terrain. From the summit, you have good views of Utah Valley but excellent ones of Mount Timpanogos to the south and Lone Peak and Pfeifferhorn ridge to the north.

After returning from the summit to the Box Elder Trail, head left (east) to return the way you came. Alternatively, you can turn right to make a clockwise loop around the mountain, eventually connecting with the Deer Creek–Dry Creek Trail to return to Granite Flat. After all, Box Elder Peak isn't just about the summit—it's a wilderness experience and an adventure in mountain solitude.

NEARBY ACTIVITIES

The city of Alpine, settled in 1850 by Mormon pioneers under the name of Mountainville, lies at the base of Box Elder Peak. Today, it's a growing residential community proud of its rural roots. Alpine's **Petersen Arboretum,** in Petersen Park at Ridge Drive and 100 East, features hundreds of trees of both native and nonnative species. Visit alpinenaturecenter.org/arboretum.html for more information.

· ·

GPS TRAILHEAD COORDINATES N40° 29.394' W111° 39.390'

DIRECTIONS From the southern intersection of I-215 and I-15 in Salt Lake City, take I-15 South about 14.4 miles to Exit 284 for Highland/Alpine. Keep left at the fork; then turn left onto UT 92 East, and drive 12.6 miles. Turn left onto UT 144/Forest Service Road 085 toward Tibble Fork. Drive 2.5 miles to the east end of Tibble Fork Reservoir; then turn left onto paved FS 010. In 0.7 mile, continue straight into Granite Flat Campground; then, in 0.2 mile, turn right into the parking area for the Sandwagon group camping area. The Box Elder trailhead (044) is at the north end of the parking lot. *Note:* Before 8 a.m., parking is available outside the campground gate.

Note: From early fall to late spring, UT 92, aka the Alpine Loop Scenic Backway, is closed to cars in the area covered by this hike, but in winter the highway is groomed periodically by **The Utah Nordic Alliance** for hikers, runners, cyclists, snowshoers, cross-country skiers, and snowmobilers. Be aware, however, that snowmobiles and other motorized vehicles are prohibited in Lone Peak Wilderness Area, which you enter just beyond the trailhead. Visit utahnordic.com/skiing/locations/sr92 for the latest information.

The trail to the caves is steep but exceptionally well maintained.

Photo: Greg Witt

THIS SPECTACULAR TRAIL is carved into and through rocky cliffs that rise high above American Fork Canyon. The trail ascends 1,000 feet of canyon wall to arrive at the entrance of Timpanogos Cave. The trail alone is worth the admission price to the cave (though you can skip the tour and hike at no cost). This is a perfect summer outing and must-see destination.

DESCRIPTION

Even if this weren't a national monument with a fascinating cave system awaiting at the end of the short paved trail, this would still be an exceptional hike. It takes you from the American Fork River on the canyon floor, up sheer rock cliffs exposing millions of years of geology, and through a subalpine forest of fir and pine, with breathtaking canyon views all along the way.

In 1887, long before anyone thought of building a trail up the canyon cliffs, settler Martin Hansen was cutting timber high on the slopes of American Fork Canyon. He noticed mountain-lion tracks leading up the hillside and followed them to a high ledge, where he found an opening in the limestone cliff to a small cave. This cave was the first of three linked caverns that contain about 2 miles of underground passages filled with colorful limestone deposits and clear-water pools.

DISTANCE & CONFIGURATION: 3-mile out-and-back

DIFFICULTY: Moderate

SCENERY: Riparian canyon with rock cliffs and subalpine slopes leading to caves

EXPOSURE: Mostly shaded to 8,000', partially shaded to 9,000', fully exposed above 9,000'

TRAIL TRAFFIC: Busy

TRAIL SURFACE: Paved

HIKING TIME: 1–2.5 hours on trail + 1 additional hour for cave tour

DRIVING DISTANCE: 31 miles from I-15/I-80 intersection

ELEVATION CHANGE: 5,638'–6,730'

ACCESS: Admission fees are charged for cave tours (see Nearby Activities, page 209). There is no charge to simply hike the trail, which is accessible daily, sunrise–sunset, mid-May–early September. Timpanogos Cave National Monument lies within American Fork Canyon, a fee-charging area (see

pages 15 and 203), but the fee applies only if you plan to explore beyond the monument.

MAPS: USGS *Timpanogos Cave;* Trails Illustrated *Uinta National Forest* (701)

FACILITIES: Restrooms, phones, water, snack stand, gift shop, and visitor center at trailhead; vault toilet along trail near cave entrance

WHEELCHAIR ACCESS: None on trail; visitor center is accessible

CONTACT: 801-756-5239, nps.gov/tica

LOCATION: American Fork Canyon, UT 92 about 7 miles east of Alpine, UT

COMMENTS: Dogs, wheelchairs, and strollers are prohibited on the trails; metal-frame backpacks and baby carriers are prohibited inside the caves. To protect the caves' bats from white-nose syndrome, a deadly fungal infection, you must consent to decontamination before entering if your clothes, shoes, or gear have ever been worn or taken inside of any other cave or mine.

Miners and early visitors stripped the center cave of many of its slow-growing formations. At one point, two railroad freight cars filled with flowstone were shipped to the east. But the discovery of two adjoining caves and the protection granted by the National Park Service in 1934 ensure that these fragile underground wonders will be available for us and future generations to enjoy.

During its approximately five-month operating season (generally mid-May–early September), Timpanogos Cave National Monument hosts around 70,000 visitors from all over the world. Most of those guests hike the trail because it's the only way to get to the cave. Thousands of additional visitors come just to hike the trail as part of a regular exercise program. The hike to the cave entrance is a good test of your conditioning and readiness for other, more strenuous hikes. If the point of your visit is to see the cave, make sure you allow yourself time to enjoy the trail and read the interpretive signs along the way.

The fact that the trail is paved doesn't detract one bit from the pristine beauty of the canyon wall. In fact, you'll appreciate the sure-footed surface, especially as you pass numerous unprotected drop-offs where a simple misstep could prove fatal. Some sections of the trail are particularly susceptible to rockfall and are marked by a red stripe; no stopping or standing is allowed in these areas.

A hike to the caves is a field course in Wasatch geology, with an open display of sedimentary and metamorphic layers, uplifted layers, and an active fault. Starting at the trailhead, you'll pass through an initial layer of quartzite, followed by distinctive

Timpanogos Cave National Monument

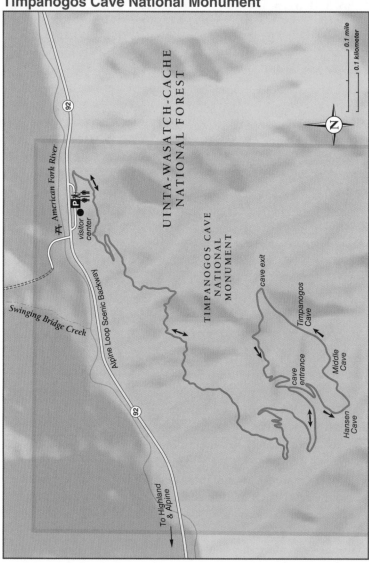

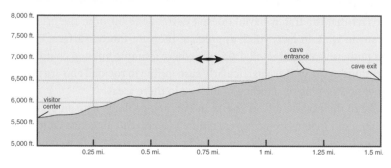

layers of shale, limestone, dolomite, and finally two layers of beautiful black limestone embedded with fossils of sea creatures and other remains of plant and animal life.

The canyon cliffs support an amazing range of conifers, many of which cling to the rocky ledges with twisted and gnarled exposed roots. Douglas-fir, white fir, and limber pine line the trail; scrub oak and bigtooth maple fill in the gaps.

Wildlife sightings on the trail are uncommon, but don't be surprised by chipmunks and squirrels along the way, or even an occasional rattlesnake on the rocky ledges. Looking across the canyon, you can often see red-tailed hawks and golden eagles soaring above. Bird-watchers may find their best opportunities on the Swinging Bridge Nature Trail across the road from the visitor center. The riverside vegetation is home to brightly colored western tanagers, Steller's jays, canyon wrens, and American dippers.

Allow 1.5–2 hours on the trail, plus an additional hour for the ranger-guided cave tour. Even when canyon temperatures hover in the 90s, the temperature in the cave remains a constant 45°F. Because you'll be in the cave for about an hour, make sure you come prepared with warm clothing for the tour. After completing the tour, you'll exit at the east end of the cave and follow a short loop back to the main trail for your descent.

NEARBY ACTIVITIES

A visit to Timpanogos Cave National Monument usually involves a **cave tour.** During the summer, tours usually sell out by early afternoon, so book your tour up to 30 days in advance by phone or online, or arrive early to buy your tickets at the visitor center (opens 7 a.m. daily in season). While waiting for your tour to depart, you can watch the introductory video at the visitor center, enjoy the picnic areas across the street, or explore the 0.25-mile nature trail. For reservations, call 877-444-6777 or go to recreation.gov/ticket/facility/249993; for more information, call 801-756-5238 or visit nps.gov/tica.

• •

GPS TRAILHEAD COORDINATES N40° 26.607' W111° 42.298'

DIRECTIONS From the southern intersection of I-215 and I-15 in Salt Lake City, take I-15 South about 14.4 miles to Exit 284 for Highland/Alpine. Keep left at the fork; then turn left onto UT 92 East, and drive 10.1 miles. The parking area and visitor center for Timpanogos Cave National Monument will be on the right. The trailhead is on the east side of the visitor center.

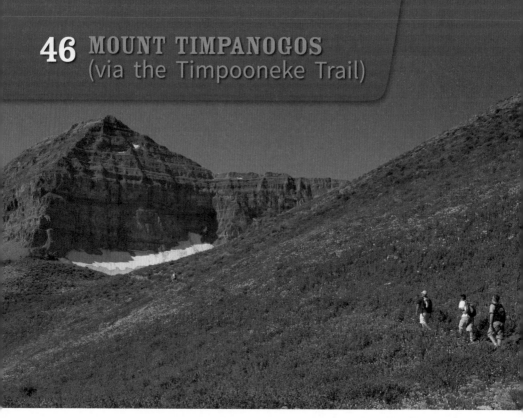

Mount Timpanogos is one of the most recognizable summits in the region.

Photo: Greg Witt

46 MOUNT TIMPANOGOS
(via the Timpooneke Trail)

THE TIMPANOGOS MASSIF dominates the skyline of Utah County. At 11,749 feet, this majestic peak is the second highest in the Wasatch (just below Mount Nebo to the south, at 11,928 feet). But looking at the steep, barren, western slope of Mount Timpanogos, it's hard to imagine the spectacular beauty to be found on the expansive, wooded eastern slopes, where trails lead past glistening lakes, flowered meadows, cascading waterfalls, and on to the summit.

DESCRIPTION

Mount Timpanogos, or "Timp" for short, is the most popular mountain-hiking destination in Utah. On any given summer Saturday, between 700 and 1,000 hikers depart from the two trailheads leading to the summit. Many have a summit destination in mind, and typically about 200–300 of those hikers make it to the top of the 11,749-foot peak. Some hikers make their ultimate destination one of the many waterfalls, meadows, or lakes, while others go as far as the saddle, less than a mile from the summit, and consider the view from the saddle as a worthy reward for their effort.

A frequent topic of discussion among Timp hikers is, "Which is the best trail to the summit: Aspen Grove or Timpooneke?" Truth is, the routes are equally popular, with about as many starting on one as the other. Each route arrives at the saddle from a different direction, but they share the final 0.9 mile to the summit. The Timpooneke Trail is

DISTANCE & CONFIGURATION: 13-mile out-and-back to saddle, 14.8-mile out-and-back to summit

DIFFICULTY: Strenuous

SCENERY: Mountain scenery, glacial basins, flowered meadows, lakes, and valley views

EXPOSURE: Mostly shaded below 8,000', partially shaded to 9,500', fully exposed above 9,500'

TRAIL TRAFFIC: Busy

TRAIL SURFACE: Dirt and rock to saddle, exclusively rock from saddle to summit

HIKING TIME: 6–11 hours

DRIVING DISTANCE: 37 miles from I-15/I-80 intersection

ELEVATION CHANGE: 7,360'–11,753'

ACCESS: UT 92, which leads to the trailhead, is closed to cars fall–late spring but is open to hikers, skiers, snowshoers, and snowmobilers at other times. While one could technically hike here anytime, *only experienced outdoorspeople should attempt to do so in winter.* The trail lies within American Fork Canyon, which charges an entrance fee: $6/1–3 days, $12/week, and $45/year; America the Beautiful passes honored (see page 15).

MAPS: USGS *Timpanogos Cave;* Trails Illustrated *Uinta National Forest* (701)

FACILITIES: Restrooms and water at trailhead; toilet near trail at Timpanogos Basin

WHEELCHAIR ACCESS: None

CONTACT: 801-785-3563, fs.usda.gov/uwcnf; check tert.org for trail conditions

LOCATION: Timpooneke Campground, FS 056 about 9 miles east of Alpine, UT

COMMENTS: Dogs allowed on leash. That said, consider your dog's fitness and stamina when planning your trip, and bring enough water and food for the both of you.

only 0.6 mile longer than the Aspen Grove Trail (see next profile), but Timpooneke has the gentler grade, as its starting elevation is 471 feet higher than that of Aspen Grove. The Timpooneke Trail ascends 593 feet per mile, while the Aspen Grove Trail ascends 714 feet per mile. Both offer comparable scenery—the Aspen Grove Trail climbs the gaping Primrose Cirque to Emerald Lake, while the Timpooneke Trail ascends the Giant Staircase to Timpanogos Basin. Aspen Grove has more accessible waterfalls and lakes along the trail, which add to the enjoyment of the hike.

Climbing Timp can make for a long day, so an early start—even before dawn—can work to your advantage. This is especially important if you're not used to the high elevations and you're forced to move a little more slowly. In summer, starting early enables you to gain most of your elevation in the shade. Also, on weekends and holidays the Timpooneke trailhead parking lot can fill by 7 a.m., so if you want a bit of mountain solitude, plan a midweek hike.

From the trailhead parking area, sign the register and begin your climb on Trail 053 through woods of Douglas-fir. The trail ascends a tiered drainage along a series of five benches known as the Giant Staircase. The Timpanogos massif is composed almost entirely of gray Oquirrh limestone, with alternating layers of limestone, sandstone, and shale exposed in the upper reaches of the mountain.

Each of the benches along the Giant Staircase becomes more open and is accompanied by a meadow of wildflowers. Finally, at the upper (Timpanogos) basin, hikers are exposed to a riot of wildflowers, with alpine aster, white columbine, Parry's primrose, and larkspur providing a colorful foreground to views of the summit

Mount Timpanogos (via the Timpooneke Trail)

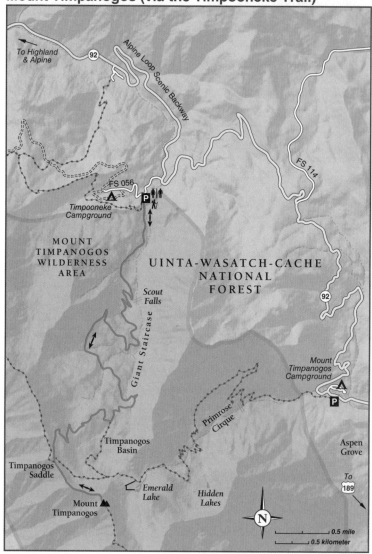

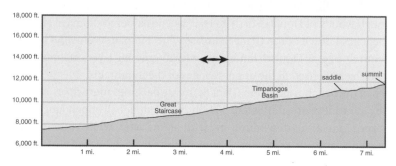

directly to the south. At this point, the elevation is 10,200 feet and the remaining hike to the summit is above tree line along rocky slopes.

On the north side of the basin, you'll come to a trail marker pointing to a backcountry toilet to the right, while the main trail continues straight ahead. Following the spur to the toilet also leads you to the wreckage of a B-25 airplane that crashed in the basin in 1955. The two engines and some sections of the fuselage remain. Continuing up a switchback on this slope, you'll come to a small cascade descending from snowmelt on an upper bowl. This is your last access to water before heading on to the summit.

As you ascend the rocky slope to the saddle, notice a steep trail descending on the left and to the south. This trail leads across a boulder field, often covered with snow, to Emerald Lake and the Aspen Grove Trail. Hikers coming up the Aspen Grove Trail to the summit typically use this steep trail to reach the saddle. A few minutes after passing this junction, you'll arrive at the saddle.

The Timpanogos saddle, at an elevation of 11,050 feet, offers excellent views of Utah Valley to the west. It's a comfortable rest stop—so comfortable that many hikers make it their final destination without going to the summit. Continuing on requires another 0.9 mile of steady and sometimes steep ascents along a well-crafted rocky trail. A steady pace should take you from the saddle to the summit in 35 minutes, but most hikers frequently stop to catch their breath, and the trip takes between 45 minutes and 1 hour to gain 700 vertical feet to the metal summit hut.

You can expect your return trip to be faster than your ascent, but be particularly careful descending the loose scree below the summit. Once below the saddle you'll find the trail provides a surefooted gradual descent, but with afternoon sun beaming down on exposed slopes, you'll want plenty of sunscreen and water.

NEARBY ACTIVITIES

The 20-mile **Alpine Loop Scenic Backway** (UT 92) goes up American Fork Canyon and continues through Uinta-Wasatch-Cache National Forest to Provo Canyon. Open late spring–late fall, the road affords wonderful views of fall colors. When snow closes part of the road, it becomes a favorite snowmobiling and cross-country-skiing trail. The narrow, winding road is not recommended for vehicles more than 30 feet long.

• •

GPS TRAILHEAD COORDINATES N40° 25.878' W111° 38.328'

DIRECTIONS From the southern intersection of I-215 and I-15 in Salt Lake City, take I-15 South about 14.4 miles to Exit 284 for Highland/Alpine. Keep left at the fork; then turn left onto UT 92 East, and drive 15.9 miles. Turn right into Timpooneke Campground on Forest Service Road 056, and drive 0.3 mile to the trailhead parking lot, on the left.

47 EMERALD LAKE AND MOUNT TIMPANOGOS (via Aspen Grove)

Emerald Lake supports a rich variety of wildflowers.

THE MOUNT TIMPANOGOS WILDERNESS AREA is full of superlatives. Whether you're hiking to a waterfall in Primrose Cirque, an alpine meadow, Emerald Lake, the Timpanogos snowfield, or on to the summit, you'll find plenty to grab your attention and make you want to go higher and farther.

DESCRIPTION

The Aspen Grove Trail, like its sister, the Timpooneke Trail (see previous profile), leads up an immense drainage to a glacial bowl, then on to the saddle and summit of Mount Timpanogos. While both are great trails and offer a challenging, spectacular, and often-overcrowded wilderness experience, the Aspen Grove Trail provides more access to water (in the form of waterfalls, streams, lakes, and snowfields) than the Timpooneke Trail. The Aspen Grove Trail also has more vertical elevation gain and is slightly shorter and steeper than the Timpooneke Trail. Finally, it offers a better chance of seeing the herd of mountain goats that call "Timp" home.

The name *Timpanogos* (timp-ah-NO-gus) comes from the Paiute name for the Provo River, meaning "rock and running water." It has nothing to do with a silly legend contrived in the early 20th century, which holds that the image of a lovesick Indian maiden who threw herself off the peak can still be seen in the mountain skyline.

DISTANCE & CONFIGURATION: 9.6-mile out-and-back to Emerald Lake, 13.6-mile out-and-back to summit

DIFFICULTY: Strenuous

SCENERY: Mountain scenery, glacial basins, flowered meadows, lakes, valley views

EXPOSURE: Partially shaded to 9,500', fully exposed above 9,500'

TRAIL TRAFFIC: Busy

TRAIL SURFACE: Asphalt for first mile, dirt and rock to Emerald Lake, mostly rock to summit

HIKING TIME: 4.5–7 hours to Emerald Lake, 7–11 hours to summit

DRIVING DISTANCE: 49 miles from I-15/I-80 intersection

ELEVATION CHANGE: 6,889'–11,753'

ACCESS: UT 92, which leads to the trailhead, is closed to cars fall–late spring but is open to hikers, skiers, snowshoers, and snowmobilers at other times. While one could technically hike here anytime, *only experienced outdoorspeople should attempt to do so in winter.* The trail lies within American Fork Canyon, which charges an entrance fee: $6/1–3 days, $12/week, and $45/year; America the Beautiful passes honored (see page 15).

MAPS: USGS *Timpanogos Cave;* Trails Illustrated *Uinta National Forest* (701)

FACILITIES: Restrooms and water at trailhead

WHEELCHAIR ACCESS: None

CONTACT: 801-785-3563, fs.usda.gov/uwcnf; check tert.org for trail conditions

LOCATION: UT 92, Provo Canyon, UT 84604

COMMENTS: Dogs allowed on leash. That said, consider your dog's fitness and stamina when planning your trip, and bring enough water and food for the both of you.

The trail departs from the north side of the large Theater in the Pines parking area and passes a small guard station, where you should sign in during the peak summer season. The trail gradually ascends the lower drainage through woods of quaking aspen and Douglas-fir. To the left is a steep slope where thousands of trees have been leveled and several lives have been lost in recent avalanches.

After entering the Mount Timpanogos Wilderness Area, the trail is paved in asphalt for the next mile. The trail arrives at a waterfall on the left, then makes a sharp turn to the right and into some switchbacks before arriving at a second waterfall. Here the asphalt ends and the trail begins a giant, gradually ascending sweep to the east along the partially shaded south-facing slope of Primrose Cirque. At about 8,000 feet in elevation, the trail turns sharply back to the west and continues its climb of the expansive cirque. Along the way, the trail traverses rocky slopes and passes by several waterfalls and small runoffs.

This section of trail can be particularly treacherous in the spring and early summer, as melting snowfields form ice bridges across the flowing water. Falling through these snowfields to the rocks and rushing water below has resulted in injuries and deaths for unprepared hikers. Use extreme caution when crossing some of the steep snowfields in this section of the trail.

After winding your way up the limestone terraces at the top of Primrose Cirque, you'll pass through a grove of Engelmann spruce (a popular camping area) at an elevation of about 9,500 feet, then move on to a high meadow laced with streams and small lakes. After several stream crossings, the trail ascends to the crest of a moraine slope and the Timpanogos Shelter comes into view, followed by views of Emerald Lake.

Emerald Lake and Mount Timpanogos (via Aspen Grove)

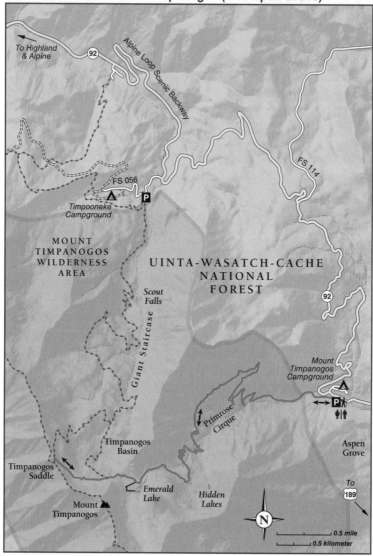

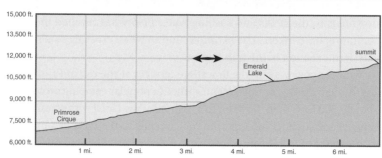

Emerald Lake is a wonderful destination if you've made a late start or want a shorter, less demanding outing. The shelter provides the only shade in the area, and a recently constructed toilet lies along a path to the northeast of the shelter.

The Timpanogos Shelter, just 100 yards to the north of Emerald Lake, was built in 1959 by the U.S. Forest Service. From 1959 to 1970, it was used as part of the Timp Hike, a community event that drew thousands to the mountain each year on a single late-July weekend. The hike was discontinued in 1970 in an effort to preserve the delicate mountain environment.

Rising to the west of Emerald Lake toward the ridgeline is the Timpanogos Glacier. Whether it's an actual glacier or not has been the subject of some debate: trip reports from the early 20th century note the existence of crevasses, indicative of a true glacier. The Dust Bowl drought of the 1930s diminished the glacier considerably, and throughout most of the 20th century it waxed and waned with variations in annual snowfall and temperatures. But in 1994, the snowfield melted sufficiently to reveal some glacial ice below the talus. Studies were inconclusive, so the debate rages on regarding whether it's a glacier, a permanent snowfield, or just a patch of snow. The snowfield can be used for both a summit ascent in the spring (typically requiring ice ax and crampons) and for a glissade descent in the summer.

Note: Glissading—sliding down a snowfield without skis, either standing up or sitting down—is a popular and fast but increasingly dangerous descent strategy. Research conditions carefully, and use caution.

The route from the shelter to the saddle crosses the meadow north of Emerald Lake to a boulder field often covered with large patches of snow. The area around Emerald Lake is your best opportunity to spot mountain goats that often graze in the meadow and find an easy retreat to the high rocky ledges of Mount Timpanogos. Mountain goats found in Utah are a nonnative species introduced in 1967 from a herd in Washington's Olympic National Park. In addition to Mount Timpanogos, they have been successfully transplanted to the Cottonwood Canyons, the Uintas, and the Tushar Mountains in southern Utah. The current population statewide is more than 1,000, with about 200 inhabiting the Timpanogos massif.

The most grueling section of trail rises from the boulder field above the Timpanogos Basin and steeply ascends to the north before joining the Timpooneke Trail and continuing to the saddle. From the saddle, it's a demanding, rocky 0.9-mile climb to the metal shelter at the 11,749-foot summit. Here you'll have commanding views of Utah Valley to the west and Heber Valley to the east.

Mount Timpanogos is arguably the best mountain hike in Utah, and certainly a classic that every local hiker should experience. As with most mountains, summit success favors those who get an early start. Once you've returned to Emerald Lake from the summit, the afternoon descent along the sunny slopes of Primrose Cirque can be long and hot, so bring plenty of water and sunscreen.

• •

GPS TRAILHEAD COORDINATES N40° 24.263' W111° 36.323'

DIRECTIONS From the southern intersection of I-215 and I-15 in Salt Lake City, take I-15 South about 27 miles to Exit 272 for UT 52/800 North. Keep left at the fork; then turn left onto West 800 North, and drive 3.7 miles. Use the left lane to take the ramp onto US 189 North, and drive 6.9 miles up the canyon. Then turn left onto UT 92, the first left after the tunnel, and drive 4.7 miles, passing Sundance Mountain Resort and Aspen Grove Family Camp on the left. After you pass the U.S. Forest Service fee booth, enter the trail-head parking lot, immediately on the left.

Hikers relax around Emerald Lake.   *Photo: Greg Witt*

Stewart Falls is the loveliest of Mount Timpanogos's cascades.

Photo: Inbound Horizons/Shutterstock

A TIERED WEDDING CAKE of cascading water set against a mountain backdrop of aspen and fir, Stewart Falls may be the most picturesque waterfall in Utah. The gentle trail is well suited for families, making this an ideal three-season day hike.

DESCRIPTION

For the thousands of Utah Valley residents living below the western slopes of the Timpanogos massif, it's easy to forget how incredibly beautiful the back side of Timp is. They should be required to pay a visit at least twice a year—spring, summer, fall, winter; it doesn't matter—to walk through the aspens, breathe the mountain air, and sit by a mountain stream at the base of a thundering waterfall. Indeed, the trail leading to Stewart Falls is one of the rare hikes where just arriving at the trailhead will prove to be one of the greatest rewards of your whole day. Regardless of where you are on this trail, the views are some of the most memorable you will ever have.

Mount Timpanogos boasts some exquisite waterfalls on all sides, and the falls along both Aspen Grove Trail and the Timpooneke Trail should be on every hiker's must-see list. But Stewart Falls, sometimes referred to as Stewarts Cascades, is the most beautiful and accessible of them all. In less than 2 miles from the trailhead,

DISTANCE & CONFIGURATION: 3.6-mile out-and-back

DIFFICULTY: Easy

SCENERY: Mountain views and waterfall

EXPOSURE: Mostly shaded for first mile, partially shaded for second

TRAIL TRAFFIC: Busy

TRAIL SURFACE: Dirt

HIKING TIME: 1.5–2.5 hours

DRIVING DISTANCE: 49 miles from I-15/I-80 intersection

ELEVATION CHANGE: 6,889'–7,200'

ACCESS: Daily, sunrise–sunset; UT 92, which leads to the trailhead, is closed to cars fall–late spring but is open to hikers, skiers, snowshoers, and snowmobilers at other times. The Aspen Grove trailhead parking area lies within the American Fork Canyon fee-access area, while the trail itself is almost entirely on Sundance Mountain Resort property. Current access fees are $6/1–3 days, $12/week, and $45/year; America the Beautiful passes honored (see page 15).

MAPS: USGS *Aspen Grove;* Trails Illustrated *Uinta National Forest* (701)

FACILITIES: Restrooms and drinking water at trailhead parking area

WHEELCHAIR ACCESS: None

CONTACT: 801-785-3563, fs.usda.gov/uwcnf; 801-225-4107, sundanceresort,com

LOCATION: UT 92 near Sundance Mountain Resort, Provo Canyon, UT 84604

COMMENTS: Dogs allowed on leash

walking along a well-groomed wooded slope, you find yourself face-to-face with tiers of cascading spring water.

From the large trailhead parking area, to the right of the restroom, take the trail that leads up Primrose Cirque, following the sign marked STEWART FALLS, TRAIL 56. As you look at the slope in front of you to the left, you can see the damage done by recent avalanches that resulted in the loss of several lives. At 0.1 mile, the trail turns sharply to the left and ascends the hillside through a forest of Douglas-fir and aspen. At 1.2 miles, the path passes through the middle of an avalanche slope where hundreds of aspens have been leveled.

Along the way you'll find a rich variety of birds in the trees and underbrush. Yellow-bellied sapsuckers, mountain bluebirds, yellow warblers, and western tanagers are just a few of the colorful varieties you may see. Squirrels make their home in the underbrush of scrub oak, bigtooth maple, and Oregon grape.

The trail reaches a peak elevation of 7,200 feet before beginning its descent toward the falls. Soon the roar of the falls can be heard even before they come into view. At 1.5 miles from the trailhead, as you come around a bend, your first view of Stewart Falls awaits. Another cascade plunges down the slope to the right.

At 1.7 miles from the trailhead, you'll come to a shale outcrop that serves as a great falls overlook. From there, take the marked trail that descends to the left. A few short switchbacks lead you to the stream level at the base of the falls. Plenty of great vantage points below the falls offer places to play in the water or enjoy a snack. However, the barren slope to the right and in front of the falls is steep and dangerous—best to avoid.

As you approach the falls from the north, you may look across the stream and see others arriving from the south. Here's an alternative approach for your next visit:

Stewart Falls

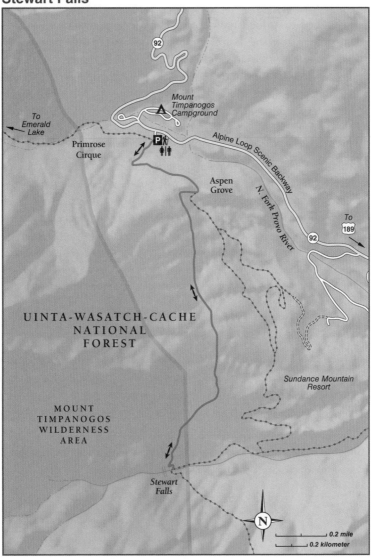

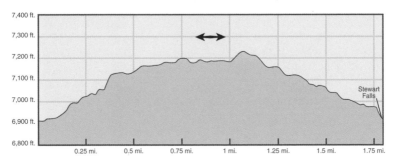

during most of the late spring, summer, and fall, the Sundance chairlift takes hikers and mountain bikers from the base elevation of 6,100 feet to the summit at 7,150 feet in a matter of minutes (prices to ride: $11 adults, $9 children ages 6–12, $8 seniors age 65 and older, free for kids under age 6 with paying adult). From the summit, a pleasant downhill stroll leads to Stewart Falls at 6,800 feet, then back to Sundance. This loop hike is especially enjoyable in fall as the hillside blazes with autumn colors.

NEARBY ACTIVITIES

Nestled at the base of Mount Timpanogos and adjacent to Stewart Falls, **Sundance Mountain Resort** (8841 N. Alpine Loop Road; 801-225-4107, sundanceresort.com) offers a diverse mountain-recreation experience year-round. Skiing, snowboarding, or cross-country skiing in winter and biking and hiking in summer all take place against a backdrop of breathtaking scenery. Lodging, fine dining, theater, and conference facilities make Sundance a favorite choice for an afternoon visit or an extended vacation.

• •

GPS TRAILHEAD COORDINATES N40° 24.263' W111° 36.323'

DIRECTIONS From the southern intersection of I-215 and I-15 in Salt Lake City, take I-15 South about 27 miles to Exit 272 for UT 52/800 North. Keep left at the fork; then turn left onto West 800 North, and drive 3.7 miles. Use the left lane to take the ramp onto US 189 North, and drive 6.9 miles up the canyon. Then turn left onto UT 92, the first left after the tunnel, and drive 4.7 miles, passing Sundance Mountain Resort and Aspen Grove Family Camp on the left. After you pass the U.S. Forest Service fee booth, enter the trailhead parking lot, immediately on the left.

Battle Creek Falls provides a popular way to beat the summer heat.

THIS POPULAR, FAMILY-FRIENDLY ROUTE runs along a creekbed in a deep canyon. The hike's payout: a 50-foot waterfall spraying down the side of a rock cliff. Hikers can bask in the spray at the bottom of the falls or quickly ascend to the top of the waterfall, which offers beautiful views of the canyon that it forms.

DESCRIPTION

The Timpanogos massif, which dominates the eastern skyline of Utah County, has several canyons along its foothills that provide water to the towns below and access to the mountain's higher slopes. From the valley, you can most easily identify Battle Creek Canyon as the one immediately to the right (or south) of the *G* on the side of the mountain. Battle Creek supplies the water that fills the large tank and irrigates the orchards you pass on the way to the trailhead. In this area on February 28, 1849, a band of Ute Indians fought Captain John Scott and his men, pursuing Scott's party into the canyon.

The parking area is large, but it often fills quickly as it's attached to a beautiful and popular park; therefore, this is a great hike to do early in the morning. From the parking area, walk toward the blue metal arch over the bridge that leads into Kiwanis Park. Find the trailhead by walking up the steep slope to your right, just a few feet before the bridge. Note the park's large picnic pavilion, drinking water, and vault

DISTANCE & CONFIGURATION: 1.6-mile out-and-back

DIFFICULTY: Easy

SCENERY: Deep-canyon waterfall and valley views

EXPOSURE: Mostly shaded

TRAIL TRAFFIC: Moderate

TRAIL SURFACE: Dirt, rock

HIKING TIME: 45 minutes–1.5 hours

DRIVING DISTANCE: 49 miles from I-15/I-80 intersection

ELEVATION CHANGE: 5,221'–5,671'

ACCESS: Daily, sunrise–sunset; no fees or permits

MAPS: USGS *Orem;* Trails Illustrated *Uinta National Forest* (701)

FACILITIES: Vault toilet near trailhead

WHEELCHAIR ACCESS: None

CONTACT: 801-785-3563, fs.usda.gov/uwcnf

LOCATION: End of 200 South just south of Kiwanis Park, Pleasant Grove, UT 84062

COMMENTS: Especially beautiful in autumn with colors and a trailbed of fallen leaves. Dogs allowed on leash. Horses and mountain bikes also use this trail.

toilet, all under the shade of giant cottonwood trees. As the trail climbs the hillside, it soon joins a jeep road on the right.

Don't expect to see any water in the creekbed to your left—because the water is diverted into underground pipes just up the canyon, it remains dry throughout the year. At 0.3 mile you'll see a water-diversion basin where Battle Creek begins its life underground. Beyond this diversion basin, follow the tumbling creek another 0.2 mile and cross to the north side of the creek over a sturdy wooden footbridge.

After it crosses the bridge, the trail steepens considerably. Shards of shale from the cliffs above cover the trail's dirt base. Still, the trail provides sure footing. At points where your confidence in the shale surface may wane, textured rubber mats help hold the small shards of rock in place. Within about 100 feet after you cross the bridge, the falls appear. Then, about 50 feet before the falls, the trail divides: the right spur descends to the base of the falls, and the main trail to the left leads to the top.

A natural spring feeds Battle Creek, augmented by snowmelt. So while the falls' spray becomes heaviest in spring, the creek and the falls are perennial. Battle Creek Falls serves as a popular escape from summer's heat, with visitors enjoying the cooling spray near its base. The water falls gently enough that even young children can safely walk and play under the main channel of water as it bounces off the rock wall. Local adventurers often rappel down the falls in summer.

The trail leading to the top of the falls continues up the canyon and joins the Great Western Trail, which surrounds much of Mount Timpanogos and connects all the canyon trails on Timpanogos's western slopes. While Battle Creek Falls is the largest of the waterfalls along this section of trail, other small cascades and falls dot the trail farther up the canyon.

At the lower elevations, below the falls, the vegetation consists of Gambel oak, sage, and cottonwoods. Conifers and aspens grow at higher elevations near the falls and above. You'll often spot pinyon jays, but scrub jays—while common—prove to be a bit more elusive.

Battle Creek Falls

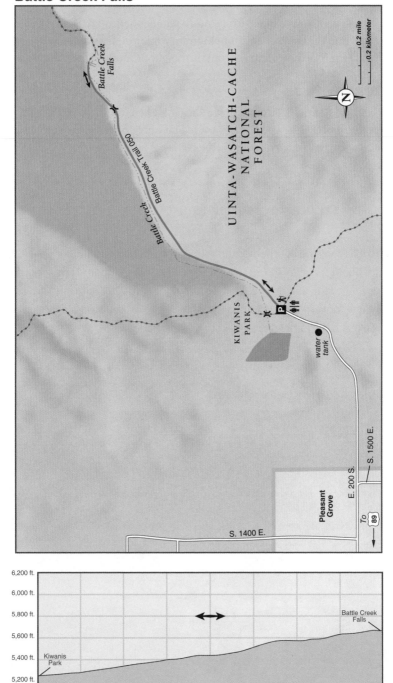

Along the way, you're likely to see more people than animals. Families out for a day hike will find the trail suitable for children, while young couples and older adults can get some exercise just minutes from the neighborhoods in the valley below.

NEARBY ACTIVITIES

The U.S. Forest Service's **Pleasant Grove Ranger Station** (801-785-3563) is on the way to the trailhead at 390 N. 100 E. (UT 146). The office offers maps and publications about recreation in Uinta-Wasatch-Cache National Forest.

• •

GPS TRAILHEAD COORDINATES N40° 21.789' W111° 42.042'

DIRECTIONS From the southern intersection of I-215 and I-15 in Salt Lake City, take I-15 South about 23 miles to Exit 275 for Pleasant Grove/Lindon. Turn left onto Pleasant Grove Boulevard, and drive 1.2 miles. Turn right onto 220 South, and drive 0.5 mile; then continue forward on 200 South, and drive 2.5 miles. You'll pass a large water tank before you reach the parking area, next to Kiwanis Park.

A wide variety of trees shades the trail to the falls.

Cascade Peak towers over the northern portion of the Provo River Parkway.

THE PROVO RIVER PARKWAY is a community treasure, connecting residents with the river, mountains, waterfalls, parks, shopping, work, and Provo's history. As the parkway follows the course of the Provo, you're constantly exposed to the life of the river—trout fishing, waterfowl, and riparian plants. Take the trail in bite-size pieces, and enjoy.

DESCRIPTION

The Provo River Parkway stretches from a deep mountain canyon through shopping centers, business parks, and neighborhoods to the shores of Utah Lake. Along its course, the trail passes through a national forest, 2 county parks, 14 city parks, and a state park.

While it's certainly possible to walk the trail from top to bottom, or vice versa, most choose to enter the parkway from one of dozens of access points and enjoy the scenic array found within just a mile or two in either direction. Officially designated as a nonmotorized multiuse trail, the parkway is widely used by families, seniors, and students as Provo's most popular venue for outdoor recreation and exercise.

On any given day, you can see hundreds of people on the trail. But think of it as a highly social trail—not a crowded one. In-line skaters, skateboarders, kids on

DISTANCE & CONFIGURATION: 15-mile point-to-point

DIFFICULTY: Easy

SCENERY: Deep canyon, mountain streams, waterfalls, towering peaks, pastures, wetlands

EXPOSURE: Partially shaded

TRAIL TRAFFIC: Busy

TRAIL SURFACE: Paved

HIKING TIME: Varies based on distance selected

DRIVING DISTANCE: 43 miles from I-15/I-80 intersection

ELEVATION CHANGE: 5,200' at trailhead, with no significant rise

ACCESS: Daily, sunrise–sunset; no fees or permits

MAPS: USGS *Bridal Veil Falls, Orem,* and *Provo*

FACILITIES: Restrooms and water at trailheads and throughout hike

WHEELCHAIR ACCESS: Yes

CONTACT: 801-852-6606, provo.org/departments /parks/trails

LOCATION: South Fork Rd. just south of US 189, Provo Canyon, UT 84604 (Vivian Park trailhead); W. North Boat Harbor Dr., Provo, UT 84601 (Utah Lake trailhead)

COMMENTS: Check for avalanche risk November– March. Dogs allowed on leash.

scooters, babies in strollers, cyclists, runners, and walkers all coexist happily, with pedestrians enjoying the right of way.

The most scenic section of the trail may be the upper 5 miles, from Vivian Park to the mouth of Provo Canyon (the intersection of US 189 and Orem 800 North). In addition to these two locations, you can enter the trail at many points in between, including Nunns Park, Canyon Glen, Mount Timpanogos Park, and Canyon View Park. These access points also offer drinking water and restroom facilities, plus tables and grates for a picnic after the hike.

Within this section the trail and the river flow together; they're never more than 20 feet apart, and they're always within view and earshot of each other. The steep canyon walls and wooded canyon floor offer abundant shade. You'll have multiple opportunities to stop and dangle your feet in the water or watch fly-fishermen try to snag a trophy cutthroat or rainbow trout.

Among the many scenic highlights in Provo Canyon, Bridal Veil Falls is a perennial crowd-pleaser. At 607 feet, this double cataract is the highest waterfall in Utah. In the spring and early summer, the water sprays onto the trail and hikers play in the runoff. In winter, the frozen falls and the Stairway to Heaven seepage to the right of the falls provide some of Utah's favorite ice-climbing routes. From Nunns Park or Bridal Veil Falls Park, the falls are just a 10-minute walk.

About 100 feet downstream from Bridal Veil Falls, located in front of an abandoned mine entrance, is a display of old mining equipment. This serves as a reminder of the mining operations that played such an important role in the canyon's development.

Another 100 yards downstream at Nunns Park are the remnants of an early hydroelectric plant built in 1897. At the time, the plant produced almost three times the electricity of any existing line in the nation and powered mining operations 32 miles to the west.

Provo River Parkway

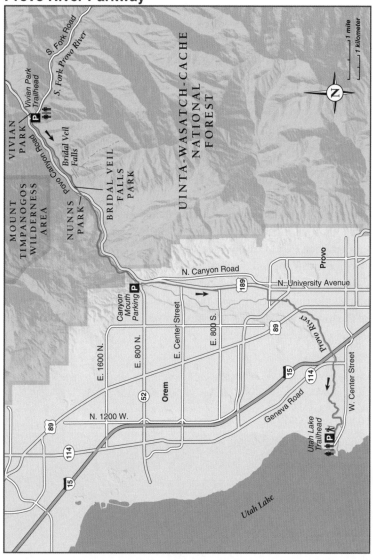

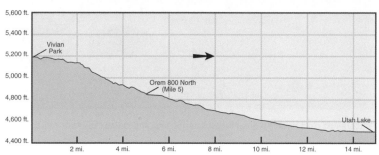

Throughout Provo Canyon you're likely to see raptors circling above, while belted kingfishers and yellow warblers flit along the riverbanks. Young children always seem fascinated by the snake grass (or horsetails), a tall, dark-green, tubular grass growing along the banks.

The lower section of the trail, from Geneva Road to Utah Lake, is every bit as beautiful as the Provo Canyon section, but in a very different way. You might even think you're on a different river in another state. As the river approaches the lake, it widens and slows. Whitewater kayaks are the upriver conveyance of choice, while below it's canoes or rowboats.

In the final 2.5 miles of the trail, the river meanders through a tunnel of mature cottonwoods. On the trail's north side are protected pastures frequented by egrets and warblers. To the south, the river and marshy lowlands host ducks, geese, and a wide variety of migrating waterfowl. You can easily reach this wetlands section of the trail from Fort Utah Park, Oxbow Park, or Utah Lake State Park.

Between the canyon and the wetlands, the Provo River Parkway passes through neighborhoods and busy shopping centers, and under city streets and I-15. While this center section of the trail lacks the scenic beauty of the canyon and the rural appeal of the lowlands, it does offer a safe, convenient place for local residents to get outdoors and enjoy a walk along the river.

The well-maintained road surface is great for cyclists, joggers, and in-line skaters as well as hikers.

Although cyclists have a 15-mph speed limit and pedestrians enjoy the right of way, you still need to keep to the right or in the marked pedestrian lane and be on guard for cyclists approaching from behind. Access to the swift-moving river is never fenced or protected, so supervise young children carefully at all times. Throughout its 15-mile length, the trail is entirely paved and well marked. The almost imperceptible incline rarely varies, so you can enter at any point for a leisurely stroll or a vigorous workout.

NEARBY ACTIVITIES

If just walking along the banks isn't enough excitement for you, try rafting the Provo River. **High Country Adventure** at Frazier Park (just downstream from Vivian Park) offers exciting trips down the Provo on mild (Class II) whitewater during the summer season. Trips down the river last about 2 hours and can be guided or unguided in a raft, tube, or kayak. Call 801-224-2500 or visit highcountryadventure.com for information and reservations.

• •

GPS TRAILHEAD COORDINATES
Utah Lake: N40° 14.277' W111° 43.922'
Vivian Park: N40° 21.327' W111° 34.448'

DIRECTIONS *Utah Lake (ending trailhead):* From the southern intersection of I-215 and I-15 in Salt Lake City, take I-15 South about 33 miles to Exit 265 for Provo Center Street/Airport. Turn right onto West Center Street, and drive 2.5 miles; then turn right onto West North Boat Harbor Drive. The parking area is immediately on your right.

Vivian Park (starting trailhead): From the Utah Lake trailhead, backtrack south on West North Boat Harbor Drive and then east on West Center Street, a total of 2.6 miles; then use the left two lanes to merge onto I-15 North. In 5.7 miles, take Exit 272 and turn right onto UT 52/800 North; then, in 4 miles, use the left lane to take the ramp onto US 189 North/East Provo Canyon Road. In 5.8 miles, turn right onto South Fork Road, and cross the South Fork Provo River; then enter the trailhead parking area, straight ahead immediately after the railroad tracks.

In addition to these starting and ending trailheads, an additional 15 official trailheads with public parking provide easy trail access.

The springs, while small, support a wide variety of plant life.

FROM THE CITY-PARK TRAILHEAD, a steady ascent follows a small creek through a broad valley to Big Springs, a natural spring flowing from the mountainside. Mountain views, abundant valley vegetation, and frequent wildlife sightings make this a popular and accessible family adventure.

DESCRIPTION

Take everything you've ever imagined about a city park—crowds, passing cars, cityscapes—and throw it all out the window. True, the land in Big Springs Hollow is largely owned by the city of Provo, and the trailhead starts in the city-park parking lot. But in less than a minute, the parking lot is out of sight and you're suddenly enveloped in a secluded mountain valley in search of the natural springs that feed the meandering creek at your side.

The main trail follows the south side of this wide, slope-sided valley as the creek crisscrosses the trail several times. Sturdy wooden bridges span all the major creek crossings. For the first 0.7 mile, the trail makes a moderate but steady climb, finally arriving at a knoll where the terrain flattens a bit. After a brief 0.1 mile of level trail, the slope steepens and the ascent returns. Mountain views of Cascade Peak and the back side of the Wasatch Front remain ahead of you to the west for most of the hike.

DISTANCE & CONFIGURATION: 5-mile out-and-back

DIFFICULTY: Easy

SCENERY: Mountain views to the west and natural springs with perennial flow; the trail follows a creek

EXPOSURE: Mostly shaded

TRAIL TRAFFIC: Moderate; go midweek for more solitude

TRAIL SURFACE: Dirt, moderate incline

HIKING TIME: 1.5–2.5 hours

DRIVING DISTANCE: 46 miles from I-15/ I-80 intersection

ELEVATION CHANGE: 5,796'–6,461'

ACCESS: Daily, sunrise–sunset; no fees or permits

WHEELCHAIR ACCESS: None

MAPS: USGS *Bridal Veil Falls;* Trails Illustrated *Uinta National Forest* (701)

FACILITIES: Restrooms and water fountain in Big Springs Park (closed/shut off in winter)

CONTACT: 801-785-3563, fs.usda.gov/uwcnf; 801-852-6000, provo.org/departments/parks /park-info

LOCATION: Big Springs Park, Spring Hollow Road about 3.6 miles southeast of US 189, Provo Canyon, UT 84604

COMMENTS: Some areas may become boggy in spring. Negligible avalanche risk in winter. Dogs allowed on leash.

Throughout the hike, quaking aspen and bigtooth maple provide most of the shade, while thickets of poplar, river birch, and willow cluster near the creek.

Following 30 minutes of steady hiking and immediately after a creek crossing, you'll come to a sign marking a fork in the trail. To the left, another 0.5 mile ahead, is Big Springs. The fork to the right leads to the Cascade Saddle at 4.1 miles. Just after you take the trail's left fork, you'll cross the creek on a wooden bridge. By the time you reach the sign, you'll have gained more than 400 feet in elevation since leaving the trailhead.

From this point on to the springs, the trail steers closer to the south side of the valley. Along this slope, stands of aspen give way to Douglas-fir and the trail soon rises above the creek, although it's never more than about 50 feet away and always within earshot.

Another 0.3 mile beyond the first sign, you'll come to a second sign at the junction of the Cascade Springs Trail. Turn right at this T-junction and continue toward Big Springs, just 0.2 mile ahead.

The trail is designated as a nonmotorized multiuse trail, meaning it's used by horse riders, mountain bikers, hikers, and—in winter—skiers and snowshoers. They all seem to get along pretty well. Hikers still predominate in summer and snowshoers in winter. The gentle side slopes of the valley make avalanche risk negligible, and there is no history or visible evidence of avalanches in the area around the trail.

As you approach Big Springs, the woods deepen and become more coniferous, with some scrub-oak underbrush. The last 0.1 mile before arriving at Big Springs proves the steepest section of trail, but not steep enough to require switchbacking or any special treatment.

Cascade Springs flows from several release points on the mountainside and fans down the slope to the left of the trail. A small water-diversion culvert to the right of the trail directs some of the water toward the main creek channel. Big Springs

Big Springs Hollow

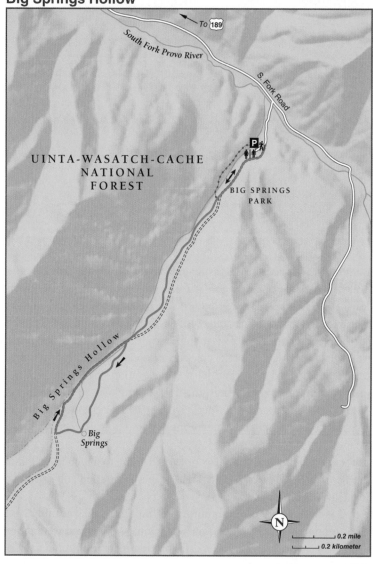

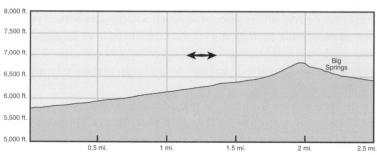

marks the high elevation point of the hike, at 6,350 feet. The water from Big Springs flows down to South Fork Creek and into the Provo River. Big Springs is the largest of many small springs, seeps, and willow bogs throughout the canyon. Some of the area's springs have been Provo drinking-water sources for more than 60 years.

From Big Springs, follow the trail down the slope to the right and cross another wooden bridge. About 0.2 mile past Big Springs, the trail merges with the Cascade Trail. This junction represents the turnaround point on the loop. Take a hard right and follow the Cascade Trail east and back to the trailhead parking area.

Continuing west on the trail will lead to the Cascade Mountain Saddle and to Rock Canyon Campground. From this trail junction, ambitious hikers could access a much larger network of trails and actually return to Provo city on foot over the Cascade Mountain Saddle and down Rock Canyon.

On the return, the north side of the loop passes a permanent site used by the Provo School District as an environmental camp for elementary students in June. You'll find a drinking fountain with chlorinated water here during the summer. The trail passes wet and dry grassy meadows with lupine, clover, violets, and mustards. A local rancher still cuts and harvests a spread of alfalfa here.

Throughout the year, hikers can expect to see deer, rabbits, and the occasional moose. Mountain lions roam the hillsides, and you'll frequently see their tracks in the winter snow, although you're unlikely to actually see this elusive species. Wild turkeys, ruffed grouse, and many songbirds can be spotted in the summer. During one recent summer, a survey of butterflies reported 60 different species in Big Springs Hollow between March and September, with western skippers and western bluetails being the most common.

Weather can change rapidly on the eastern slopes of the Wasatch. Once the sun sets or the clouds roll in, particularly in the fall and winter, afternoon temperatures can drop quickly.

After returning to the parking area, you'll find the tables, fire grates, and covered group sites to be inviting spots for relaxing or enjoying an afternoon picnic or cookout. With their higher elevations, mountain shade, and cooler temperatures, South Fork Canyon and Big Springs Hollow are a popular summer retreat.

NEARBY ACTIVITIES

Utah County residents use Provo Canyon as a year-round playground. Anglers, river runners, and hikers can find lots to keep them busy through most of the year. In the depths of winter, you'll often spot ice climbers ascending the frozen overspray of **Bridal Veil Falls. Vivian Park** (see previous hike), at the mouth of South Fork Canyon, is a popular picnic area that serves as the starting point for the historic **Heber Valley Railroad.** The billowing steam engine takes tourists up Provo Canyon from Vivian Park to Soldier Hollow and the Heber Valley. Call 435-654-5601 or visit hebervalleyrr.org for schedules, special events, and information.

• •

GPS TRAILHEAD COORDINATES N40° 19.938' W111° 31.456'

DIRECTIONS From the southern intersection of I-215 and I-15 in Salt Lake City, take I-15 South about 27 miles to Exit 272 for UT 52/800 North. Keep left at the fork; then turn left onto West 800 North, and drive 3.7 miles. Use the left lane to take the ramp onto US 189 North, and drive 5.8 miles; then turn right onto South Fork Road, and drive 3.3 miles. Turn right onto Spring Hollow Road, entering Big Springs Park. Continue 0.2 mile to the upper-level parking area, where you'll find the trailhead in the lot's southwest corner.

Big Springs Hollow affords stunning views of area peaks.

From Buffalo Peak you're rewarded with unobstructed views of Mount Timpanogos.

IF YOU'RE AFTER a great view with very little effort, Buffalo Peak is the easiest, most accessible summit on the Wasatch Front. Within minutes of the trailhead, you're overlooking Utah Valley from an elevation of more than 8,000 feet. And you'll likely have the trail and the summit to yourself.

DESCRIPTION

If you were to fill Provo's LaVell Edwards Stadium to capacity with 65,000 local residents, then ask them where Buffalo Peak is, you might find only a handful who could point it out. From the valley floor, Buffalo Peak is a fairly nondescript rounded knoll, north of the more striking Squaw Peak and west of Cascade Peak. It doesn't appear in the USGS Geographic Names Information System database, yet at 8,025 feet in elevation, it's higher than many popular peaks on the Wasatch Front. It's unfortunate that this peak has gone unrecognized for so long, because Buffalo Peak stands out as one of the best short hikes in Utah County. You'll enjoy an easy stroll to some dazzling views, all against the solitude of a mountainous backdrop.

At the unmarked trailhead, you can park at the side of the dirt road and easily crawl over or under the log fence. You almost feel like you're sneaking onto private property, but the hike lies within the Uinta-Wasatch-Cache National Forest. From

DISTANCE & CONFIGURATION: 1-mile out-and-back

DIFFICULTY: Easy

SCENERY: Sweeping views of Utah Valley and surrounding peaks

EXPOSURE: Partially shaded

TRAIL TRAFFIC: Light

TRAIL SURFACE: Dirt with shale near summit

HIKING TIME: 30 minutes–1 hour

DRIVING DISTANCE: 46 miles from I-15/I-80 intersection

ELEVATION CHANGE: 7,738'–8,025'

ACCESS: Daily, sunrise–sunset; no fees or permits.

Squaw Peak Road/FS 027, which leads to the trailhead, is closed to cars late fall–late spring but is accessible by snowmobile.

WHEELCHAIR ACCESS: None

MAPS: USGS *Bridal Veil Falls*

FACILITIES: None

CONTACT: 801-785-3563, fs.usda.gov/uwcnf

LOCATION: Squaw Peak Road/FS 027 about 7.3 miles south of US 189, Provo Canyon, UT 84604

COMMENTS: You'll enjoy this trail most on a clear day in late spring with wildflowers in bloom, or in early fall as trees start to turn colors at high elevations. Bring a camera or binoculars. Dogs allowed on leash.

the fence, continue up the trail through a grassy meadow sprinkled in spring with violet-blue larkspur and yellow bursts of wyethia.

Deer and cougars visit these dry mountain slopes infrequently. Ground squirrels prove to be more-active inhabitants, and with some luck you'll see a black-headed grosbeak or mountain chickadee.

At 100 yards, the trail leaves the grassy clearing and enters a clump of aspen and oak. As the trail continues its gradual ascent, you come to some early partial views of Utah Valley below, with the trail laid out clearly ahead of you. Be sure, however, to turn around as you ascend the slope.

The best views from this trail are not of Utah Valley but rather of the mountains and hills to the north and west. In fall you'll be rewarded with a seemingly endless spread of colorful hillsides that you're unlikely to soon forget. Along the trail you will spot a few campsites. Even though the hike is short, its lack of notoriety makes this a quick and convenient getaway for Utah Valley residents looking for a quiet night under the stars.

At 0.3 mile a trail forks to the right, but your summit lies directly ahead. Soon the trail dramatically steepens, as the path is sprinkled with chips of shale. The final 0.1-mile push to the summit requires you to negotiate a steep slope of shale and dirt.

Even though the final stretch is short, the strenuous push gives hikers equipped with cameras the perfect excuse to stop and snap some photos of the mountains behind and the valley below, while their pulse returns to a more manageable rate.

After just 0.5 mile of walking from the trailhead, you come to the Buffalo Peak summit, a balding shale outcrop crowned with curly-leaf mountain mahogany, maple, and Gambel oak. In autumn, these hillsides take on the look of a patchwork quilt with lemon-colored aspen, fiery maples, and golden oaks. Take in the excellent views stretching from Mount Nebo on the south to the Salt Lake Valley on the

Buffalo Peak

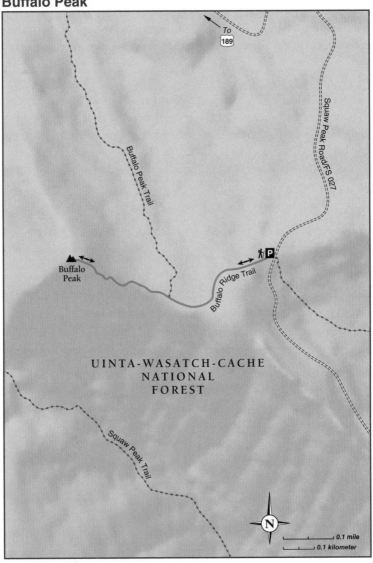

To
189

Squaw Peak Road/FS 027

Buffalo Peak Trail

Buffalo
Peak

Buffalo Ridge Trail

UINTA-WASATCH-CACHE
NATIONAL
FOREST

Squaw Peak Trail

N

0.1 mile
0.1 kilometer

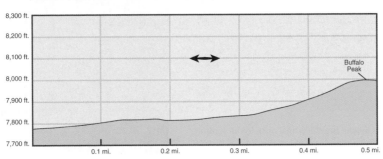

8,300 ft.
8,200 ft.
8,100 ft.
8,000 ft.
7,900 ft.
7,800 ft.
7,700 ft.

Buffalo
Peak

0.1 mi.   0.2 mi.   0.3 mi.   0.4 mi.   0.5 mi.

north. You overlook Squaw Peak (7,877') directly to the south, with the summit of Cascade Peak (10,760') directly to the east, just 1.6 miles away as the crow flies.

NEARBY ACTIVITIES

Utah Valley's traditional lovers' lane, the **Squaw Peak Overlook** is a mandatory stop on your way to or from Buffalo Peak. At an elevation of 6,707 feet, it's the perfect drive-to viewpoint for day or evening views of the valley below. From the signed intersection of Squaw Peak Road/Forest Service Road 027 and FS 199, about 0.3 mile west of Hope Campground, turn right on FS 199 and continue 0.3 mile to the overlook parking area.

• •

GPS TRAILHEAD COORDINATES N40° 16.973' W111° 36.313'

DIRECTIONS From the southern intersection of I-215 and I-15 in Salt Lake City, take I-15 South about 27 miles to Exit 272 for UT 52/800 North. Keep left at the fork; then turn left onto West 800 North, and drive 3.7 miles. Use the left lane to take the ramp onto US 189 North, and drive 1.9 miles; then turn right onto Squaw Peak Road/FS 027. Drive 4.1 miles; then bear left at the intersection, following the signs for Hope Campground. Drive 0.4 miles to where the pavement ends, and then continue an additional 2.9 miles on the dirt road to the unmarked trailhead, with a log-rail fence on the right and a fire-prevention sign on the left side of the road. Note that this unpaved stretch of road is rough and bumpy, so drive carefully (a high-clearance vehicle would be helpful here).

Hikers ascend the steep final push to the summit.

Goats hang out on the upper reaches of Squaw Peak.

ONE OF THE MOST POPULAR SUMMIT HIKES in Utah County, the climb to the top of Squaw Peak offers memorable highlights such as the dramatic rock walls of Rock Canyon, a climb through a wooded hillside, and panoramic views from the summit. You'll particularly enjoy the hike after the aspens have leafed out in the spring or when they turn a fiery yellow in the fall.

DESCRIPTION

At just 7,876 feet in elevation, Squaw Peak is considered one of the lesser peaks of the Wasatch Range, but it cuts an unmistakable profile as it rises above the craggy cliffs on Provo's east bench. It's also one of the most deservedly popular day hikes on the Wasatch Front.

The trail to the summit can be broken into three distinctive chunks: the canyon approach, the hillside ascent, and the summit stretch. Each section has its own characteristic appeal, and all combine to form a challenging hike offering varied features and highlights. The first 1.5 miles follow the Rock Canyon Trail (060) east up Rock Canyon; then the route turns north onto the Squaw Peak Trail to the summit.

From the large trailhead parking lot, the trail is paved for the first 0.4 mile as it leads toward the mouth of Rock Canyon through a covering of sage and Gambel oak. After a few hundred feet, the asphalt road forks. The forks (one asphalt, the other surfaced

DISTANCE & CONFIGURATION: 7-mile out-and-back

DIFFICULTY: Moderate

SCENERY: Rock formations, canyon, hillside forest, mountain meadow, panoramic views at summit

EXPOSURE: Mostly shaded

TRAIL TRAFFIC: Busy

TRAIL SURFACE: Paved for first 0.4 mile, rocky for next 1.2 miles, then dirt to summit

HIKING TIME: 3.5–5 hours

DRIVING DISTANCE: 41 miles from I-15/ I-80 intersection

ELEVATION CHANGE: 5,167'–7,876'

ACCESS: Daily, sunrise–sunset; no fees or permits

WHEELCHAIR ACCESS: None

MAPS: USGS *Bridal Veil Falls*

FACILITIES: Restrooms and water at trailhead

CONTACT: 801-785-3563, fs.usda.gov/uwcnf

LOCATION: Just east of the intersection of 2300 North and 1450 East, Provo, UT 84604

COMMENTS: The mouth of Rock Canyon provides a great place to watch or participate in rock climbing. Dogs allowed on leash.

with roadbed) soon rejoin, but bear right if you want to stay on the surfaced road. Easy access to some great routes makes Rock Canyon one of the most popular rock-climbing areas in Utah County. The first rock face on your right is the popular Black Rose wall, with Red Slab to the right. Just after the pavement ends, the trail passes through a metal gate and leads to a small cove of climbing faces on the right called The Kitchen.

Beyond the gate, the rocky trail steadily ascends the dry creekbed and passes through a wide canyon. At 0.5 mile past the gate, you'll come to the first of five wooden footbridges crossing the creek. At this point, with the higher elevation, conifers first appear.

On the north side of the creek, at 1.1 miles past the Kitchen gate, you'll come to a brown plastic flap-pole Forest Service sign indicating a trail up the hillside draw to the left, known as the First Left Fork. This begins the second chunk of the hike—the hillside ascent—which begins at an elevation of 6,100 feet. After 1.1 miles of steady climbing, you'll reach a meadow at 7,240 feet. No switchbacks offer relief. But the trail surface is well worn and smooth, and the setting is a thick forest of Gambel oaks and quaking aspens. The climb is steep, the experience rewarding.

In the hillside forest you may spot deer and small cats. Mountain lions and even bears make an occasional appearance in Rock Canyon, but they are rare. You're much more likely to see mountain chickadees—which often nest and breed above 8,000 feet—along the hillside trail in spring and summer.

Crossing the high meadow begins the third chunk of the hike—the summit stretch. The trail curves to the left along the southern rim of the meadow through a stand of aspens. Leaving the meadow, the path now heads south toward the summit ahead. You'll climb steadily, but the trail is not quite as steep as the hillside section behind you.

On the way to the summit, the oak cover becomes shorter and juniper dots the hillside. Here you'll first glimpse both the valley to the east and the higher peaks

Squaw Peak

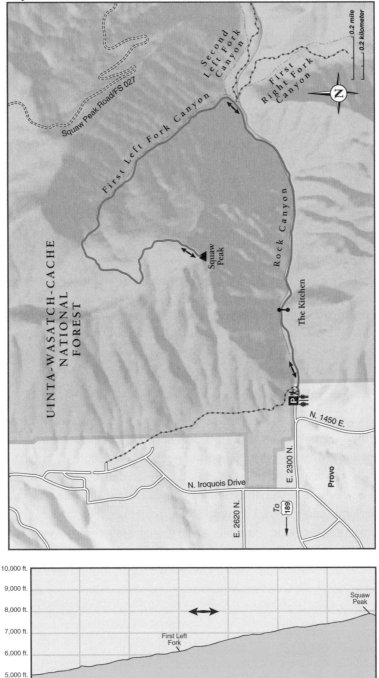

to the west (which are snowcapped well into June). Deer often graze above the meadow; you may even spot them at or near the summit.

Generally, Utah Valley to the west provides the most popular view from the summit. You may feel like you're looking straight down at the trail below, and, interestingly, the trail near the mouth of the canyon is about 2,500 feet to the south, with a vertical drop of 2,700 feet. On most days, you can see Mount Nebo to the south and Mount Timpanogos to the north.

As long as you're taking in the panorama, don't forget the peaks behind you to the east. Cascade Mountain (10,908') is the rounded peak with the striated face to the northeast. Lightning Peak is the triangular (11,044') peak in the background to the east, and Provo Peak (11,068') is in the forefront to the southeast. Squaw Peak's summit offers plenty of large, flat rocks that make the perfect table for a summer picnic with a view.

NEARBY ACTIVITIES

With its steep ascents, Squaw Peak supplies a good workout in spring, summer, and fall. During the winter, you may be relegated to **Brigham Young University**'s indoor jogging track in the Smith Fieldhouse. Near the corner of 1060 North and 150 East in Provo, the fieldhouse also hosts BYU volleyball games and other events.

• •

GPS TRAILHEAD COORDINATES N40° 15.879' W111° 37.791'

DIRECTIONS The trail begins at the mouth of Rock Canyon, about 0.4 mile east of the LDS Temple in Provo. From the southern intersection of I-215 and I-15 in Salt Lake City, take I-15 South about 29 miles to Exit 269, and turn left onto UT 265 East/West University Parkway. Drive 3.2 miles; then turn left onto 2230 North, and drive 1.2 miles. Turn left onto North Temple Drive/2300 North; then, in 0.8 mile, continue forward onto the Rock Canyon entrance road. The trailhead parking lot is just ahead on your left.

The view from the Y showcases the Brigham Young University campus and the Utah Valley beyond.

THE IMMENSE CONCRETE LETTER *Y* on the mountainside directly east of Brigham Young University in Provo is visible for miles around Utah Valley. The trail to the Y is a series of a dozen switchbacks offering splendid views of the valley along the way. It's a popular workout or training hike.

DESCRIPTION

At 380 feet high and 130 feet wide, Y Mountain's namesake is the largest collegiate symbol in the US—even larger than the HOLLYWOOD sign in the Los Angeles hills. While it can be seen throughout much of Utah Valley, it's also a great place from which to view the valley itself.

The trailhead also provides public access to the Bonneville Shoreline Trail and to the extended Y Mountain Trail for those hikers wanting to continue beyond the Y and on to the summit.

The wide, well-marked trail is a series of 10 steep switchbacks leading to the bottom of the Y, plus three more for those continuing to the top of the Y. Interpretive signs at each turn provide light-hearted encouragement alongside information about the local wildlife. The trail is on private land owned by BYU up to the second switchback, after which you enter Uinta-Wasatch-Cache National Forest. The city of Provo maintains the trailhead parking area.

DISTANCE & CONFIGURATION: 2.2-mile out-and-back

DIFFICULTY: Moderate

SCENERY: Continuous views of Utah Valley below

EXPOSURE: No shade

TRAIL TRAFFIC: Busy

TRAIL SURFACE: Compacted dirt and rock

HIKING TIME: 1–2 hours

DRIVING DISTANCE: 44 miles from I-15/I-80 intersection

ELEVATION CHANGE: 5,148'–6,221'

ACCESS: Daily, sunrise–sunset; no fees or permits. Ample free parking at trailhead.

WHEELCHAIR ACCESS: None

MAPS: USGS *Provo*

FACILITIES: Restrooms and water at trailhead

CONTACT: 801-785-3563, fs.usda.gov/uwcnf

LOCATION: 0.2 mile southeast of Terrace Drive, Provo, UT 84604

COMMENTS: This popular trail is well trod by local families and BYU students. Short but steep. Dogs allowed on leash.

Because the trail ascends more than 1,000 feet in just over a mile, this is a popular workout hike, with many residents climbing the path several times a week. No bikes are allowed on the trail, so hikers can move at their own pace and not feel chased. Throughout the hike you have views of the valley below, with no trees to block the view—or the afternoon sun. In the heat of summer you'll see why this hike is popular in the early morning, before the sun crests over the peaks above.

The first two switchbacks are the longest and cover nearly 0.4 mile. For those climbing to the top of the Y, the sign at the 5th switchback marks the halfway point for both distance and elevation gain. The 10th switchback is a good rest stop where you can study the photographic panel identifying local peaks and landmarks in the valley below. From this point it's another 0.1 mile to the bottom of the Y. Finally, taking just three more short switchbacks 0.3 mile up the mountain leads you to the top of the Y.

Y Mountain juts out from the western slopes of the Wasatch Range to deliver sweeping views of Utah Valley, from Mount Nebo in the south to Lone Peak in the north. Across Utah Lake to the northwest are the Oquirrh Mountains, and the Lake Mountains rise up from the western shores of Utah Lake. The freestanding mountain on the southwest shore of Utah Lake is West Mountain.

The Y was first placed on the mountain in 1906 and enhanced in 1907 with a layer of rock. In 1911 it was enlarged to its present size and fortified with a base of rock, sand, and concrete. Viewed straight-on from the air, the letter appears elongated, but it was designed that way so it would look normal from the valley floor. In order to reduce both ongoing maintenance costs and the risk of falling, hikers are encouraged not to climb onto the Y itself.

Scrubby Gambel oak, sage, and grasses cover the mountain slope. Because the trail is steep and lacks dense vegetation, hikers must stay on the path to minimize erosion. While the trail is steep, it's safe even for young children, with most drop-offs protected by log-rail fencing.

Y Mountain

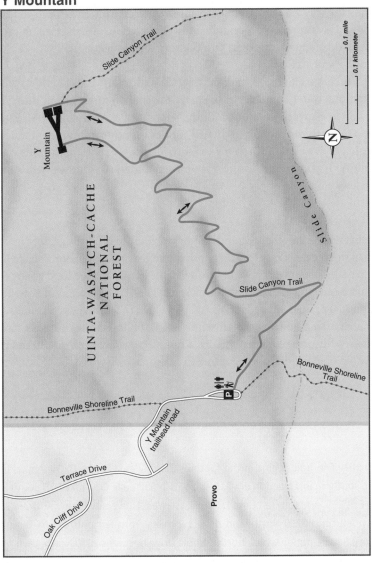

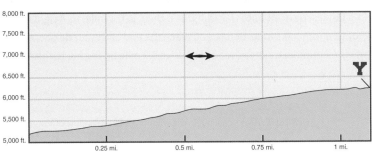

Along the way, chukars frequently cross the trail from their nests in the brush. Magpies and jays appear year-round at lower elevations. Deer graze on the mountain slopes throughout the year, and bighorn sheep occasionally make their way down to the trail area.

Most hikers make the Y their destination and return the way they came up. If you have time, water, and energy to spare, the trail continues from the Y, heading south to Slide Canyon, then north to the summit of Y Mountain at 8,569 feet. It's another 3 miles to the summit (a total of 8 miles round-trip from the trailhead). For those going to the summit, it's nice to know that the steepest part of the trail is all below the Y. If you go just to the Y, you've had a great workout with some well-earned views along the way.

NEARBY ACTIVITIES

The **Brigham Young University** campus sprawls below the trailhead. After you've hiked to the Y, a stop at the Creamery on Ninth for an ice cream cone or a shake is a well-deserved guilty pleasure. The Wilkinson Center houses a large food court, the BYU Store, and a bowling alley on the lower level. The BYU Museum of Art showcases an exceptional permanent collection and plays host to world-class traveling exhibits. The Monte L. Bean Life Science Museum (645 E. Phillips Lane) houses a fascinating and extensive display of animal life. It's a fun place where both adults and children can view regional wildlife and big game from around the world.

• •

GPS TRAILHEAD COORDINATES N40° 14.690' W111° 37.632'

DIRECTIONS The trail begins in the foothills directly east of the BYU campus in Provo. From the southern intersection of I-215 and I-15 in Salt Lake City, take I-15 South about 29 miles to Exit 269, and turn left onto UT 265 East/West University Parkway. Drive 3.2 miles; then turn left onto 2230 North, and drive 1.2 miles. Turn left onto North Temple Drive, and drive 0.8 mile, during which North Temple Drive becomes 2300 North; then bear right onto 1450 East where the entrance road into Rock Canyon (see previous hike) continues straight. In 1.1 miles, turn left onto Oak Cliff Drive; then, in 0.1 mile, turn right onto Terrace Drive, and drive another 0.1 mile. Before you reach the end of the cul-de-sac, turn left onto the unmarked Y Mountain trailhead road, and drive 0.2 mile up the hill to the parking area.

OPPOSITE: Hikers chill out in the wildflower-filled shadow of Mount Timpanogos.
(See Hikes 46 and 47, pages 210 and 214.)   Photo: Greg Witt

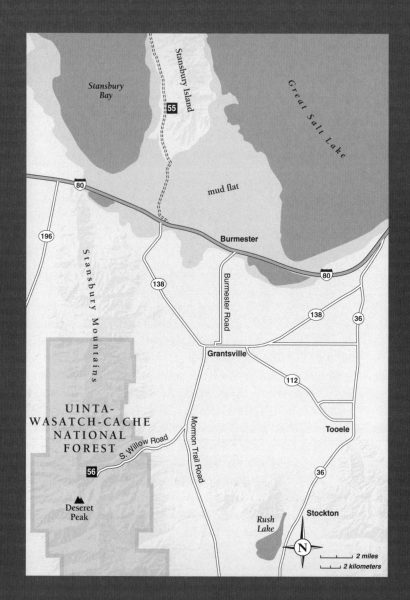

WEST
(Tooele County)

Salt-evaporation ponds lie to the south as Deseret Peak (see next hike) rises in the distance. *Photo: Greg Witt*

STANSBURY ISLAND PROVIDES a fascinating glimpse into the geology and natural history of the Great Salt Lake. This loop hike gains all of its elevation in the first mile before following the ancient shoreline of a much larger lake. Solitude, salt, and sweeping lake views define the experience.

DESCRIPTION

When Jim Bridger first saw the Great Salt Lake on an expedition in the winter of 1823–24, he thought it was an arm of the Pacific Ocean. In reality, the Great Salt Lake is the remnant of Lake Bonneville, a much larger prehistoric freshwater lake that was the size of Lake Michigan and covered most of northern Utah. Unless you're armed with some knowledge of the ancient Bonneville shoreline, this could be a fairly mundane desert hike. Let's take a moment to review.

About 15,000 years ago, the elevation of Lake Bonneville was about 5,200 feet. This shoreline left a visible "bench," which is prominent along much of the Wasatch Front. Then, about 14,500 years ago, the lake washed away a natural dam near Red Rock Pass in southeastern Idaho, which resulted in a catastrophic flood, draining the lake to a much smaller size. Over the course of a year, the Lake Bonneville shoreline dropped to a lower level, known as the Provo shoreline, which had an elevation of about 4,840 feet—380 feet lower than the earlier Bonneville shoreline.

DISTANCE & CONFIGURATION: 9.5-mile loop

DIFFICULTY: Moderate

SCENERY: Great Salt Lake, geology of Lake Bonneville shoreline

EXPOSURE: No shade

TRAIL TRAFFIC: Light

TRAIL SURFACE: Dirt, rock

HIKING TIME: 3.5–4.5 hours

DRIVING DISTANCE: 46 miles from I-15/I-80 intersection

ELEVATION CHANGE: 4,275'–4,894'

ACCESS: Daily, sunrise–sunset; no fees or permits. Trail is open to hikers, cyclists, and equestrians.

MAPS: USGS *Corral Canyon* and *Plug Peak*

FACILITIES: None

WHEELCHAIR ACCESS: None

CONTACT: 801-539-4001, blm.gov/utah

LOCATION: Stansbury Island, on the Great Salt Lake west of Salt Lake City

COMMENTS: Driving to the trailhead, you'll pass salt-evaporation ponds. Morton, Cargill, and other companies extract about 2.5 million tons of salt from the lake annually. Dogs allowed off-leash.

Stansbury Island provides the best-preserved and most visible example of the Provo shoreline. Our hike follows this shoreline around the southern end of the island as it winds along the level contour of several large canyons.

When Howard Stansbury, a government surveyor, first explored the island in 1849, water entirely surrounded it. Since then, the Great Salt Lake has retreated from its 1875 high-water level, leaving Stansbury Island as a peninsula.

As you take the road to the trailhead, watch for the many migratory shorebirds found in the wetlands and pools at the south end of the lake. Once on the island, the shorebirds disappear, replaced by meadowlarks and other range and field birds.

From the trailhead, follow the trail to the south, across the alluvial plain and up a rocky slope. At 1.2 miles, you've arrived at the high elevation for the hike, just under 5,000 feet. After crossing the saddle, you drop a little more than 100 feet in elevation, and the trail begins its 4-mile love affair with the Provo shoreline. As the contour of the shoreline enters canyons and rounds hillsides, the trail never gains or loses more than 10 feet in elevation. It sticks with the shoreline until making its final descent back to lake level.

The first canyon you skirt is the fairly small Bomber Canyon. At 1.8 miles you come around the bend to enter Tabbys Canyon. After following the deep and clearly visible shoreline contour of Tabbys Canyon for 2.8 miles, you round the hillside to wide-open views of the Great Salt Lake and the Oquirrh Mountains to the east. To the south are the Stansbury Mountains and Deseret Peak..

At 5.2 miles you'll find yourself at the head of No Name Canyon, on the southeast side of the island. At a fork in the trail, take the faint path to the right that descends the slope directly for 0.5 mile to a jeep road that loops back to the trailhead along the flat desert terrain just above lake level.

Once you reach the dirt road, the signs do a good job of guiding you back to the trailhead, although it's a pretty intuitive route. If you want to avoid hiking on jeep

Stansbury Island

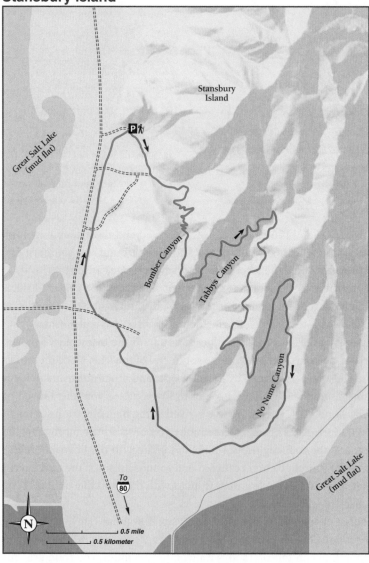

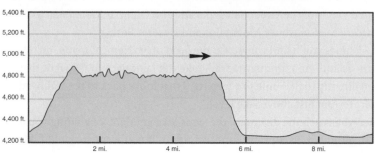

trails, you can leave a shuttle vehicle at the mouth of No Name Canyon and make this a one-way 6.4-mile hike.

Stansbury Island offers a field course in geology. Along the way you'll pass outcrops of shale, limestone, quartzite, and conglomerates that look for all the world like concrete—but they're not. The calcium carbonate deposits that form much of the Provo shoreline, known as tufa rock, were formed by precipitation from the high dissolved-calcium content of Lake Bonneville. Tufa rock was used to construct many early Utah homes in areas such as Bountiful and Pleasant Grove.

Although the trail is hikable year-round, the best time to visit is in early spring, when the sheep grass is green and the sage and juniper are at their most aromatic. By mid-May, the range grasses have turned dry and brown in the desert heat.

With every step of the hike, you'll have great views of the Great Salt Lake and distant mountains. To the south you'll be looking down on the evaporation ponds used for the commercial production of salt. More than 4.5 billion tons of salt are dissolved and suspended in the Great Salt Lake, which has no outlet. About 2.2 million tons of salt enter the lake annually from surface and ground-water flow, while commercial extraction yields about 2.5 million tons of salt and other elements from the lake each year. As you look out over a lake that was once 1,000 feet deep, it's interesting to note that today the Great Salt Lake has a maximum depth of only 35 feet, with an average depth of just 14 feet.

NEARBY ACTIVITIES

On the shores of the Great Salt Lake, **Saltair** (435-243-7258, thesaltair.com) is a former beach resort that was once described as "the Coney Island of the West." Today it hosts concerts and special events. To the west of Saltair is **Great Salt Lake State Park,** whose amenities include camping, hiking, a seasonal restaurant, and a marina (801-828-0787, stateparks.utah.gov/parks/great-salt-lake).

• •

GPS TRAILHEAD COORDINATES N40° 48.377' W112° 31.234'

DIRECTIONS From the western intersection of I-80 and I-215 in Salt Lake City, take I-80 West about 33 miles to Exit 84 for UT 138/Grantsville; turn left onto the access road, following the signs for Stansbury Island. Drive 7.2 miles, during which this road quickly becomes Stansbury Island Road. Turn right and follow a dirt road 0.2 mile to the Bureau of Land Management trailhead.

Note: If on the access road you come to a cattle grate followed by a NO TRESPASSING sign, you've gone too far north—turn around and go back 0.4 mile to the dirt road leading to the trailhead.

Deseret's 11,031-foot summit towers over other peaks in the vicinity.

Photo: Greg Witt

AT 11,031 FEET, Deseret Peak is the highest point in Tooele County and the centerpiece of the Deseret Peak Wilderness Area. It's also a magnificent expanse of both semiarid and alpine scenery—glacial basins, mountain streams, woodland, and high meadows—rising from the middle of the desert. This loop hike captures some of that surprising variety and affords views across the Bonneville Salt Flats and into Nevada.

DESCRIPTION

The Great Basin, which covers western Utah and most of Nevada, consists of dozens of north-to-south-trending mountain ranges and basins. Best known for their impact on local weather patterns and their jagged profile revealed with each sunset, the Oquirrh Mountains bound the Salt Lake Valley on the west. The Stansbury Mountains, which lie just to the west of the Oquirrhs and Tooele Valley, don't attract as much attention. Wasatch hikers rarely climb Deseret Peak, the jewel of the Stansbury Mountains. And that's a shame, because the area has so much to offer.

The drive to the trailhead captures the transformation from desert to mountain as the road ascends an alluvial plain into the mouth of the canyon. You'll drive through two narrows with barely enough room for both the road and the stream to pass through the high rock walls rising above. Nearing the trailhead, you're likely to

DISTANCE & CONFIGURATION: 8.5-mile balloon

DIFFICULTY: Strenuous

SCENERY: Wooded approach, high-mountain terrain, excellent views

EXPOSURE: Mostly shaded below 10,000', fully exposed above 10,000'

TRAIL TRAFFIC: Light

TRAIL SURFACE: Dirt, rock

HIKING TIME: 5–7 hours

DRIVING DISTANCE: 50 miles from I-15/I-80 intersection

ELEVATION CHANGE: 7,428'–11,031'

ACCESS: Daily, sunrise–sunset; FS 171/South Willow Canyon Road, which leads to the trailhead, is closed late fall–late spring but is open to snowmobilers and other winter-recreation seekers. No fees or permits.

MAPS: USGS *Deseret Peak East* and *Deseret Peak West*

FACILITIES: Restrooms at trailhead

WHEELCHAIR ACCESS: None

CONTACT: 801-733-2660, fs.usda.gov/uwcnf

LOCATION: Loop Campground, FS 171/S. Willow Canyon Rd., Dugway, UT 84022

COMMENTS: Most of the hike past the trailhead lies within the Deseret Peak Wilderness Area, where motorized vehicles and bicycles are prohibited. Dogs allowed on leash.

see wild turkeys and deer along the roadside. On its way to the trailhead, the road gains nearly 2,500 feet of elevation, giving hikers a good head start on the summit.

From the trailhead, a dense forest of aspen and conifers quickly immerses you. This section of the trail provides a vivid example of the aspen-to-conifer succession cycle. Aspen appear early in a woodland life cycle. Conifers, which initially are shaded and protected by aspen, eventually shade out the aspens. Many of the large, mature aspens have fallen in this area, while the conifers remain.

At 0.7 mile from the trailhead, you'll reach a stream crossing. Immediately after the crossing, the trail dips momentarily before coming to a sign and trail junction. Take the trail on the left to Deseret Peak. This junction marks the start of a clockwise loop that will take you up one drainage, along much of the Deseret Peak ridgeline to the summit, and then bring you back by way of another drainage.

At 1.1 miles from the trailhead, you'll enter the lower level of Mill Fork, a large glacial valley ringed by Douglas-firs. The trail leads to the top of a steep glacial bowl, gaining nearly 2,200 feet of elevation in 2.3 miles. After a series of switchbacks near the top of the bowl, you'll arrive at the ridge and enjoy your first views of the Great Basin to the west. On this ridge, at a four-way junction, a sign points the way to Bear Fork on the left, Antelope Canyon directly ahead, and Deseret Peak to your right. Take the trail to the right as it leads almost directly up a shadeless slope to a higher rocky ridge. The trail skirts some false summits before arriving at the true summit nearly a mile from the junction. Along the way, you'll gain an appreciation for the hardy limber pines and subalpine firs that survive a tortured existence at 11,000 feet. In late spring and summer, wildflowers line the rocky trail all the way to the summit.

You'll share the summit with cliff swallows as they swoop and dart around the rocky ledges. Because the Stansbury Mountains are an isolated, stand-alone range,

Deseret Peak

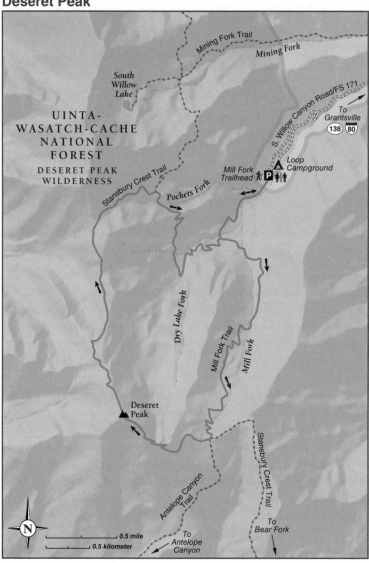

UINTA-WASATCH-CACHE NATIONAL FOREST

DESERET PEAK WILDERNESS

Mining Fork Trail

Mining Fork

South Willow Lake

S. Willow Canyon Road/FS 171

To Grantsville

138 80

Loop Campground

Mill Fork Trailhead

Stansbury Crest Trail

Pockets Fork

Dry Lake Fork

Mill Fork Trail

Mill Fork

Deseret Peak

Antelope Canyon Trail

Stansbury Crest Trail

To Bear Fork

To Antelope Canyon

N

0.5 mile
0.5 kilometer

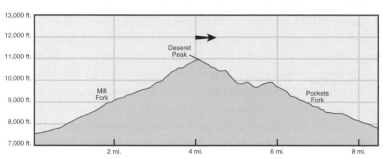

Deseret Peak has nothing nearby to block the view. On a clear day, which in summer is nearly every day, you can see Pilot Peak in Nevada more than 60 miles to the northwest. Mount Nebo is visible to the southeast.

Most Wasatch peak-baggers never see the Bonneville Salt Flats from a summit, but they're easily viewed from Deseret Peak. This 6,000-square-mile bed of salt, known as the flattest place on earth, is the site of numerous land speed records.

To make the return loop, continue north as you descend along the summit ridge. After 0.3 mile, the trail drops well below the ridge on the west side. When you've hiked 1.5 miles from the summit, the trail makes a sharp turn to the right and continues its descent of the east side of the ridge in a series of short switchbacks. At 2.2 miles from the summit, having descended Pockets Fork, you'll come to a sign pointing to South Willow Lake to the left and Loop Campground, your return route, to the right. As the trail sweeps along a bowl, making a gradual descent, you'll have picture-postcard views of the ridge above and to the west. Soon you enter the familiar aspen–spruce woodland that leads back to the stream-crossing junction and down to the trailhead.

The Deseret Peak loop offers abundant scenery, a real appreciation for the immense size of the wilderness area, and a sense of how much is available to explore.

NEARBY ACTIVITIES

The Tooele Valley is home to the **Deseret Peak Complex** (2930 UT 112 W., Grantsville; 435-843-4020 or visit deseretpeakcomplex.com). This multipurpose public recreation venue features one of Utah's largest swimming pools as well as professionally designed and maintained tracks for motocross, BMX, ATV, and horse racing. Within the complex you'll also find soccer fields, softball diamonds, pitch-and-putt golf, playgrounds, an archery park, indoor and outdoor arenas, pavilions, and two museums.

• •

GPS TRAILHEAD COORDINATES N40° 28.978' W112° 36.398'

DIRECTIONS From the western intersection of I-80 and I-215 in Salt Lake City, take I-80 West about 33 miles to Exit 84 for UT 138/Grantsville. Turn left onto the access road; then, in 0.3 mile, make another left onto UT 138 East, and drive 9.5 miles to Grantsville. Turn right onto South West Street, and drive 5.1 miles, during which West Street becomes Mormon Trail. Turn right onto Forest Service Road 171/South Willow Canyon Road, and drive about 7 miles to Loop Campground. Look for the Mill Fork trailhead at the top of the campground loop, to the right of the vault toilets.

Note: The last 4 miles of FS 171 are unpaved, and during the snowy season the road is closed where the pavement ends, in which case you'll need to park outside the gate.

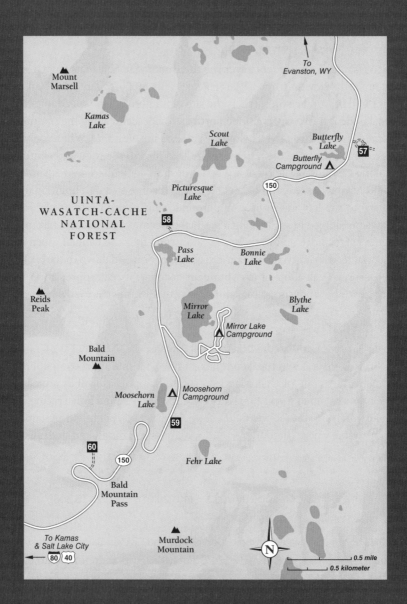

Mount
Marsell

Kamas
Lake

Scout
Lake

Butterfly
Lake

Butterfly
Campground

57

UINTA-
WASATCH-CACHE
NATIONAL
FOREST

Picturesque
Lake

150

58

Pass
Lake

Bonnie
Lake

Reids
Peak

Mirror
Lake

Blythe
Lake

Mirror Lake
Campground

Bald
Mountain

Moosehorn
Lake

Moosehorn
Campground

59

60

150

Fehr Lake

Bald
Mountain
Pass

To Kamas
& Salt Lake City

80   40

Murdock
Mountain

To
Evanston, WY

N

0.5 mile

0.5 kilometer

EAST
(Summit County and Uintas Mountains)

The Provo River begins humbly in the High Uintas.

ROLLING THROUGH A basin of woods, meadows, and scenic lakes, this hike lies almost entirely above 10,000 feet in elevation. While the complete loop with spur trails to nearby lakes can cover more than 20 miles, it can easily be adapted to a shorter 12-mile hike. But the gentle, flowing nature of the trail makes you want to go on to the next lake or meadow.

DESCRIPTION

The beauty of the Uinta Mountains is as likely to be found in its complex network of basins and drainages as in its quartzite peaks. Here, unlike the canyons of the Wasatch, you're never quite sure of where the water comes from or the direction in which it flows. Naturalist Basin, which lies east of the Mirror Lake Scenic Byway, generally flows south into the Duchesne River. But the rolling, meandering nature of the trail never makes that clearly visible to the hiker.

Naturalist Basin sits to the south of Mount Agassiz, named for the great Swiss-American naturalist Louis Agassiz. Most of the lakes in the basin were named after Agassiz's students at Harvard and Cornell, many of whom went on to become prominent scientists and naturalists in their own right: David Starr Jordan, Nathaniel Shaler, Joseph LeConte, Charles Walcott, and Alpheus Packard. Agassiz's legacy can be found in the names of many American species and natural landmarks.

DISTANCE & CONFIGURATION: 12- to 18-mile balloon

DIFFICULTY: Strenuous

SCENERY: Lakes and ponds, spruce forests, wildflowers, surrounding mountains

EXPOSURE: Mostly shaded to Naturalist Basin, fully exposed on upper basin above tree line

TRAIL TRAFFIC: Moderate

TRAIL SURFACE: Dirt, some rock

HIKING TIME: 6–10 hours

DRIVING DISTANCE: 74 miles from I-15/I-80 intersection

ELEVATION CHANGE: 10,376'–10,946'

ACCESS: Daily, sunrise–sunset. UT 150/Mirror Lake Scenic Byway, which leads to the trailhead, is closed to cars late fall–late spring but is open to snowmobilers and other winter-recreation seekers. Mirror Lake Scenic Byway is a U.S. Forest Service fee-charging area. Current access fees are $6/1–3 days, $12/week, and $45/year; pick up a recreation pass at the Kamas Ranger Station or at one of the self-service fee stations along the byway. America the Beautiful passes are also honored (see page 15).

MAPS: USGS *Hayden Peak;* Trails Illustrated *High Uintas Wilderness* (711)

FACILITIES: Restrooms, picnic tables, and drinking water at trailhead

WHEELCHAIR ACCESS: None

CONTACT: 435-783-4338, fs.usda.gov/uwcnf

LOCATION: UT 150 in Uinta-Wasatch-Cache National Forest east of Salt Lake City, about 21 miles south of the Utah–Wyoming state line

COMMENTS: Dogs allowed off-leash

Naturalist Basin is accessed from the Highline Trail (083), which crosses the Uintas from east to west. Almost all of the trail's 60-mile length is above 10,000 feet in elevation, and much of it is above tree line. The large trailhead parking area to the south serves hikers, while the parking area to the north has loading ramps and facilities for horses and stock.

From the trailhead, the trail descends 200 feet in elevation through a forest of Engelmann spruce to a junction with the Mirror Lake Trail at 0.7 mile. Continue on the Highline Trail to the southeast. At about 2 miles from the trailhead, you'll pass Scudder Lake to the south and continue another mile before arriving at a junction with the Packard Lake Trail (059), which leads south on a 1.4-mile optional spur to Wilder, Wyman, and Packard Lakes.

In these woods you're likely to see woodpeckers and pine grosbeaks. One species you're not likely to see is the bark beetle, an insect about the size of a piece of rice; but you'll certainly see the damage it's done to trees throughout the Uintas. Bark beetles are native insects that kill individual trees but do not threaten the entire tree species. Healthy trees normally produce enough defensive pitch to flush out the attacking beetles. But when trees are stressed and weakened, they're unable to produce sufficient amounts of pitch. In recent years, more trees have been killed by bark beetles than by forest fires.

Continuing along the Highline Trail for another 1.2 miles, you'll arrive at a marked junction where the trail forks. Go left and to the north into Naturalist Basin. (The Highline Trail continues to the right.) The trail makes a gradual ascent for about a mile into Naturalist Basin, eventually crossing a stream and arriving at an open meadow with a backdrop of Uinta cliffs and 12,428-foot Mount Agassiz to the northwest.

Naturalist Basin

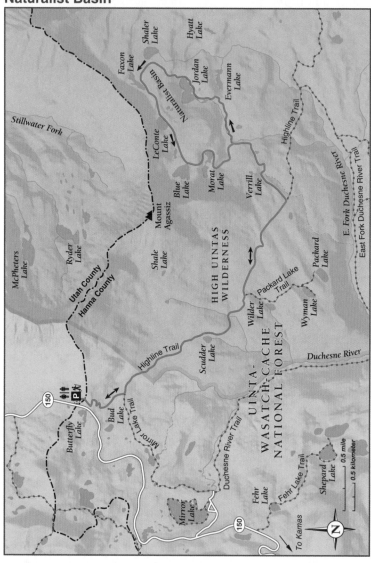

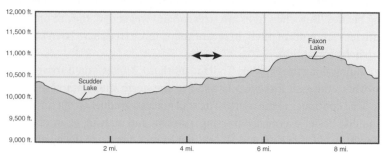

At this point, you've hiked a little more than 5 miles from the trailhead and you're at the edge of Naturalist Basin. Jordan Lake (10,625'), a popular fishing destination, is another mile up the trail to the northeast. Morat Lakes (10,757'), about a mile to the northwest, also attract the anglers. But if you got off to an early start and still have plenty of energy, consider taking the loop to the upper basin. Few hikers take this loop, as it ascends beyond the tree line into a more remote and rugged alpine ecosystem, but it is certainly worth the effort. To reach this upper basin, take a faint trail leading from the east side of Jordan Lake up a rocky slope to Shaler Lake (10,920'). As you ascend just 300 feet of elevation, you move from a subalpine to an alpine ecosystem, where everything changes. You'll find different animals, birds, wildflowers, and trees as you explore this high-alpine shelf.

From Shaler Lake, the loop continues on to Faxon Lake (10,946'), LeConte Lake (10,925'), Blue Lake (10,945'), and Morat Lakes (10,757'). Passing Morat Lakes, the trail descends 300 feet to return to the junction and stream crossing where you first entered Naturalist Basin. From here you can pick up the trail that returns you to the Highline Trail and on to the trailhead, another 5 miles to the west.

Naturalist Basin is popular but never really busy. The trail is well traveled but never crowded. It's relaxing, meandering, and therapeutic, and in spite of its long distance and high elevation it's suitable for hikers of various skill levels. For the most part the route is intuitive, but you should take a GPS or a map and compass, and be proficient in their use.

NEARBY ACTIVITIES

The **Samak Smoke House** is a favorite one-stop shopping destination for visitors to the Mirror Lake Scenic Byway. Just 2 miles east of Kamas at 1937 Mirror Lake Highway, the country store and restaurant is a convenient place to pick up your recreation pass and any provisions you might need for the hike. On the return trip, stop and try their famous jerky, and smoked salmon or trout. Shop for gifts and gourmet foods or dine out on the patio. For orders and information, call 435-783-4880 or shop online at samaksmokehouse.com.

• •

GPS TRAILHEAD COORDINATES N40° 43.325' W110° 51.842'

DIRECTIONS From the western intersection of I-80 and I-215 in Salt Lake City, take I-80 East about 17.5 miles to Exit 146 for Heber/Vernal. Follow the ramp onto US 40 East, and drive 3.2 miles. Take Exit 4 for Park City/Kamas, turn left onto UT 248 East, and drive 11.4 miles. Turn left onto Main Street in Kamas and, in 0.2 mile, turn right onto UT 150 East/East Center Street. Drive 34.2 miles to the Hayden Pass–Highline trailhead parking area on the right, just past mile marker 34.

Reaching elevations over 11,000 feet, this hike offers sweeping views of the valleys below.

LOFTY LAKE LOOP has something for everyone: lakes, streams, deep woods, meadows, ridge routes, mountain passes, and scenic views, all within a convenient loop. There are a few steep ascents and descents, but they're never too long. Some route-finding and map-reading are required, but it's never too challenging. The hike is well suited to families and children capable of hiking 4 miles over varied and sometimes rugged terrain. The entire hike is above 10,000 feet in elevation, so be on guard for symptoms of altitude sickness.

DESCRIPTION

Lofty Lake Loop is the perfect introduction to all of the scenic beauty that the Uinta Mountains have to offer. And because it's a loop hike (as you've probably already guessed), you never have to retrace your route. New territory and fresh sights wait around every corner.

The trail can be hiked in either direction, but the clockwise loop described here seems to be the general preference for several reasons: If you get an early start, the wildlife-viewing is likely to be better in the clockwise direction. Also, the steepest sustained grade on the trail occurs as a descent near the end if done clockwise. The trail leading clockwise from the trailhead to Kamas Lake generally offers more

DISTANCE & CONFIGURATION: 4.1-mile loop

DIFFICULTY: Moderate

SCENERY: Alpine lakes, streams, meadows, mountains

EXPOSURE: Mostly shaded below 10,500', partially shaded above 10,500'

TRAIL TRAFFIC: Moderate

TRAIL SURFACE: Dirt, rock

HIKING TIME: 3–4 hours

DRIVING DISTANCE: 73 miles from I-15/I-80 intersection

ELEVATION CHANGE: 10,154'–11,074'

ACCESS: Daily, sunrise–sunset. UT 150/Mirror Lake Scenic Byway, which leads to the trailhead, is closed to cars late fall–late spring but is open to snowmobilers and other winter-recreation seekers. Mirror Lake Scenic Byway is a U.S. Forest Service fee-charging area. Current access fees are $6/1–3 days, $12/week, and $45/year; pick up a recreation pass at the Kamas Ranger Station or at one of the self-service fee stations along the byway. America the Beautiful passes are also honored (see page 15).

MAPS: USGS *Mirror Lake;* Trails Illustrated *High Uintas Wilderness* (711)

FACILITIES: Restroom at trailhead

WHEELCHAIR ACCESS: None

CONTACT: 435-783-4338, fs.usda.gov/uwcnf

LOCATION: UT 150 in Uinta-Wasatch-Cache National Forest east of Salt Lake City, about 23 miles south of the Utah–Wyoming state line

COMMENTS: A section of trail passes through Camp Steiner, the highest-elevation Boy Scout camp in the United States. Dogs allowed off-leash.

solitude than the section from Lofty Lake back to the parking lot, which passes through the Boy Scout camp.

The trail starts near the restroom, at the southwest side of the parking lot, and ends just 100 feet away, on the north side of the lot. In addition to the Lofty Lake Trail, the trailhead serves the Weber River and Cuberant Lake Trails. You'll know you're on the right trail when, 50 feet into the woods, you come to a sign directing you to Holiday Park (7 miles) and Cuberant Lake (3 miles).

At this sign, take the trail to Holiday Park and Cuberant Lake, to the right. At 0.3 mile you'll come to another fork, where you'll take the Cuberant Lake Trail to the right. You'll find occasional muddy surfaces along these lower sections of the trail. Wildflowers abound all along the trail, with Parry's primrose and alpine asters among the most common. Watch for Queen Anne's lace with its bursts of tiny white flowers; as a member of the carrot family, it has leaves that look just like carrot tops.

At 0.7 mile the trail crosses a small brook, then skirts the north side of a large, open, marshy area known as Reids Meadow. At 0.9 mile you leave the meadow by climbing a rocky slope to the north. At 1.2 miles from the trailhead, you come to another fork in the trail pointing to Cuberant Lake on the left and Kamas and Lofty Lakes to the right. Continue up and to the right another 0.4 mile, along a rocky grade made up of chunky quartzite, and you'll soon arrive at a crest with Kamas Lake spread out immediately in front of you. The total distance from the trailhead to Kamas Lake is 1.6 miles. At this point you've descended just 150 feet from the trailhead to Reids Meadow, yet you've gained 520 feet in the climb up to Kamas Lake, at 10,520 feet in elevation.

Kamas Lake is a great place to rest before continuing on along the shore to a small man-made dam at the northwest end of the lake. From the dam, another steep,

Lofty Lake Loop

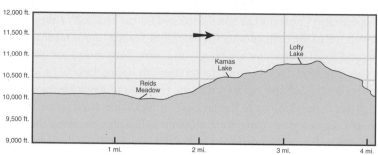

rocky ascent leads to a high meadow laced with small ponds and brooks and ringed with fir and spruce. Another steep ascent of a rocky slope leads to a crest above the meadow at an elevation of 10,700 feet and some dreamlike views of Teal, Cutthroat, and Jewel Lakes to the north.

At this midpoint, just 0.5 mile beyond Kamas Lake, the trail begins to head south, crossing a high-alpine plateau sprinkled with wildflowers and Engelmann spruce. At the south end of the plateau you'll come to a small rise before dipping down to Lofty Lake, a shimmering jewel ringed by wildflowers. At an elevation of 10,840 feet, Lofty Lake is 2.5 miles from the starting trailhead.

Leading away from Lofty Lake, the trail rises and peaks at an elevation of 10,920 feet along a rock outcrop. Below is Scout Lake, easily identifiable by the boat dock, which serves the Scouts at Camp Steiner. From this high elevation point, it's just 1.4 miles back to the parking lot, and nearly all of it is downhill. The steepest part is right in front of you as you descend 520 feet in elevation down a rocky slope to the shores of Scout Lake.

The area around Picturesque Lake, which lies immediately south of Scout Lake, can be buggy and is the only portion of the trail where insect repellent may come in handy, especially in July. As with other hikes in the Uintas, afternoon thundershowers can appear quickly. If you see a storm gathering, find the quickest and safest route possible leading away from high, rocky elevations and back to the trailhead.

Leaving Picturesque Lake, the trail crosses a camp service road and continues along a gentle descent back to the parking area.

NEARBY ACTIVITIES

For visitors on the Mirror Lake Scenic Byway, **Provo River Falls** is a must-see destination waterfall. It's actually a series of three distinct falls separated from each other by about 100 feet. From the parking and picnic area at the upper falls, take the paved trail to the second falls. An easy scramble leads to the river below the third falls. The falls parking area is on the left (west) side of the Mirror Lake Scenic Byway, just before milepost 24.

• •

GPS TRAILHEAD COORDINATES N40° 42.848' W110° 53.582'

DIRECTIONS From the western intersection of I-80 and I-215 in Salt Lake City, take I-80 East about 17.5 miles to Exit 146 for Heber/Vernal. Follow the ramp onto US 40 East, and drive 3.2 miles. Take Exit 4 for Park City/Kamas, turn left onto UT 248 East, and drive 11.4 miles. Turn left onto Main Street in Kamas and, in 0.2 mile, turn right onto UT 150 East/East Center Street. Drive 32 miles to the parking area for the Pass Lake trailhead, on the left (north) side of the road.

59 FEHR LAKE TRAIL

Area peaks loom large over this relatively low-elevation hike.

THE FEHR LAKE TRAIL descends along a route that skirts three alpine lakes and passes through woods and meadows, and along ponds and small streams. You can hike this trail as a short 1-mile stroll to Fehr Lake or continue to Shepard and Hoover Lakes for a 3-mile round-trip walk—all in the shadow of Murdock Mountain to the southwest.

DESCRIPTION

This Uintas classic explores descending tiers of charming, jewel-like lakes. The lakes along the Fehr Lake Trail are part of the Duchesne River drainage, which eventually flows into the Green River and on to the Colorado River. The lakes to the south of the Bald Mountain summit flow into the Provo River and down to Utah Lake before terminating in the Great Salt Lake. This short hike can also be used as the starting point of an extended backpacking trip deep into the High Uintas Wilderness.

From the trailhead parking area, the trail departs southeast across a small wooden bridge over a marshy meadow. Soon the trail leaves the meadow and drops into a forest of fir and Engelmann spruce. Along the way you'll be treated to splashes of blue gentian, shooting star, elephant head, Parry's primrose, and other brightly hued wildflowers.

DISTANCE & CONFIGURATION: 3.4-mile out-and-back

DIFFICULTY: Easy

SCENERY: Lakes and ponds, spruce forests, wildflowers, mountains

EXPOSURE: Mostly shaded

TRAIL TRAFFIC: Moderate

TRAIL SURFACE: Dirt, some rock

HIKING TIME: 1.5–3 hours

DRIVING DISTANCE: 70 miles from I-15/I-80 intersection

ELEVATION CHANGE: 10,377'– 9,220'

ACCESS: Daily, sunrise–sunset. UT 150/Mirror Lake Scenic Byway, which leads to the trailhead, is closed to cars late fall–late spring but is open to snowmobilers and other winter-recreation seekers. Mirror Lake Scenic Byway is a U.S. Forest Service fee-charging area. Current access fees are $6/1–3 days, $12/week, and $45/year; pick up

a recreation pass at the Kamas Ranger Station or at one of the self-service fee stations along the byway. America the Beautiful passes are also honored (see page 15).

MAPS: USGS *Mirror Lake;* Trails Illustrated *High Uintas Wilderness* (711)

FACILITIES: None at trailhead; water and restrooms across the highway at Moosehorn Campground

WHEELCHAIR ACCESS: None

CONTACT: 435-783-4338, fs.usda.gov/uwcnf

LOCATION: UT 150/Mirror Lake Scenic Byway in Uinta-Wasatch-Cache National Forest east of Salt Lake City, about 24 miles south of the Utah–Wyoming state line

COMMENTS: A rare mountain hike where the trailhead is at the higher elevation and each lake along the way takes you down the basin to a lower elevation—so save some energy for your return trip. Dogs allowed off-leash.

At first, the trail loses elevation slowly but noticeably. At 0.2 mile you come to an unmarked junction, where you continue on the trail as it bears right. After crossing two more wooden bridges, you'll arrive at the shore of Fehr Lake (10,273'), which is less than 0.4 mile from the trailhead.

As you loop around Fehr Lake's eastern shore, the trail becomes faint as it crosses a low meadow and departs the lake. As is the case with many of the hikes in the Mirror Lake region, insects can be a problem early in the season, so come prepared with appropriate repellent.

At 1 mile from the trailhead, a small pond appears on the left. The trail soon drops along a rocky channel, the rate of descent increasing as it enters the basin holding Shepard Lake. It's easy to lose the trail in this wooded stretch, but as long as you keep descending, you'll be on course. Soon, at 1.4 miles from the trailhead, you arrive at Shepard Lake (9,987'), a body of water about twice the size of Fehr Lake.

As you skirt the northeast shore of Shepard Lake, the trail leaves the lake and, just 100 feet east, rises to a small crest. Looking down the slope, you'll see the largest of the three lakes, Hoover Lake (9,220'), through the trees. Within 3 minutes you'll be at its shore. At this point you'll have hiked 1.7 miles from the trailhead.

The lakes are all stocked with fish, including arctic grayling, brook trout, brown trout, rainbow trout, and cutthroat trout. On a busy weekend, you are likely to see anglers at each of the lakes along the trail (and any of the lakes that dot the Mirror Lake region of the High Uintas). If you have the mandatory license, be sure to bring

Fehr Lake Trail

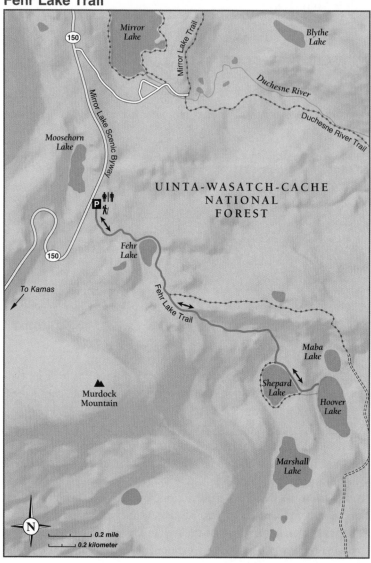

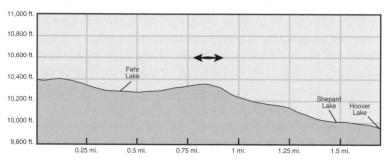

along your fishing rod, and add another dimension to your enjoyment of the region. Beyond the aquatic life, common sights around the lakes include deer and moose, chipmunks, ground squirrels, and the occasional black bear.

High Uinta trails are notoriously winding and exceptionally scenic. Fehr Lake provides the perfect opportunity to dip into this lush wooded land of glistening alpine lakes.

NEARBY ACTIVITIES

As the Mirror Lake Scenic Byway passes through the western Uintas from Kamas, Utah, to Evanston, Wyoming, you'll find dozens of easily accessible developed campgrounds and inviting picnic areas for both day and overnight use. Additionally, you can choose from among hundreds of primitive backcountry campsites throughout the general forest area, many just a mile or two from the highway. For camping reservations, call 877-444-6777 or visit recreation.gov.

• •

GPS TRAILHEAD COORDINATES N40° 41.572' W110° 53.503'

DIRECTIONS From the western intersection of I-80 and I-215 in Salt Lake City, take I-80 East about 17.5 miles to Exit 146 for Heber/Vernal. Follow the ramp onto US 40 East, and drive 3.2 miles. Take Exit 4 for Park City/Kamas, turn left onto UT 248 East, and drive 11.4 miles. Turn left onto Main Street in Kamas and, in 0.2 mile, turn right onto UT 150 East/East Center Street. Drive 30.4 miles to a small, unpaved, unmarked parking area, on the right—if you see the Moosehorn Campground entrance on your left, you've gone about 100 yards too far.

The approach to Bald Mountain is steep and strewn with boulders.

WITH A CONVENIENT TRAILHEAD and a well-groomed trail to the summit, Bald Mountain is an ideal climb, especially for children and inexperienced hikers who want to experience the thrill of climbing a high mountain summit. A National Recreation Trail recognized for its outstanding scenery, the Bald Mountain Trail offers wildflowers and breathtaking views of lakes and surrounding peaks in the High Uintas.

DESCRIPTION

The Uinta Mountains are part of a rare mountain range in the Western Hemisphere that runs east–west rather than north–south. At the western edge of the Uintas, Bald Mountain is a freestanding rounded peak that begs to be climbed. With a summit elevation of 11,943 feet, it's the most easily accessible high peak in Utah, higher than any peak in the Wasatch Range, and well worth climbing. Other Uinta peaks to the east are higher—including the highest point in Utah, 13,528-foot Kings Peak—but none are more suitable for a day hike.

Bald Mountain provides more than just bragging rights for making it to the top, though. It delivers spectacular summit views and gives hikers the opportunity to move from a subalpine environment to a high-alpine zone while experiencing an amazing variety of wildflowers along the way. A herd of mountain goats

DISTANCE & CONFIGURATION: 3-mile out-and-back

DIFFICULTY: Moderate

SCENERY: Wildflowers, high-alpine vegetation, exceptional Uintas views from summit

EXPOSURE: No shade

TRAIL TRAFFIC: Busy

TRAIL SURFACE: Dirt, rock

HIKING TIME: 1.5–3 hours

DRIVING DISTANCE: 69 miles from I-15/ I-80 intersection

ELEVATION CHANGE: 10,764'–11,943'

ACCESS: Daily, sunrise–sunset. UT 150/Mirror Lake Scenic Byway, which leads to the trailhead, is closed to cars late fall–late spring but is open to snowmobilers and other winter-recreation seekers. Mirror Lake Scenic Byway is a U.S. Forest Service fee-charging area. Current access fees are $6/1–3 days, $12/week, and $45/year; pick up

a recreation pass at the Kamas Ranger Station or at one of the self-service fee stations along the byway. America the Beautiful passes are also honored (see page 15).

MAPS: USGS *Mirror Lake;* Trails Illustrated *High Uintas Wilderness* (711)

FACILITIES: Restrooms and picnic area at trailhead; water at Mirror Lake Campground

WHEELCHAIR ACCESS: None

CONTACT: 435-783-4338, fs.usda.gov/uwcnf

LOCATION: UT 150/Mirror Lake Scenic Byway, in Uinta-Wasatch-Cache National Forest east of Salt Lake City, about 26 miles south of the Utah–Wyoming state line

COMMENTS: Bald Mountain is the highest peak in this book, yet it's one of the easiest peaks to climb. It's normal to feel winded at this elevation, but watch for more-severe signs of altitude sickness, which include headache, nausea, vomiting, and dizziness. Dogs allowed off-leash.

inhabits the slopes of the mountain and can often be spotted on the plateau and above the tree line.

From the trailhead, at the edge of a meadow of lavender alpine aster, the trail passes through a small stand of spruce before hitting the rocky slope leading up the mountain. The trail, though unmarked, is well traveled and easy to follow. The distinct texture and plant cover make this trail visually unique amongst its regional peers.

At 0.6 mile, as the path approaches the tree line, you enter a large, rocky tundra plateau. The trail continues its ascent across this upper shelf, but at a more gentle gradient. As you reach the higher elevation, the alpine asters become noticeably smaller but just as vibrant. They are joined by moss campion, fiery Indian paintbrush, blue skypilot, and dozens of other wildflower species. At this high elevation, you'll find wildflowers you're unlikely to see in the Wasatch or in other areas of Utah. Subalpine fir makes its last appearance at about 11,400 feet, but the wildflowers continue to the summit. Perhaps most memorable, though, are the lichen-mottled boulders that surround you. These age-old organisms are every bit as colorful and beautiful as the wildflowers of the area. You can't help but wonder, as you step across these rocks, just how ancient each vibrant spot is.

At 0.9 mile the trail steepens to ascend a false summit. As you crest this mound, the true summit comes into view just 100 yards ahead. This last section of trail crosses a flat stretch of quartzite before climbing a short stairway of large, angular blocks. You'll encounter some big steps, but no scrambling is required.

Bald Mountain

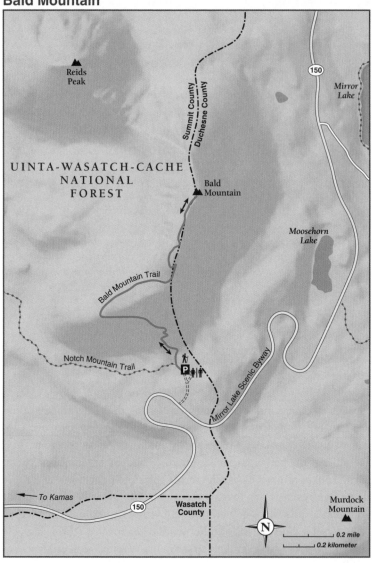

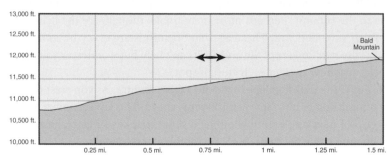

Just 1.5 miles from the trailhead, you reach the expansive summit dome, with Reids Peak immediately to the northwest. The large, rounded peak to the east is Mount Agassiz (12,428'), while Hayden Peak (12,479') is the jagged peak to the northeast. On a clear day, you won't be able to count all of the lakes that lie in the basins below, but Moosehorn Lake lies immediately below, between the highway and the eastern slopes of Bald Mountain. Mirror Lake is the larger lake to the north, on the east side of the highway.

Climb Bald Mountain early in the day. During the short summer season, afternoon thundershowers and lightning commonly occur in the Uintas. If such a storm appears to be brewing, you'd be wise to turn around and make a quick retreat to the parking area.

NEARBY ACTIVITIES

The **Kamas Ranger Station,** at 50 E. Center St. in Kamas (435-783-4338), makes an excellent starting point for a trip along the Mirror Lake Scenic Byway. The station has an interpretive center and offers an excellent assortment of books, maps, and resource materials for area trails, campgrounds, and activities.

• •

GPS TRAILHEAD COORDINATES N40° 41.348' W110° 54.238'

DIRECTIONS From the western intersection of I-80 and I-215 in Salt Lake City, take I-80 East about 17.5 miles to Exit 146 for Heber/Vernal. Follow the ramp onto US 40 East, and drive 3.2 miles. Take Exit 4 for Park City/Kamas, turn left onto UT 248 East, and drive 11.4 miles. Turn left onto Main Street in Kamas and, in 0.2 mile, turn right onto UT 150 East/East Center Street. Drive 29.1 miles to the Bald Mountain trailhead–picnic area, on your left. The trailhead is at the northwest corner of the large loop parking lot.

APPENDIX A: Outdoors Shops

BLACK DIAMOND
blackdiamondequipment.com
2092 E. 3900 S.
Salt Lake City, UT 84124
801-278-0233

CABELA'S
cabelas.com
391 Cabela's Drive
Farmington, UT 84025
801-939-3700

2502 W. Cabela's Blvd.
Lehi, UT 84043
801-766-2500

KIRKHAM'S OUTDOOR PRODUCTS
kirkhams.com
3125 S. State St.
Salt Lake City, UT 84115
801-486-4161

OUT N BACK
outnback.com
418 N. State St.
Orem, UT 84057
801-224-0454

PATAGONIA
patagonia.com
2292 S. Highland Drive
Salt Lake City, UT 84106
801-466-2226

RECREATION OUTLET
recreationoutlet.com
615 E. State Road
American Fork, UT 84003
801-763-7722

3160 S. State St.
Salt Lake City, UT 84115
801-484-4800

2326 Washington Blvd.
Ogden, UT 84401
801-409-9994

REI
rei.com
3285 E. 3300 S.
Salt Lake City, UT 84109
801-486-2100

230 W. 10600 S., Ste. 1700
Sandy, UT 84070
801-501-0850

SPORTSMAN'S WAREHOUSE
sportsmanswarehouse.com
165 W. 7200 S.
Midvale, UT 84047
801-567-1000

1075 S. University Ave.
Provo, UT 84601
801-818-2000

1137 W. Riverdale Road
Riverdale, UT 84405
801-334-4000

USGS topographic maps are available at the following locations and at most of the stores in Appendix A (opposite).

UINTA-WASATCH-CACHE NATIONAL FOREST
fs.usda.gov/uwcnf

- **Kamas Ranger District Office**
50 E. Center St.
Kamas, UT 84036
435-783-4338

- **Salt Lake Ranger District Office**
6944 S. 3000 E.
Cottonwood Heights, UT 84121
801-733-2660

- **Pleasant Grove Ranger District Office**
390 N. 100 E.
Pleasant Grove, UT 84062
801-785-3563

UTAH DEPARTMENT OF NATURAL RESOURCES MAP & BOOKSTORE
utahmapstore.com
1594 W. North Temple
Salt Lake City, UT 84116
801-537-3395, 888-UTAHMAP
(888-882-4627)

APPENDIX C:
Hiking Clubs

The **Salt Lake City area** is home to a wide variety of hiking clubs, catering to all interest and skill levels. In addition to the organized groups mentioned below, you can also look for hiking groups through social media sites such as Meetup and Facebook.

BRIGHAM YOUNG UNIVERSITY OUTDOORS UNLIMITED
outdoors.byu.edu
2201 N. Canyon Road
Provo, UT 84602
801-422-2708

LIVE AND THRIVE
liveandthrive.com
Sheryl McGlochlin, Director
Salt Lake City, UT
801-278-5313

MOUNTAIN TRAILS FOUNDATION
mountaintrails.org
PO Box 754
Park City, UT 84060
435-649-6839

SIERRA CLUB, OGDEN GROUP
utah.sierraclub.org/ogden
PO Box 1821
Ogden, UT 84402

SIERRA CLUB, UTAH CHAPTER
utah.sierraclub.org
2159 S. 700 E., Ste. 210
Salt Lake City, UT 84106
801-467-9297

UNIVERSITY OF UTAH OUTDOOR RECREATION PROGRAM
utah.edu/campusrec
George S. Eccles Student Life Center
1836 Student Life Way
Salt Lake City, UT 84112
801-581-8898

UTAH VALLEY UNIVERSITY OUTDOOR ADVENTURE CENTER
uvu.edu/oac
800 W. University Parkway, SC103H
Orem, UT 84058
801-863-7052

WASATCH MOUNTAIN CLUB
wasatchmountainclub.org
1390 S. 1100 E., Ste. 103
Salt Lake City, UT 84105
801-463-9842

WEBER PATHWAYS
weberpathways.org
PO Box 972
Ogden, UT 84402
801-393-2304

WEBER STATE UNIVERSITY WILDERNESS RECREATION CENTER
weber.edu/wrc
4022 Taylor Ave.
Ogden, UT 84408
801-626-6373

ALPINE Having to do with mountains; often describes plants, animals, and scenery found in mountainous regions.

ALPINE ZONE A life zone found in regions above 11,500 feet that is characterized by arctic-alpine tundra.

AVALANCHE A mass of snow, ice, and accompanying debris that slides down a mountain or over a cliff.

BERM A natural or human-made raised bank of earth that forms a low ridge.

BONNEVILLE SHORELINE (AKA BONNEVILLE BENCH) The geologic features visible at the 5,090-foot level on the mountains surrounding Salt Lake City. These deposits were left by the shoreline of ancient Lake Bonneville 15,000 years ago.

BOULDER-HOPPING Hiking that involves walking and sometimes jumping across sections with large rocks.

BOWL A large depression that is left in the earth by a retreating glacier; often part of a cirque (see below).

BUSHWHACK To clear a path through thick woods or undergrowth where no official hiking trail exists.

CAIRN A stack of rocks created as a trail marker. Hikers often construct cairns to mark the way on faint trails.

CANOPY A layer formed by the leaves and branches of the forest's tallest trees.

CIRQUE A deep-walled, glacier-carved basin on a mountain usually forming the blunt upper end of a valley.

CONIFER Trees and shrubs that are typically cone-bearing and evergreen. In Utah, common conifers are spruce, fir, pine, and juniper.

COULOIR A steep mountainside chute or gully that often retains snow until late in the season.

DRAINAGE A land area—specifically, a basin—that is generally bounded by ridges or slopes, encompassing a watershed.

EXPOSURE The potential for physical harm in the event of a fall; can also refer to the amount of tree cover or shade on a particular hike.

FORB A broad-leafed flowering plant other than grass that is often found growing in fields and meadows.

GLACIER A large body of ice moving down a slope or mountain.

GLISSADE To slide in a standing or sitting position down a snow-covered slope without using skis. Glissading is dangerous in areas prone to avalanches.

KNIFE EDGE A mountain ridge, often close to the summit, characterized by a narrow passage and slopes that drop sharply on both sides.

(continued on next page)

KRUMMHOLZ Trees and other wooded vegetation found near tree line that have been twisted and stunted by wind and severe weather.

MASSIF A compact portion of a mountain range containing one or more summits. Mount Timpanogos, for example, is a massif within the larger Wasatch range.

MONTANE ZONE Life zone found at elevations from 8,000 to 9,500 feet and characterized (in the Salt Lake City area) by aspen and Douglas-fir.

MORAINE The rocks and soil carried and deposited by a glacier.

OUTCROP The exposed part of a rock formation that can be seen above the ground.

RIPARIAN Along or near a stream or river.

ROUTE FINDING Navigating in the backcountry or wilderness without using GPS, a compass, or maps.

SADDLE A ridge between two peaks.

SCRAMBLING A type of climbing that does not entail the use of ropes; instead, hands and legs are used to provide propulsion and balance.

SCREE Debris consisting of small loose rocks, usually fist-size or smaller.

SIDE CANYON A tributary or branch of a larger canyon. Broads Fork and Mineral Fork, for example, are side canyons of Big Cottonwood Canyon.

SNOWFIELD An expanse of snow cover that can either be permanent or last well beyond the winter season. The accumulation above Emerald Lake on Mount Timpanogos, for instance, is considered a permanent snowfield.

SUBALPINE ZONE Life zone found at elevations from 9,500 feet to tree line (about 11,000 feet) and characterized by spruce forests.

SWITCHBACK A trail that zigzags up the side of a steep slope or mountain. Allows for a more gradual and less strenuous ascent.

TALUS A sloping mass of rock debris at the base of a cliff.

TARN A mountain lake formed by a glacier.

TECHNICAL CLIMBING Rock or mountain climbing that involves the use of ropes and other protective equipment.

TRANSITION ZONE The foothills at an elevation of 5,500–8,000 feet, characterized (in the Salt Lake City area) by oak and maple shrublands.

TRAVERSE A section of trail that moves across a slope or ridge in a horizontal direction.

TREE LINE (TIMBERLINE) The elevation where the trees end and subalpine or alpine vegetation begins. The elevation of tree line varies with latitude and climate. In northern Utah, the tree line is around 11,000 feet.

TUNDRA The treeless vegetation found in high-alpine and arctic terrain, consisting of lichens, mosses, grasses, and low shrubs.

WATERSHED A land area that drains water into a larger river system or other body of water.

The 60 featured hikes are identified with bracketed numbers (e.g., Adams Canyon [6]) that correspond to their respective hike numbers in the book.

Photo: Celeste Elain Witt

Greg Witt has lived the adventures he writes about and shares with audiences around the world. His journeys have taken him to every corner of the globe. He has guided mountaineering expeditions in the Alps and Andes and paddled wild rivers in the Americas. He has dropped teams of adventurers into golden slot canyons; trudged through deep jungles in Africa, Central America, and Asia; and guided archaeological expeditions across the parched Arabian Peninsula.

After earning degrees from the University of California and Brigham Young University, Greg had an early career in human-resources management. Preferring high adventure to the high-rise, he traded his wingtips for hiking boots decades ago and has never looked back.

Some weeks Greg hikes more miles than he drives, which means he wears out his boots faster than he wears out his tires. He has crossed the Grand Canyon on foot more than a dozen times and climbed Colorado's three highest peaks in three days. Each summer in the Swiss Alps, he hikes more than 700 miles and gains nearly 100,000 vertical feet of elevation as he guides guests of Alpenwild (alpenwild.com), a company he owns and operates.

Greg loves leading readers on the most breathtaking hikes and exciting outdoor adventures on the globe. He comes ready to discuss the geology, history, archaeology, weather patterns, culture, flora, and fauna of the exciting locales he loves. His other books include *Exploring Havasupai* (Menasha Ridge Press), *Ultimate Adventures: A Rough Guide to Adventure Travel* (Rough Guides), and *50 Best Short Hikes: Utah's National Parks* (Wilderness Press).

Greg's research and exploration continue to uncover adventures just waiting to be experienced. If you join him, you'll be guaranteed a phenomenal journey.

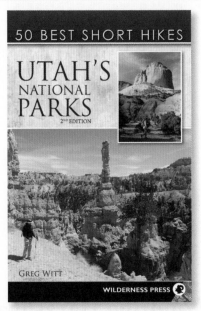

Check out this other great title from
— Menasha Ridge Press! —

Exploring Havasupai

By Greg Witt
ISBN: 978-1-63404-070-9
$19.95, 2nd edition

6 x 9, paperback
Full color, 208 pages
Maps, photographs, index

Deep in the Grand Canyon lies a place of unmatched beauty—a place where blue-green water cascades over fern-clad cliffs into travertine pools, where great blue heron skim canyon streams, and where giant cottonwoods and graceful willows thrive in the shade of majestic sandstone cliffs. Havasupai is a paradise enveloped in one of the earth's most rugged and parched landscapes.

Exploring Havasupai, by Greg Witt, is the essential destination guide for those visiting the area. This updated guidebook is filled with insider tips, fascinating background, and essential information. It identifies many new hikes, mines, springs, and historical sites never before revealed in a Grand Canyon or Havasupai guidebook. Details on canyon geology, weather patterns, and the unique flora and fauna add depth to a hiker's experience.

Exploring Havasupai includes detailed maps, trail descriptions, stunning full-color photographs, and intriguing historical insights. This is the must-have guide for canyon visitors, whether they're arriving by helicopter, on horseback, or on foot.

MENASHA RIDGE PRESS
menasharidge.com

DEAR CUSTOMERS AND FRIENDS,

SUPPORTING YOUR INTEREST IN OUTDOOR ADVENTURE, travel, and an active lifestyle is central to our operations, from the authors we choose to the locations we detail to the way we design our books. Menasha Ridge Press was incorporated in 1982 by a group of veteran outdoorsmen and professional outfitters. For many years now, we've specialized in creating books that benefit the outdoors enthusiast.

Almost immediately, Menasha Ridge Press earned a reputation for revolutionizing outdoors- and travel-guidebook publishing. For such activities as canoeing, kayaking, hiking, backpacking, and mountain biking, we established new standards of quality that transformed the whole genre, resulting in outdoor-recreation guides of great sophistication and solid content. Menasha Ridge Press continues to be outdoor publishing's greatest innovator.

The folks at Menasha Ridge Press are as at home on a whitewater river or mountain trail as they are editing a manuscript. The books we build for you are the best they can be, because we're responding to your needs. Plus, we use and depend on them ourselves.

We look forward to seeing you on the river or the trail. If you'd like to contact us directly, visit us at menasharidge.com. We thank you for your interest in our books and the natural world around us all.

SAFE TRAVELS,

Bob Sehlinger

BOB SEHLINGER
PUBLISHER